Collins

Maths Matters 4

Prabha Sethy

Published by Collins India
A division of HarperCollins*Publishers* India Limited
HarperCollins *Publishers*
A-75, Sector 57, Noida, Uttar Pradesh 201301, India
1 London Bridge Street, London, SE1 9GF, United Kingdom
Hazelton Lanes, 55 Avenue Road, Suite 2900, Toronto, Ontario M5R 3L2
and 1995 Markham Road, Scarborough, Ontario M1B 5M8, Canada
25 Ryde Road, Pymble, Sydney, NSW 2073, Australia
195 Broadway, New York, NY 10007, USA

Browse the complete Collins catalogue at **www.collins.in**

First published in 2016
Latest reprint edition 2017

ISBN: 978-93-5136-888-5

Artwork and layout by **Mukesh Technologies Pvt. Ltd.**

Printed and bound in India by Thomson Press India Ltd.

MRP: ₹ 230

Acknowledgements

Cover: WEKWEK, iStockphoto

Title Page: WEKWEK, iStockphoto

Maths Matters 4

Prabha Sethy

Preface

Maths Matters is a series of eight books for Classes 1 to 8. The primary school series follows a universal approach whereas the middle school series is based on the syllabus prescribed by the Inter-State Board for Anglo-Indian Education.

Maths Matters focuses on developing thinking and reasoning skills in students. It enables students to comprehend the application of mathematics in real life. In addition, the coherent and structured approach is valuable for teachers as it helps the lesson flow from one level to the next. Sufficient number of solved examples, exercises and mental maths questions are provided to ensure a holistic grasp of the mathematical thought processes.

Some Key Features

Let's Get Started to revise the concepts learnt earlier

Mental Maths to sharpen the calculation skills and logical reasoning

Hints and Tips for better conceptual understanding

Try These to test student's understanding of the topic covered

Note brings the focus to certain important points

Remember to highlight key points of the concept discussed

Exercise to revise the topics just learnt

Revision Exercise for a well-integrated review of the concepts covered in a chapter

For the Curious Mind to encourage students to think beyond the textual knowledge

Worksheet to reinforce practice with fun exercise

Project to extend the concept learnt to real–life applications

Mixed Review for cumulative revision after every few chapters

Test Papers at the end of the book to comprehensively test the concepts

We would like to take this opportunity to thank all the teachers who reviewed the books and provided their valuable feedback. Special thanks to Ms Indrani Shome, formerly a teacher of Lakshmipat Singhania Academy, Kolkata, for giving her suggestions, which helped in improving the quality of the content.

Any suggestions or constructive criticism from the users are welcome. We shall try to incorporate those in the future editions.

Authors

Key Features

Let's Get Started

To revise the concepts learnt earlier

> **Let's Get Started**
>
> What comes to your mind when you hear
> How often do you come across numbers i
>
> Numbers are not only used to count, bu
> measure and label. For example, numb

Mental Maths

To hone the calculation skills and logical reasoning.

> **Mental Maths**
>
> 1. Write the place value of the underlined digits:
>   a. <u>9</u>782485 ______
>   b. 7<u>6</u>81984

Try These!

To test student's understanding of the concept

> **Try These!**
>
> 3 × 2 = ____
> 5 × 2 = ____
> 7 × 2 = ____
> 9 × 2 = ____

Note

To bring the focus to certain important points

> **Note**
>
> Bigger objects may not necessarily be heavier than smaller objects. A lock is heavier than a pencil box

Hints and Tips

To provide hints and tips for better understanding of the concept

> **Hints and Tips**
>
> Distinguish between the terms Cost Price and Actual Cost. Always remember that if overhead expenses are mentioned in the question, then Actual cost = CP + Overhead expenses.

Remember

To highlight key points of the concept discussed

> **Remember**
>
> When we subtract 0 from a number, the value of the number remains the same; it does not decrease.
>
> 12345 – 0 = 12345
> 56789 – 0 = 56789

Exercises

To revise the concepts just learnt

> **Exercise 9.2**
>
> 1. A lamp costs ₹835 and a book costs cost?
>
> | | H | T | O |
> |---|---|---|---|
> | Lamp costs | | | |
> | Book costs | | | |
>
> Thus, both the things cost ₹ ______
>
> 2. Ram has ₹750. Shyam has ₹525. Hov have than Shyam?
>
> Ram has ₹ ______
> Shyam has ₹ ______
> Thus, Ram has ₹ ______ more

Revision Exercise

At the end of each chapter for a comprehensive review of the concepts

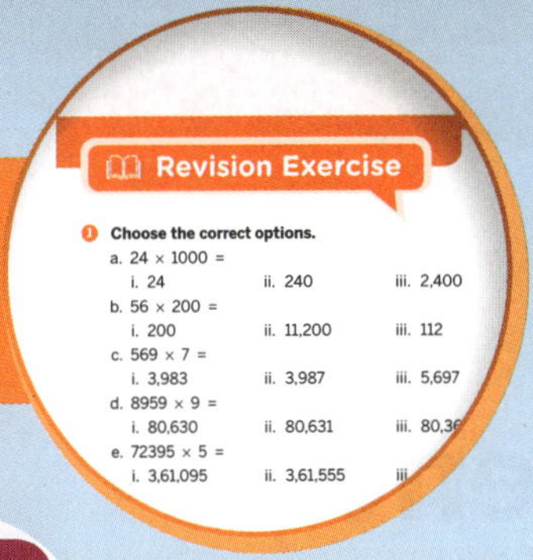

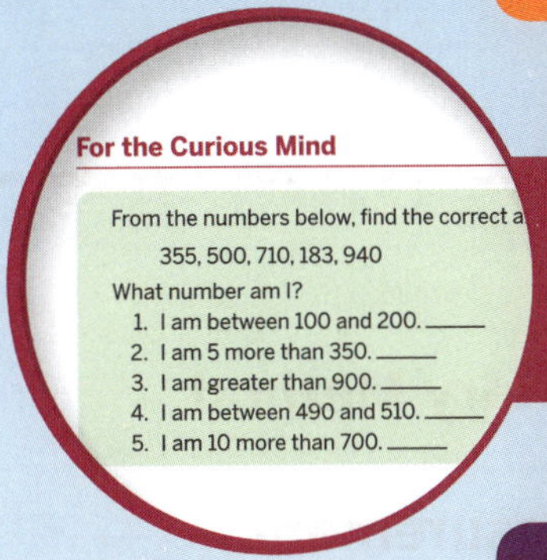

For the Curious Mind

To encourage students to think beyond the textual knowledge

Worksheet

To reinforce practice with fun exercise

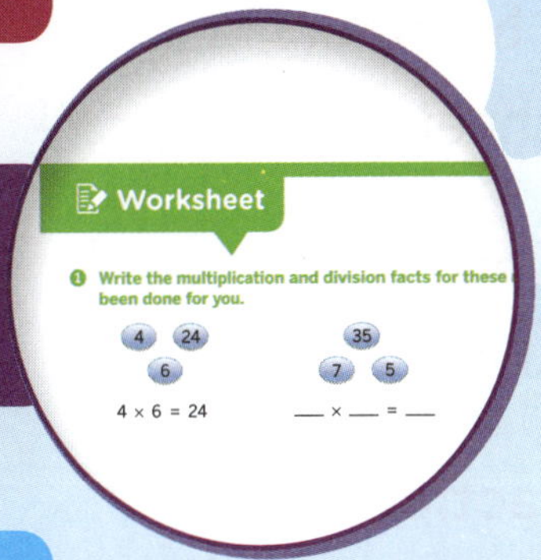

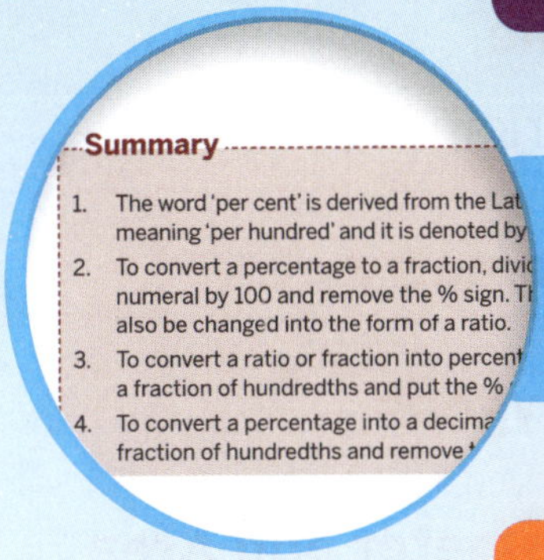

Summary

To provide the gist of the chapter for quick revision

Project

To extend the concept learnt to real-life applications

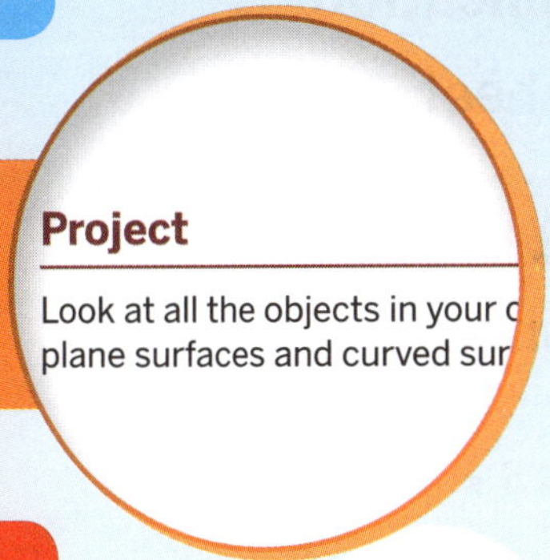

Mixed Review

To provide more practice after every few chapters

Collins DigiSuite is an innovative digital solution for teachers. It contains four modules delivering classroom content that can be used to effectively integrate the teaching and evaluation tools with the coursebooks.

The **E-book** includes animations, interactive exercises and worksheets. The E-book reader also includes interactive teaching tools like pen tool, text highlighter, page zoom, search and bookmark.

The **Test Generator** is a question bank with a variety of questions for effective evaluation. It is an easy-to-use assessment tool for the teachers to create test papers and worksheets.

The **Teacher's Resource** consists of lesson plans, answer keys and teaching techniques for the teachers.

This module has a PDF of the **Collins dictionary** appropriate for each level with all the words and definitions one needs.

Contents

Large Numbers

1

We have studied 5-digit numbers in Class 3. Now let us learn about 6- and 7-digit numbers.

Place Value Chart

In Class 3, we discussed place values up to ten thousands. These place values are categorized into different groups known as periods.

The ones, tens and hundreds places come under the **Ones** period. The thousands and ten thousands places come under the **Thousands** period.

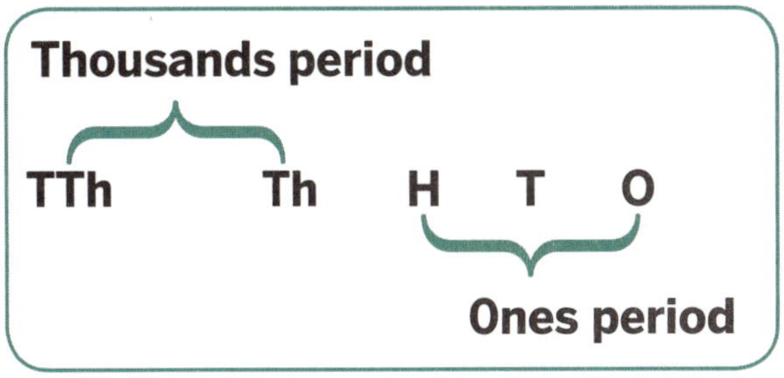

6-digit Numbers

We have learned that the largest 5-digit number is 99,999. On adding 1 to 99,999, we get the number 1,00,000. This number has six digits and is read as **one lakh**.

The new place is known as the **lakhs** place and it is denoted by **L**.

A comma is used after the lakhs digit to distinguish it from other periods.

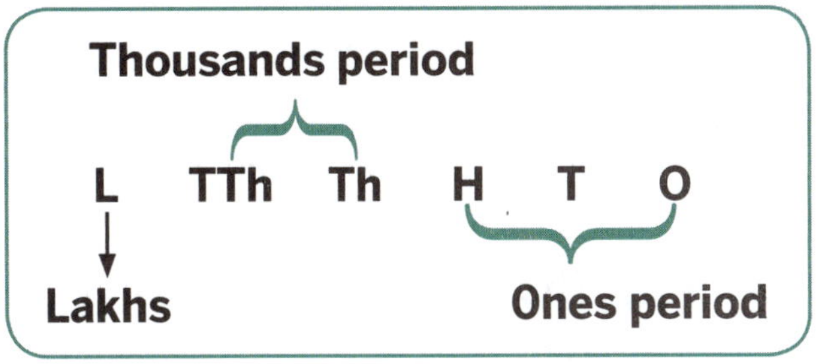

Understanding 6-digit Numbers in Indian System of Numeration

Lakhs	Ten thousands	Thousands	Hundreds	Tens	Ones
↓	↓	↓	↓	↓	↓
L	TTh	Th	H	T	O

The chart given above shows the different place values of a 6-digit number in the Indian system of numeration.

In this system, the first comma is placed after three digits from the right and then after every two digits, moving to the left.

While reading a number, we first read the lakhs place. Then, we read the thousands period and lastly, we read the ones period.

Place Value

The position of a digit in a number determines its place value. The place value of a digit in a number is the product of the digit and the value of that place.

For example, the place value of 6 in the number 64,932 = 6 × 10,000 = 60,000.

	Thousands		Ones		
L	**TTh**	**Th**	**H**	**T**	**O**
8,	6	4,	9	3	2

The number name for the number 8,64,932 is eight lakh sixty-four thousand nine hundred thirty-two.

Its expanded form is

8,00,000 + 60,000 + 4,000 + 900 + 30 + 2

Note

The smallest 6-digit number is 1,00,000.

The largest 6-digit number is 9,99,999.

Example 1: Write the number name and the expanded form of 1,59,726.

L	TTh	Th	H	T	O
1	5	9	7	2	6

Number name: One lakh fifty-nine thousand seven hundred twenty-six

Expanded form of 1,59,726 =

1,00,000 + 50,000 + 9000 + 700 + 20 + 6

Writing Numerals for Number Names

Consider the number name four lakh twenty-five thousand seven hundred eighty-two. The numeral for it is

L	TTh	Th	H	T	O
4	2	5	7	8	2

Example: The number representing the expanded form 7,00,000 + 40,000 + 300 is 7,40,300

7-digit Numbers

We have learned that the largest 6-digit number is 9,99,999. On adding 1 to 9,99,999, we get the number 10,00,000. This number has seven digits and is read as **ten lakhs**.

It is denoted by **TL**. Ten lakhs and lakhs together constitute the period of lakhs.

A comma is used after the lakhs period to distinguish it from the other periods.

Lakhs period		Thousands period		Ones period		
TL	**L**	**TTh**	**Th**	**H**	**T**	**O**

Understanding 7-digit Numbers in Indian System of Numeration

Ten Lakhs	Lakhs	Ten thousands	Thousands	Hundreds	Tens	Ones
↓	↓	↓	↓	↓	↓	↓
TL	**L**	**TTh**	**Th**	**H**	**T**	**O**

The chart given above shows the different place values of a 7-digit number. Here also the first comma is placed after three digits from the right and then after every two digits, moving to the left.

Lakhs		**Thousands**		**Ones**		
TL	**L**	**TTh**	**Th**	**H**	**T**	**O**
5	4	2	1	9	4	7

While reading a number, we first read the lakhs period together. Then, we read the thousands period together and lastly, we read the ones period.

The number name for the above number is fifty-four lakh twenty-one thousand nine hundred forty-seven.

Its expanded form is

50,00,000 + 4,00,000 + 20,000 + 1,000 + 900 + 40 + 7

Example 2: Write the number name and the expanded form of 10,97,816.

TL	**L**	**TTh**	**TH**	**H**	**T**	**O**
1	0	9	7	8	1	6

Number name: Ten lakh ninety-seven thousand eight hundred sixteen

Expanded form: 10,00,000 + 90,000 + 7,000 + 800 + 10 + 6

Remember

Put a comma after 3 digits from the right and then after every two digits.

Example: The number representing the expanded form 90,00,000 + 7,00,000 + 4000 + 300 = 97,04,300.

Writing Numerals for Number Names

Consider the number name seventy-nine lakh twenty-two thousand five hundred sixty-one. The numeral for it is

TL	**L**	**TTh**	**TH**	**H**	**T**	**O**
7	9	2	2	5	6	1

Similarly, the numeral for the number name eighty-nine lakh forty-four thousand four hundred thirty-four is

TL	**L**	**TTh**	**TH**	**H**	**T**	**O**
8	9	4	4	4	3	4

International System of Numeration

M	HTh	TTh	Th	H	T	O
↓	↓	↓	↓	↓	↓	↓
Millions	Hundred thousands	Ten thousands	Thousands	Hundreds	Tens	Ones

The chart given above shows the different place values of a 7-digit number in the International system of numeration.

Millions period			Thousands period			Ones period		
HM	**TM**	**M**	**HTh**	**TTh**	**Th**	**H**	**T**	**O**

Here, the place values as well as the periods are different from those in the Indian system of numeration.

The ones, tens and hundreds places come under the **Ones** period.

The thousands, ten thousands and hundred thousands places come under the **Thousands** period.

The millions, ten millions and hundred millions places come under the **Millions** period. In this number system, we put a comma after every three digits, starting from the right. In this system, the millions period also will have three places. We will learn about numbers having ten millions and hundred millions later.

Writing Number Names

In order to read a number in the International system of numeration, first read the digits in the millions period together. Then, read the digits in the thousands period and finally the digits in the ones period.

Million	Thousands			Ones		
M	**HTh**	**TTh**	**Th**	**H**	**T**	**O**
5	8	6	4	9	3	2

The number name for the above number is five million eight hundred sixty-four thousand nine hundred thirty-two.

Example 3: Write the number name for 5,264,583.

M	HTh	TTh	Th	H	T	O
5	2	6	4	5	8	3

The number name is five million two hundred sixty-four thousand five hundred eighty-three.

Note

Indian system	Number	International system
10,000 Ten thousand	10000 (5-digit numbers)	10,000 Ten thousand
1,00,000 One lakh	100000 (6-digit number)	100,000 One hundred thousand
10,00,000 Ten lakh	1000000 7-digit number	1,000,000 One million

Example 4: Write the number name for 4,003,490.

M	HTh	TTh	Th	H	T	O
4	0	0	3	4	9	0

The number name is four million three thousand four hundred ninety.

Writing Numbers from Number Names

In order to write the number corresponding to a given number name, first identify the periods and then write the digits corresponding to each period. For example, let us write the number corresponding to five million eight hundred twenty-four thousand four hundred nine.

Step 1: Identify the periods. Here, there are three periods namely, millions, thousands and ones.

Millions			Thousands			Ones		
Hundred Million	Ten Million	Million	Hundred Thousand	Ten Thousand	Thousand	Hundred	Ten	One

Step 2: Write the digits in each period.

Millions			Thousands			Ones		
Hundred Million	Ten Million	Million	Hundred Thousand	Ten Thousand	Thousand	Hundred	Ten	One
		5	8	2	4	4	0	9

Step 3: Place the commas after each period. 5,824,409

Exercise 1.1

1. **Write the number names of the following in the Indian system of numeration.**

   a. 5,64,769 b. 12,12,905 c. 6,48,928 d. 5,30,629
   e. 13,42,700 f. 29,06,221 g. 50,50,550 h. 34,49,962

2. **Write the expanded forms of the following.**

   a. 2,34,562 b. 45,93,287 c. 8,49,438 d. 54,71,037

3. **Write the numerals for the following number names.**

   a. Sixteen thousand two hundred ninety-four
   b. Five lakh twenty-three thousand eight hundred nine
   c. Eighty-seven lakh fifty-three thousand nine hundred twenty-seven
   d. Ninety-six lakh fifty thousand seven hundred eighty-one
   e. Sixty-seven lakh five thousand two hundred seventy-two
   f. Nine lakh seven hundred twelve
   g. Seventeen lakh eighteen thousand
   h. Two lakh five thousand three

4. **Write the number names of the following in the International system of numeration.**

   a. 468,981 b. 5,624,729 c. 709,400 d. 5,800,016
   e. 3,520,001 f. 462,963 g. 8,008,008 h. 9,999,999

5. **Write the numerals for the following number names.**

   a. Five thousand two hundred forty-nine
   b. Three thousand fifty
   c. Two thousand two hundred
   d. Fifteen thousand nine hundred ninety
   e. Nine million two hundred seventy-five thousand six hundred twenty
   f. Three million five hundred thousand seven
   g. Four million nine hundred five thousand two hundred thirty-one
   h. Two million seven hundred nine thousand one

6. **Write the number names of the following numbers. Check the comma placement in each number and decide which number system is to be used.**

   a. 2,48,974 b. 19,89,456 c. 1,792,450 d. 873,002
   e. 29,321 f. 8,000,006 g. 9,00,453 h. 6,000,127

7 Write the numerals of the following number names.

a. Three lakh forty-two thousand five hundred twenty
b. Four hundred thirty-two thousand five hundred twenty
c. Seventeen lakh twenty-three thousand two hundred seven
d. Three million two hundred twenty-one thousand four hundred nine
e. Ninety lakh four thousand five
f. Five million five thousand twenty-nine
g. Fifteen lakh fourteen thousand eight hundred thirty-one
h. One million five hundred twenty-eight thousand three hundred sixty-two

Difference between Place Value and Face Value

Place value of a digit is the digit followed by the same number of zeros as the number of digits on the right side of the digit concerned in the original number.

Face value of a digit is the digit itself.

Example 5: In 2,34,872

Place value of 2 = 2,00,000	Face value of 2 = 2
Place value of 3 = 30,000	Face value of 3 = 3
Place value of 4 = 4000	Face value of 4 = 4
Place value of 8 = 800	Face value of 8 = 8
Place value of 7 = 70	Face value of 7 = 7
Place value of 2 = 2	Face value of 2 = 2

Example 6: Find the place value and face value of the underlined digit in the following number.

23,45,671

Place value of 5 = 5,000

Face value of 5 = 5

Example 7: Find the place value and face value of the underlined digit in the following number.

45,39,210

Place value of 5 = 5,00,000

Face value of 5 = 5

Mental Maths

1. Write the place value of the underlined digits.
   a. 9782485 ____________
   b. 7681984 ____________
2. Circle the digit with the place value of nine hundred.
   9 0 9 9 9 9 0 ____________

Comparing Numbers

Comparing Numbers With Different Number of Digits

While comparing two numbers, in order to find out which one is greater, we first check the number of digits in both the numbers. If the number of digits in both the numbers is not the same, then the one with more digits is the greater number.

Example 8: 6,87,534 > 9,987 because the first number has more digits.

Comparing Numbers With Same Number of Digits

If the number of digits is the same in both the numbers, then we compare the first digit (from left) of both the numbers. The number that has the greater first digit is the greater number.

If the first digit is the same in both the numbers, then we compare the second digit of both the numbers. The number that has the greater second digit is the greater number.

If the second digit is the same in both the numbers, then we compare the third digit in both the numbers. This process is carried out till we find the greater digit. If all the digits are the same, then the numbers are equal.

Example 9: 4,91,293 < 4,91,345 because the first three digits are the same but the fourth digit is bigger in the second number.

Example: 23,495 = 23,495

Because all the digits are equal in both the numbers.

Ascending Order and Descending Order

Hints and Tips

The trick to remember is that the word 'ascending' starts with the letter A, which is the first letter of the English alphabet. So, in ascending order, we start from the smallest number.

Ascending Order

↓

A, B, C, D, E ...

1, 2, 3, 4, 5 ...

In ascending order, we write numbers from the smallest to the largest and in descending order, we write numbers from the largest to the smallest.

Example 10: Arrange 3,45,953, 6234, 5643 and 9870 in ascending and descending orders.

Ascending order – 5643, 6234, 9870, 3,45,953

Descending order – 3,45,953, 9870, 6234, 5643

Successor and Predecessor

Successor of a number is the number we get after adding 1 to the original number.

$$\begin{array}{r} 5\ 3\ 2\ 1\ 9\ 8 \\ +1 \\ \hline 5\ 3\ 2\ 1\ 9\ 9 \\ \hline \end{array}$$

Example 11: The successor of 5,32,198 is 5,32,199.

Predecessor of a number is the number we get after subtracting 1 from the original number.

$$\begin{array}{r} 5\ 3\ 2\ 1\ 9\ 8 \\ -1 \\ \hline 5\ 3\ 2\ 1\ 9\ 7 \\ \hline \end{array}$$

Example 12: The predecessor of 5,32,198 is 5,32,197.

Smallest and Largest Numbers

Given below are the smallest and the largest 2-, 3-, 4- and 5-digit numbers.

	Smallest	**Largest**
2-digit number	10	99
3-digit number	100	999
4-digit number	1,000	9,999
5-digit number	10,000	99,999

Forming Smallest and Largest Numbers

To form the smallest 6-digit or 7-digit number out of a given set of digits, we arrange the digits in increasing order.

To form the largest 6-digit or 7-digit number out of a given set of digits, we arrange the digits in decreasing order.

Example 13: Form the smallest and the largest 6-digit numbers using the digits 3, 9, 5, 1, 6 and 8.

The smallest 6-digit number using the given digits is 1,35,689 (arranging the digits in increasing order).

The largest 6-digit number using the given digits is 9,86,531 (arranging the digits in decreasing order).

Example 14: Form the smallest and the largest 7-digit numbers using the digits 2, 6, 4, 1, 0, 5 and 8.

To form the smallest 7-digit number, we have to start placing the digits in increasing order. But we cannot place 0 at the beginning as in that case, the number will be a 6-digit number. So, we start by placing the next smallest digit at the first place, that is, 1. Then, we arrange the rest of the digits in increasing order.

So, we get 10,24,568 as the smallest 7-digit number using the given digits.

The largest 7-digit number formed by the above digits is 86,54,210 (arranging the digits in decreasing order).

Exercise 1.2

1. **Write the place value and the face value of the underlined digits in the following numbers.**

   a. 6,3$\underline{8}$,294 b. 6,$\underline{2}$9,460 c. $\underline{7}$,16,285 d. 5,63,2$\underline{9}$8

2. **Fill in the blanks with >, < or =.**

   a. 6,43,298 ________ 6,43,297 b. 2,45,394 ________ 24,53,891

   c. 4,96,432 ________ 4,96,734 d. 5,92,561 ________ 59,25,610

   e. 6,13,900 ________ 60,39,990 f. 5,93,748 ________ 5,83,748

   g. 9,97,217 ________ 9,97,216 h. 2,95,934 ________ 2,95,934

3. **Arrange the following numbers in ascending order.**

   a. 6,93,212 6,93,200 6,93,220 6,93,240

   b. 53,21,424 7,32,844 9,97,879 88,88,129

   c. 9,00,000 8,99,990 99,98,998 9,99,999

4. **Arrange the following numbers in descending order.**

   a. 5,75,320 5,75,340 5,75,310 5,75,300

   b. 69,32,189 69,32,180 6,93,210 6,93,219

   c. 9,999 99,999 9,99,999 99,99,999

5. **Write the successors of the following numbers.**

   a. 6,39,421 b. 5,69,999 c. 85,69,009 d. 73,29,999 e. 59,60,009

6. **Write the predecessors of the following numbers.**

   a. 7,49,852 b. 6,38,900 c. 5,39,218 d. 69,99,980 e. 69,99,000

7. **Write the smallest and the largest 6-digit numbers formed using each of the given digits only once.**

   a. 3, 9, 6, 8, 1, 5 b. 4, 0, 3, 9, 8, 2

   c. 6, 0, 0, 7, 9, 1 d. 9, 8, 2, 0, 4, 7

Roman Numerals

Roman number system was used in ancient Rome. It had some basic symbols which were combined to form numbers. The basic symbols were:

Hindu-Arabic Numerals	1	5	10	40	50	100	500	1000
Roman Numerals	I	V	X	XL	L	C	D	M

Roman numerals from 1 to 39 are given below.

1 = I	11 = XI	21 = XXI	31 = XXXI
2 = II	12 = XII	22 = XXII	32 = XXXII
3 = III	13 = XIII	23 = XXIII	33 = XXXIII
4 = IV	14 = XIV	24 = XXIV	34 = XXXIV
5 = V	15 = XV	25 = XXV	35 = XXXV
6 = VI	16 = XVI	26 = XXVI	36 = XXXVI
7 = VII	17 = XVII	27 = XXVII	37 = XXXVII
8 = VIII	18 = XVIII	28 = XXVIII	38 = XXXVIII
9 = IX	19 = XIX	29 = XXIX	39 = XXXIX
10 = X	20 = XX	30 = XXX	40 = XL

Listed below are a few rules for writing numbers in Roman numerals.

1. When a symbol appears on the right side of a larger symbol, it is added.
   Example: XI = 10 + 1 = 11
2. When a symbol appears on the left side of a larger symbol, it is subtracted.
   Example: IX = 10 – 1 = 9
3. The same symbol is not repeated more than three times.
4. When symbols are placed next to each other, we first identify the basic symbol and then add or subtract the other symbol.

   Example: VIII

   V is the basic symbol and we add III to it.

   That is, 5 + 3 = 8.

   Example: IX

   X is the basic symbol and we subtract I from it.

   That is, 10 – 1 = 9.

Exercise 1.3

1 Write the Roman numerals for the following numbers.

a. 6 b. 10 c. 9 d. 11 e. 18 f. 20
g. 21 h. 25 i. 30 j. 41 k. 3 l. 13

2 Write the Hindu-Arabic numerals for the following Roman numerals.

a. VIII b. XVI c. XX d. XXX e. XXXIX f. X
g. XXIX h. XIX i. XXV j. XXXVI k. XXXXI l. XXVIII

Revision Exercise

1 **Choose the correct options.**

a. Twenty-nine lakh forty-seven thousand one hundred three is the number name of

i. 2,947,103 ii. 29,40,703 iii. 29,47,103 iv. 2,947,1003 ☐

b. Which one of the following numbers is written in the International system of numeration?

i. 5,29,362,109 ii. 834,71,256 iii. 165,382,47 iv. 129,480,267 ☐

c. In 6,498,102, the difference between the place value of 8 and the place value of 1 is

i. 7,900 ii. 8,000 iii. 100 iv. 8,100 ☐

d. Which of the following numbers is the largest?

i. 7,00,007 ii. 7,70,000 iii. 7,07,777 iv. 7,00,999 ☐

e. In descending order, we write the numbers from

i. the smallest to the largest ii. the largest to the smallest ☐

f. The predecessor of the smallest 6-digit number is

i. 1,00,000 ii. 9,99,999 iii. 10,000 iv. 99,999 ☐

g. Which is the smallest 7-digit number formed using the digits 1, 0, 9, 8, 5, 3 and 7 only once?

i. 0,135,789 ii. 03,15,789 iii. 98,75,310 iv. 10,35,789 ☐

h. Which is the greatest 6-digit number formed using the digits 2, 9, 4, 0, 7 and 6 only once?

i. 0,24,679 ii. 2,04,679 iii. 9,76,240 iv. 9,76,420 ☐

i. Which is the number corresponding to the expanded form 5,00,000 + 6,000 + 4,00 + 7?

i. 5647 ii. 50,647 iii. 65,407 iv. 5,06,407 ☐

j. The Roman numeral for 5 + 8 is equal to

i. VI ii. XIII iii. XI iv. IX ☐

2 Twenty-four lakh sixty-seven thousand nine hundred thirty-five written in the International system of numeration will be ____________________.

3 The difference between five million six hundred forty-nine thousand two hundred three and eight lakh five hundred is ____________________.

4 The place value of 5 multiplied by the face value of 2 in 1,65,209 is

____________________.

5. **Write >, < or =.**

   a. 5,00,000 ________ 50,00,000 b. 8,98,998 ________ 8,98,989

6. **Write the following numbers in ascending order.**

   9,00,099 9,00,009 99,99,999 90,00,999 9,90,099

7. The successor of 999790 is ________________.

8. The difference between the successor of 1,99,900 and the predecessor of 5,00,001 is ________________.

9. What is the sum of the largest 6-digit number and the smallest 6-digit number?

10. What is the smallest 6-digit number formed by using the digits 6, 0, 8, 0, 9 and 7 only once?

11. Write the expanded form of 8,95,321.

12. Write the number from the expanded form 60,00,000 + 90,000 + 2.

13. **Write True or False.**

    a. The Roman numeral for 16 is XVI. ________________

    b. The Roman numeral for 28 is XVIII. ________________

14. **Match the following.**

1.	VII	a.	19
2.	XXIX	b.	3
3.	XIX	c.	29
4.	III	d.	33
5.	XXXIII	e.	7

For the Curious Mind

1. There are ________________ thousands in one lakh.

2. There are ________________ thousands in one million.

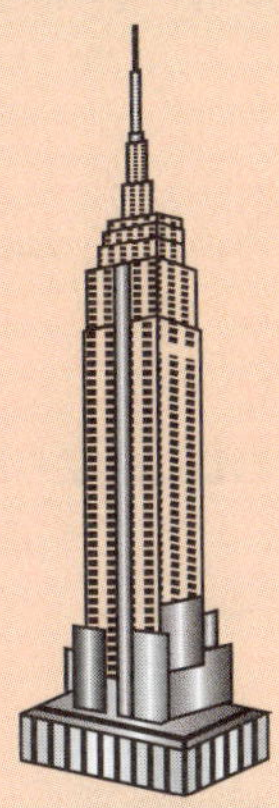

Did you know?

The Empire State Building at New York was built with ten million bricks!

Worksheet

1. **In 12,79,846, the numeral in the ten lakhs place is ______________.**

2. a. Write fifty lakh forty-one thousand six hundred as a number. ______________

   b. Write five million four hundred thousand two as a number. ______________

3. a. The number name for 49,00,001 is ______________________________.

   b. The number name for 5,892,001 is ______________________________.

4. **In 5,69,438, the place value of 9 is ______________ and the face value of 9 is ______________.**

5. **Write >, < or = in the blanks.**

   a. 5,99,999 ______ 9,99,995 b. 1,00,003 ______ 10,00,003

   c. 6,43,212 ______ 6,43,212

6. **The smallest 6-digit number formed by using the digits 5, 3, 0, 4, 9 and 1 only once is ______________.**

7. **The predecessor of 8,99,999 is ______________.**

8. **The successor of 19,99,899 is ______________.**

9. a. The number representing the expanded form

   50,00,000 + 4,00,000 + 30,000 + 9 = ______________.

   b. The expanded form of 9,60,402 = ______________________________.

10. **Circle the correct digit in each number to match the value.**

    Example: 2 0 6 7 ③ 9 5 three hundred

    a. 2 9 6 9 9 2 1 nine lakh b. 7 2 2 4 0 2 5 twenty thousand

    c. 3 3 6 3 2 8 0 thirty lakh d. 8 5 5 0 1 5 9 7 five lakh

11. **Solve using Roman numerals.**

    a. XX + X = ______________ b. XXXVIII – XXXV = ______________

12. **Fill in the blanks. Two have been done for you.**

	Smallest	Largest		Smallest	Largest
2-digit number	10	99	5-digit number	______	______
3-digit number	100	999	6-digit number	______	______
4-digit number	______	______	7-digit number	______	______

Addition

2

We have learned how to add 4-digit and 5-digit numbers. Now, let us use the same method to add 6-digit numbers.

Adding 6-digit Numbers Without Carrying

6-digit numbers are added in the same way as smaller numbers. We first add the digits in the ones place, then we add the digits in the tens place, followed by those in the hundreds, the thousands, the ten thousands and the lakhs places. The numbers that are being added are called addends and the result obtained after adding the numbers (addends) is called the sum.

Remember

1. The symbol '+' is used when we add numbers.
2. Numbers added in any order give the same answer.
3. When we add 0 to a number, the answer is the number itself.

Example 1:

	L	TTh	Th	H	T	O
Addend →	1	3	4	2	4	8
Addend →	+ 8	6	4	5	3	1
Sum →	9	9	8	7	7	9

Sum = 9,98,779

Adding 6-digit Numbers With Carrying

Here, we use the same method as above. However, in this case, we carry forward numbers to the next higher place value, wherever required.

Example 2:

	L	TTh	Th	H	T	O
	$^{1}5$	$^{1}4$	9	6	2	3
+	3	6	5	2	7	4
	9	1	4	8	9	7

Sum = 9,14,897

Remember

Add the digits at different places (O/T/H/Th/TTh/L) and regroup, if required. Carry forward to the next higher place value.

Example 3:

	TL	L	TTh	Th	H	T	O
		$^{1}7$	$^{1}9$	4	$^{1}3$	$^{1}2$	8
		5	3	2	0	7	4
+		1	1	6	3	0	2
	1	4	4	2	7	0	4

Sum = 14,42,704

Exercise 2.1

Solve the following.

1. a. 5 + 8 = 8 + ________ b. 35 + 3 = 3 + ________
   c. 0 + 141 = ________ d. 2331 + 0 = ________
2. a. 13 + 5 + 7 = ________ b. 16 + 1 + 4 = ________
   c. 18 + 9 + 2 = ________ d. 25 + 2 + 5 = ________

3.

	3	4	4	3	2	1
+	6	5	3	5	6	8

4.

	9	4	3	2	8	1
+	6	2	4	5	0	7

5.

	5	3	9	2	1	2
+	3	4	0	3	8	5

6.

	2	3	8	6	5	9
+	6	4	2	3	4	0

7.

	5	4	6	8	4	6
+	7	2	3	1	5	2

8.

	6	3	9	4	2	5
+	8	7	0	2	3	4

9.

	3	2	9	5	5
	6	1	6	8	3
+	1	3	2	9	0

10.

	1	3	4	9	3
	2	4	6	1	2
	1	3	3	2	0
+		4	6	9	4

⑪

	3	4	5	3	2	1
			6	9	8	2
			7	9	4	8
+			2	5	7	9

⑫

		2	0	9	3	6
	1	2	5	7	9	3
	6	9	4	8	9	2
+	1	0	0	0	0	3

⑬ 4968 + 62941 + 132496 + 9836 = ____________

⑭ 43921 + 6943 + 962136 + 480 = ____________

⑮ 634900 + 59321 + 23423 + 56926 = ____________

⑯ 732196 + 139 + 439690 + 6370 = ____________

Word Problems on Addition

Word problems on addition are solved in the same manner as they were in the previous classes except, now, the numbers are larger.

Hints and Tips

Whenever we have to find the total, we add.

Example 4: For flood relief, students of Class 4 collected ₹2468, those of Class 5 collected ₹1100 and those of Class 6 collected ₹1220. What was the total amount collected?

Amount collected by Class 4	= ₹2 4 6 8
Amount collected by Class 5	= ₹1 1 0 0
Amount collected by Class 6	= ₹1 2 2 0
Total amount collected	= ₹4 7 8 8

Thus, the total amount collected was ₹4788.

Note

1. It is important to write short statements. This helps us to understand what we are doing and also to avoid mistakes.
2. The answer to word problems must always be written in the statement form.

Example 5: A factory sold 3,94,680 cycles in January, 1,02,300 cycles in February and 4,01,010 cycles in March. What was the total number of cycles the factory sold in these three months?

Number of cycles sold in January	=	3 9 4 6 8 0
Number of cycles sold in February	=	1 0 2 3 0 0
Number of cycles sold in March	=	4 0 1 0 1 0
Total cycles sold	=	8 9 7 9 9 0

Thus, the total number of cycles the factory sold in these three months was 8,97,990.

Example 6: Mr Gupta saved ₹5,96,800 in 2011, ₹3,24,780 in 2012 and ₹1,90,900 in 2013. How much money did he save in these three years?

Amount saved in 2011	=	₹5 9 6 8 0 0
Amount saved in 2012	=	₹3 2 4 7 8 0
Amount saved in 2013	=	₹1 9 0 9 0 0
Total amount saved	=	₹11 1 2 4 8 0

Thus, Mr Gupta saved ₹11,12,480 in these three years.

Exercise 2.2

Solve the following word problems.

1. A man travelled 16,346 km by plane, 9349 km by train and 729 km by car. What was the total distance he travelled?
2. A movie hall sold 69,385 tickets in January, 56,392 tickets in February and 4,692 tickets in March. How many tickets were sold in these three months?
3. A city has 6,29,480 men, 4,32,958 women and 7,38,201 children. What is the total population of the city?
4. A furniture shop sold 3800 tables to School A, 4320 tables to School B and 7389 tables to School C. How many tables did the shop sell in all?
5. Sonam Wangchuk spent ₹69,325 maths books, ₹2936 on history books and ₹70,869 on English books for his school library. How much money did he spend in all?

6. Mr Ahuja spent ₹9,50,000 to buy a shop, ₹90,000 to get the wood work done and ₹2,20,000 on electrical fittings. How much did Mr Ahuja spend in all?

Revision Exercise

1 Choose the correct options.

a. 125060 + 9 = ________________ + 125060

i. 12 ii. 9 iii. 21 iv. 0 ☐

b. 198765 + 0 = ________________

i. 198765 ii. 0 iii. 200000 iv. 1987650 ☐

c. 150000 + 9999 + 500 = ________________

i. 156500 ii. 159,499 iii. 165000 iv. 160499 ☐

d.

6	5	3	5	6	2
+ 1	3	1	3	5	4

i. 7158906 ii. 615842 iii. 784916 iv. 715844 ☐

e.

7	3	2	4	3	5
+ 2	3	4	9	8	4

i. 967410 ii. 967435 iii. 967489 iv. 967419 ☐

f.

5	3	9	2	8	4
+ 2	4	8	1	7	0

i. 789454 ii. 798454 iii. 787450 iv. 787454 ☐

g. 342976 + 13520 + 999 = ________________

i. 357945 ii. 354795 iii. 375495 iv. 357495 ☐

h. Raman has ₹2,35,680. His father gives him ₹15,720 more. How much money does Raman have now?

i. ₹2,51,400 ii. ₹2,41,500 iii. ₹2,45,100 iv. ₹2,54,100 ☐

i. Mr Gupta spent ₹651,000 to buy a car, ₹82,000 to repair it and ₹12,000 to paint it. How much did Mr Gupta spend in all?

i. ₹9,92,000 ii. ₹6,91,000 iii. ₹7,45,000 iv. ₹7,17,000 ☐

j. The population of Town A is 7,35,482, that of Town B is 9,00,100 and that of Town C is 2,50,000. What is the total population of these three towns?

i. 18,85,528 ii. 18,85,258 iii. 18,85,582 iv. 18,25,582 ☐

Add the following (Q2 to Q10).

2.

	4	3	8	9	1	2
		1	0	1	2	4
+		9	6	4	3	6

3.

	5	9	6	8	6	7
		1	8	9	9	3
+		4	8	9	6	0

4.

	1	0	9	2	5	9
			4	6	8	9
+			9	3	4	8

5.

	2	5	3	4	2	6
		6	1	3	4	2
+			2	1	3	6

6.

	1	6	4	9	2	5
+	6	2	8	1	7	3

7.

	1	3	8	9	4	8
	2	4	3	1	2	0
+	9	8	0	0	0	4

8. 449684 + 55429 + 986 + 1024 = ____________

9. 324109 + 262356 = ____________

10. 786000 + 200000 = ____________

11. In one month, a company spends ₹5,23,420 on salaries, ₹2,50,000 on raw material and ₹1,00,000 on other expenses. What is the total amount the company spends on these three items in one month?

12. Jyoti spent ₹2,46,900 on a shop, ₹5,25,000 on a car and ₹1,30,000 on travelling. How much did she spend in all?

13. Rahim spent ₹6,99,000 to buy a house. He further spent ₹1,20,000 on white wash and ₹50,000 on furniture. What is the total amount Rahim spent?

14. For a flood relief fund, company A collected ₹4,55,000 and company B collected ₹7,90,500. What is the total amount collected by the two companies?

Worksheet

1 **Fill in the blanks.**

a. 6876 + 3345 = 3345 + ____________

b. 19421 + 5000 = ____________

c. 10000 + 18 = ____________

d. 27019 + 0 = ____________

e. 6 + 3 + 9000 = ____________

f. 4 + 5 + 100000 = ____________

g. 7200 + 280000 = ____________

h. 9999 + 10000 = ____________

i. 123456 + 543210 = ____________

j. 5296 + 4703 = ____________

2 Nitika has ₹4,60,000 in her bank account. She puts ₹40,000 and her father puts ₹1,90,000 in her account. What is the total amount in Nitika's account now?

3 Tick the option(s) which gives the answer as 10,00,000.

a. 99,999 + 1

b. 10,000 + 99,900

c. 4,50,000 + 5,50,000

d. 8,00,000 + 20,000

4 Tick the correct statement.

a. 2,66,900 + 3,45,000 = 6,10,900

b. 7,89,000 + 78,899 = 8,67,899

c. 1,00,002 + 2,00,001 = 3,00,003

d. 4,00,000 + 40,000 + 4,000 = 4,44,444

For the Curious Mind

1 Mr Sethi buys a car for ₹7,96,809. He wants to sell it after increasing the price by ₹2,00,000. For how much should he sell it?

2 Raman has ₹5,56,000 with him. He asks his brother to lend him ₹1,50,000. His brother only manages to give him 1,25,000. He borrows ₹75,000 from his friend. How much money does Raman manage to collect?

Subtraction

3

We have learned to subtract numbers with 5 digits. Now, let us use the same method to subtract numbers with more than 5 digits.

Subtracting 6-digit Numbers Without Borrowing

We first subtract the digits in the ones place, then we subtract the digits in the tens place, followed by those in the hundreds, the thousands, the ten thousands and the lakhs places.

Example 1:

	L	TTh	Th	H	T	O
	6	9	2	8	5	7
−	2	5	0	7	1	6
	4	4	2	1	4	1

Answer = 4,42,141

Remember

When we subtract 0 from a number, the answer is the number itself.

12345 − 0 = 12345

56789 − 0 = 56789

Subtracting 6-digit Numbers With Borrowing

Here, we use the same method as above, but wherever required, we borrow numbers from the next higher place value.

Example 2:

	L	TTh	Th	H	T	O
		14	15			
	7 ~~8~~	4 ~~5~~	5 ~~6~~	12 ~~2~~	8 ~~9~~	17 ~~7~~
−	2	8	6	4	1	8
	5	6	9	8	7	9

Answer = 5,69,879

Try These!

1.

	5	6	9	3	2	1
	−	8	9	6	3	0

2.

	8	7	0	9	6	9
−	5	9	9	9	9	9

Exercise 3.1

Solve the following

1. a. 999999 – 0 = ________

   b. 435678 – 0 = ________

2.
```
  8 9 5 9 2 7
– 2 7 3 4 1 3
```

3.
```
  8 3 2 1 9 8
–   1 6 7 9 3
```

4.
```
  7 9 3 2 8 1
– 2 4 9 6 3 5
```

5.
```
  9 3 2 9 1 5
  4 0 0 9 6 7
```

6.
```
  6 0 0 0 0 0
  3 0 9 9 9 9
```

7.
```
  9 8 3 5 0 0
– 2 3 4 5 6 9
```

8.
```
  9 3 4 9 6 0
–   6 9 3 8 9
```

9.
```
  9 4 6 9 8 7
– 2 4 9 9 9 9
```

10. 734921 – 64320 = ________

11. 946893 – 84963 = ________

12. 900000 – 46938 = ________

13. 700000 – 299999 = ________

Word Problems on Subtraction

Example 3: How much should be added to 5,39,876 to get 7,49,432?

Number to be added = 7,49,432 – 5,39,876

```
      18 13 12
    3  8  3  2 12
  7 4  9  4  3  2 ⟶ [Larger number at the top]
– 5 3  9  8  7  6
  2 0  9  5  5  6
```

Thus, 2,09,556 should be added to 5,39,876 to get 7,49,432.

Example 4: Rajat had ₹5,73,840. He spent ₹2,39,290. How much money was left with him?

```
                       6 13 7 14
Amount Rajat had = ₹ 5 7  3 8  4 0
Amount he spent  = ₹ 2 3  9 2  9 0
                     3 3  4 5  5 0
```

So, ₹3,34,550 was left with Rajat.

Note

Whenever we have to find the difference, we subtract.

Always subtract the smaller number from the larger number. In vertical subtraction, the larger number is placed at the top.

Remember

1. It is important to write short statements. It helps us to understand what we are doing and to avoid mistakes.
2. The answer to word problems must always be written in the statement form.

Example 5: Manzar first deposited ₹5,93,700 in the bank and then withdrew ₹4,20,800. How much of his money was left in the bank?

Amount Manzar deposited =	₹	5	9	3→2	7→17	0	0
Amount he withdrew =	−₹	4	2	0	8	0	0
		1	7	2	9	0	0

So, ₹1,72,900 was left in the bank.

Exercise 3.2

Solve the following word problems.

1. How much should be added to 5,23,980 to get 7,37,000?
2. By how much is 2,35,296 greater than 1,59,260?

3. A stadium has 1,66,250 seats, out of which 55,120 seats are occupied. How many seats are vacant?
4. The sum of two numbers is 9,89,340. One of the numbers is 69,898. What is the other number?
5. The sum of two numbers is 7,49,650. One of the numbers is 1,00,500. What is the other number?

6. John wants to buy a house which costs ₹8,25,000. He has ₹4,39,200 in his bank account. How much more money does he require to buy the house?
7. The population of a town is 9,56,000. Out of this, 5,00,000 are men. How many are not men?

8. In one year, two trains cover 2,19,000 km in total. If one train alone covers 1,24,340 km, find the distance covered by the other train.
9. Afzal buys a house for ₹5,98,000. He sells it for ₹9,69,898. How much more money does he get?
10. In a refugee camp, there were 2,39,460 people. 2,23,560 blankets were distributed. How many people did not get blankets?

Revision Exercise

1 Choose the correct options. Write the option in the box provided.

a. 1234321 – 0 =

i. 11 ii. 0 iii. 20 iv. 1234321 ☐

b. 225000 – 5000 =

i. 25 ii. 5 iii. 220000 iv. 15 ☐

c.
```
   4 9 3 4 5 0
 –   2 1 3 2 0
 -------------
 -------------
```

i. 472150 ii. 472130 iii. 72120 iv. 21330 ☐

d.
```
   8 4 3 2 1
 – 1 9 6 7 0
 -----------
 -----------
```

i. 64601 ii. 64629 iii. 64671 iv. 64651 ☐

e.
```
   1 6 7 8 3 2
 –   1 6 9 4 1
 -------------
 -------------
```

i. 150892 ii. 150891 iii. 50981 iv. 50982 ☐

f.
```
   8 4 9 6 3 2
 – 1 6 9 7 3 2
 -------------
 -------------
```

i. 670099 ii. 679090 iii. 670909 iv. 679900 ☐

g. What should be subtracted from 7,23,924 to get 5,10,000?

i. 2,57,465 ii. 2,13,924 iii. 2,57,654 iv. 2,13,645 ☐

h. What should be added to 3,42,315 to get 5,00,916?

i. 1,58,600 ii. 1,58,601 iii. 1,85,601 iv. 1,65,801 ☐

i. By how much is 9,35,201 greater than 9,35,200?

i. 2 ii. 200 iii. 201 iv. 1 ☐

j. By how much is two lakh eighty-five thousand four hundred greater than one lakh fifty-nine thousand?

i. 2,85,400 ii. 2,45,800 iii. 1,26,400 iv. 2,00,000 ☐

Solve the following (Q2 to Q7).

2. a. 100000 – 9000 = ____________________

   b. 292535 – 122535 = ____________________

3.

	7	3	9	8	0	0
–	5	1	6	7	5	5

4.

	8	2	2	4	3	7
–		2	8	9	6	1

5.

	9	9	6	2	4	1
–	2	9	6	8	0	0

6.

	8	9	5	4	6	3
–		2	4	1	8	5

7. a. 800000 – 149 = ____________ b. 600000 – 20000 = ____________

8. Ajay needs ₹4,50,000 to buy a car. He has ₹2,02,500. How much more money does he need?

9. The sum of two numbers is 3,99,000. One of the numbers is 99,999. What is the other number?

10. By how much is 8,66,090 greater than 5,55,550?

11. Rahul buys a television and a washing machine for ₹1,30,900. If the cost of television is ₹67,800, what is the cost of the washing machine?

12. Mitali has ₹4,40,000 in her bank account. She withdraws ₹3,33,600. How much money is left in her account?

13. Saima wants to buy a gold necklace worth ₹2,98,000. She has ₹1,78,000 with her. How much more money does she need to buy the necklace?

14. The school authorities decide to collect ₹180,000 from the students to contribute to the flood victims. If ₹1,28,500 has been collected so far, how much more needs to be collected?

For the Curious Mind

I subtracted 35 from a number. Then, I subtracted 135 from it and was left with 287. What was the original number?

Mixed Review 1

1. **Write the number names of the following numbers in the Indian system of numeration.**

   a. 15,75,209   b. 90,00,001

2. **Write the number names of the following numbers in the International system of numeration.**

   a. 4,681,292   b. 8,020,007

3. **Write the following number names in numerals.**

   a. Eighteen lakh five hundred three

   b. Three million fifty-one

4. What is the sum of the place value and the face value of 2 in 92,874?

5. Write the following numbers in descending order.

   195684, 932, 45685, 23456

6. Find the sum of the successor of the largest 3-digit number and the smallest 2-digit number.

7. Write the smallest 4-digit number using the digits 0, 3, 6 and 7.

8. Write the number form of 9,00,000 + 70 + 2.

9. Zoya bought a pair of gold earring for ₹2,60,000 and a diamond necklace for ₹5,70,000. What is the total amount of money spent by Zoya?

10. Mr Sharma bought a house for ₹3,75,460 and later sold it for ₹5,23,000. How much extra money did he get?

11. By how much is 3,35,207 greater than 1,88,290?

12. Mr Gulati bought a car for ₹2,25,500. He spent ₹10,800 to repair it. How much did the car cost him?

13. The sum of two numbers is 5,98,650. One of the numbers is 3,00,019. What is the other number?

14. In a refugee camp, there were 2,57,121 people. 1,00,999 more people came. How many people were there at the camp?

Multiplication

4

Multiplication of Numbers

Remember

0 multiplied by any number is equal to 0.

$5 \times 0 = 0$

$91 \times 0 = 0$

$0 \times 135 = 0$

Note

When a number is multiplied by 1, the product is that number itself.

$5 \times 1 = 5$

$91 \times 1 = 91$

$7 \times 1 = 7$

$135 \times 1 = 135$

Multiplication is the process of adding a number to itself many times. When we multiply two numbers, we get a product.

If we want to add 4 to itself 3 times, then we multiply 3 by 4 (that is, 3×4) to make the calculation easier.

$4 + 4 + 4 = 12$

3 times 4 is equal to 12.

$3 \times 4 = 12$

Also, $4 \times 3 = 12$

Terms of Multiplication

In multiplication, we need to know the following terms.

1. **Product** – Product is the result obtained by multiplying two or more numbers.

   Example: The product of 2 and 3 is 6. That is, $2 \times 3 = 6$.

   The product of 12 and 8 is 96. That is, $12 \times 8 = 96$.

2. **Multiplier and Multiplicand** – When we multiply two numbers, the number to be multiplied is called the multiplicand and the number of times the number is multiplied is called the multiplier.

   But as the order in which the numbers are multiplied does not change the product, they are generally called **factors**. We will learn about them later.

   7 × 4 = 28

   7 → Multiplier; 4 → Multiplicand; 28 → Product

3. **Multiple** – Multiple of a number is the product of the number with other number.

Example:

2 × 1 = **2**	
2 × 2 = **4**	→ These are the multiples of 2.
2 × 3 = **6**	
2 × 4 = **8**	
2 × 5 = **10**	

and so on.

Recalling Multiplication Tables

Complete the multiplication tables from 4 to 12 given below. The first three products for each have been written for you.

1 × 4 = 4	1 × 5 = 5	1 × 6 = 6
2 × 4 = 8	2 × 5 = 10	2 × 6 = 12
3 × 4 = 12	3 × 5 = 15	3 × 6 = 18
4 × 4 = ___	4 × 5 = ___	4 × 6 = ___
5 × 4 = ___	5 × 5 = ___	5 × 6 = ___
6 × 4 = ___	6 × 5 = ___	6 × 6 = ___
7 × 4 = ___	7 × 5 = ___	7 × 6 = ___
8 × 4 = ___	8 × 5 = ___	8 × 6 = ___
9 × 4 = ___	9 × 5 = ___	9 × 6 = ___
10 × 4 = ___	10 × 5 = ___	10 × 6 = ___
1 × 7 = 7	1 × 8 = 8	1 × 9 = 9
2 × 7 = 14	2 × 8 = 16	2 × 9 = 18
3 × 7 = 21	3 × 8 = 24	3 × 9 = 27
4 × 7 = ___	4 × 8 = ___	4 × 9 = ___
5 × 7 = ___	5 × 8 = ___	5 × 9 = ___
6 × 7 = ___	6 × 8 = ___	6 × 9 = ___
7 × 7 = ___	7 × 8 = ___	7 × 9 = ___
8 × 7 = ___	8 × 8 = ___	8 × 9 = ___
9 × 7 = ___	9 × 8 = ___	9 × 9 = ___
10 × 7 = ___	10 × 8 = ___	10 × 9 = ___
1 × 10 = 10	1 × 11 = 11	1 × 12 = 12
2 × 10 = 20	2 × 11 = 22	2 × 12 = 24
3 × 10 = 30	3 × 11 = 33	3 × 12 = 36
4 × 10 = ___	4 × 11 = ___	4 × 12 = ___
5 × 10 = ___	5 × 11 = ___	5 × 12 = ___
6 × 10 = ___	6 × 11 = ___	6 × 12 = ___
7 × 10 = ___	7 × 11 = ___	7 × 12 = ___
8 × 10 = ___	8 × 11 = ___	8 × 12 = ___
9 × 10 = ___	9 × 11 = ___	9 × 12 = ___
10 × 10 = ___	10 × 11 = ___	10 × 12 = ___

Exercise 4.1

1 Solve the following.

a. $17 \times 0 =$ ______   b. $0 \times 495 =$ ______   c. $366 \times 1 =$ ______

d. $1 \times 593 =$ ______   e. $69 \times 0 =$ ______   f. $473 \times 1 =$ ______

g. $538 \times 0 =$ ______   h. $0 \times 682 =$ ______   i. $294 \times 1 =$ ______

j. $1 \times 240 =$ ______   k. $465 \times 0 =$ ______   l. $381 \times 1 =$ ______

2 Fill in the blanks.

a. When we multiply two numbers, the result is known as the ______ of the two numbers.

b. The order in which the numbers are multiplied ______ change the product.

c. When we multiply a number with ______, we get the same number as the product.

3 Fill in the blanks.

a. $5 \times 2 = 2 \times$ ______   b. $7 \times 9 = 9 \times$ ______

c. $11 \times 12 =$ ______ $\times 11$ d. $23 \times 9 =$ ______ $\times 23$

Multiplying by 10, 100, 1000 and so on

It is easy to find the product when a number is multiplied by 10, 100, 1000 and so on. The product is the multiplier on the left, followed by the same number of zeros as in the multiplicand.

Remember

Any change in the order in which the numbers are multiplied does not change the product.

$2 \times 4 = 4 \times 2$

$5 \times 3 = 3 \times 5$

$6 \times 7 = 7 \times 6$

Examples:

8×10	$= 80$	35×10	$= 350$
8×100	$= 800$	35×100	$= 3500$
8×1000	$= 8000$	35×1000	$= 35000$
8×10000	$= 80000$	35×10000	$= 350000$

Multiplying by Multiples of 10

When a number is multiplied by 10 or multiples of 10, that is, 20, 100 and so on, we multiply the number by the first digit and then add the zeros.

Example 1: 35×20

First, write the product of 35 and 2. Then, write 0 to its right because 20 has one zero.

$$^{1}35 \times 20 = 700$$

Example 2: 15 × 300

First, write the product of 15 and 3. Then, write 00 to its right because 300 has two zeros.

$$^{1}15 \times 300 = 4500$$

Example 3:

$$^{1}493 \times 2000 = 986\underbrace{000}_{\text{since 2000 has 3 zeros.}}$$

Mental Maths

439 × 10 = ______

439 × 100 = ______

439 × 1000 = ______

439 × 10000 = ______

Exercise 4.2

1. Multiply the following numbers by 10, 100, 1000 and 10,000.

a. 9   b. 16   c. 20   d. 35

e. 92   f. 30   g. 40   h. 50

2. Solve the following.

a. 42 × 20   b. 32 × 50   c. 29 × 30   d. 432 × 20

e. 163 × 40   f. 1623 × 30   g. 2714 × 50   h. 2349 × 200

i. 5234 × 300   j. 1629 × 4000   k. 2384 × 6000   l. 123 × 7000

Long Multiplication

The method of long multiplication is used when the numbers are too big to be multiplied using shorter methods.

Multiplying by 1-digit Numbers

Without Carrying Forward

Example 4: 432 × 2

```
 4 3 2 ——→ Multiplier
   × 2 ——→ Multiplicand
 -----
 8 6 4 ——→ Product
 -----
```

Answer = 864

With Carrying Forward

Example 5: 694 × 6

```
  5 2
  6 9 4
    × 6
 -------
 4 1 6 4
 -------
```

6 × 4 = 24. So, we write 4 below 6 and carry forward 2. We write 2 on top of 9.

Then, 6 × 9 = 54. We add 2 to 54 and get 56. We write 6 under 9 and carry forward 5. We write 5 on top of 6.

Then, 6 × 6 = 36. We add 5 to 36 and get 41. We write 41 under 6. The answer is 4164.

Answer = 4164

Hints and Tips

To understand better,
122×34 is the same as
$122 \times (30 + 4)$.
$122 \times 4 = 488$
$122 \times 30 = 3660$
So, $122 \times 34 = 488 + 3660$
$= 4148$

Multiplying by 2-digit Numbers

Without Carrying Forward

Example 6: 122×34

$$\begin{array}{r} 1\,2\,2 \\ \times 3\,4 \\ \hline {}^{1}4\,8\,8 \\ +{}^{1}3\,6\,6\,0 \\ \hline 4\,1\,4\,8 \\ \hline \end{array}$$

First multiply 122 by 4.

Put a 0 under 8 and then multiply 122 by 3.

Answer = 4148

Multiplying by 2 or More Digits With Carrying Forward

Example 7: 6293×52

$$\begin{array}{r} \text{①④①} \\ 6\,{}^{1}2\,9\,3 \\ \times 5\,2 \\ \hline 1\,{}^{1}2\,{}^{1}5\,8\,6 \\ +3\,1\,4\,6\,5\,0 \\ \hline 3\,2\,7\,2\,3\,6 \\ \hline \end{array}$$

We first multiply 6293 by 2 and write the carried forward number on top.

Next, we put a 0 under 6 and multiply 6293 by 5. The numbers carried forward this time are encircled and written on top of the previous ones to avoid confusion.

Then, we add to get the answer.

Answer = 3,27,236

Example 8: 1934×234

$$\begin{array}{r} \text{①}\quad\quad \\ \text{②①①} \\ {}^{3}1\,{}^{1}9\,{}^{1}3\,4 \\ \times 2\,3\,4 \\ \hline {}^{1}7\,7\,3\,6 \\ {}^{2}5\,8\,0\,2\,0 \\ +{}^{1}3\,8\,6\,8\,0\,0 \\ \hline 4\,5\,2\,5\,5\,6 \\ \hline \end{array}$$

We first multiply 1934 by 4.

Next, we put a 0 under 6 and multiply 1934 by 3.

Next, we put a 0 under 0 and 2 and multiply 1934 by 2, putting the numbers carried forward above the earlier ones every time. Then, we add to get the answer.

Answer = 4,52,556

Exercise 4.3

1. **Solve the following.**

a. 332×3 b. 593×5 c. 729×4 d. 692×7

e. 593×6 f. 829×3 g. 4290×2 h. 9324×3

i. 5389×5	j. 7736×5	k. 9267×9	l. 1429×7
m. 23432×3	n. 68293×7	o. 34621×3	p. 78321×8
q. 43294×6	r. 69346×9		

2 Solve the following.

a. 539×21	b. 429×36	c. 682×43	d. 535×27
e. 297×35	f. 229×49	g. 5329×23	h. 9329×76
i. 7295×42	j. 8321×87	k. 9329×24	l. 9326×65

3 Solve the following.

a. 216×212	b. 732×135	c. 1349×239
d. 6234×539	e. 6235×248	f. 7293×475

Words Problems on Multiplication

Word problems on multiplication are solved in the same manner as they were in the previous classes except, now, the numbers are bigger. When the value of 1 item is given and we have to find the value of more items, we multiply.

Example 9: If the cost of 1 pen is ₹20, what is the cost of 12 pens?

Cost of 1 pen = ₹20

Cost of 12 pens = 20 × 12

= 240

So, 12 pens will cost ₹240.

Note

In this question, we have to find the cost in rupees. So, the cost should be on the right side of our statements.

Example 10: 1 year is equal to 12 months. How many months are there in 135 years?

1 year = 12 months

135 years = 12 × 135 years

$$\begin{array}{r} 1\,{}^{1}3\,5 \\ \times\ 1\,2 \\ \hline {}^{1}2\,7\,0 \\ +1\,3\,5\,0 \\ \hline 1\,6\,2\,0 \\ \hline \end{array}$$

So, in 135 years, there are 1620 months.

> **Note**
> Before solving the question, we convert 5 years into months because the value given in the question is in months.

Example 11: A factory pays ₹60,000 as salaries every month. What is the total amount it pays in 5 years?

1 year = 12 months

So, 5 years = $12 \times 5 = 60$ months

Amount paid in 1 month = ₹60,000

Amount paid in 60 months

$= 60{,}000 \times 60 = 36{,}00{,}000$

So, in 5 years, the factory pays ₹36,00,000.

> **Note**
> Notice that in this statement we write 60 months. In the answer, we write 5 years as given in the question.

> **Note**
> February 2012 is a leap year because 2012 is divisible by 4. In a leap year, February has 29 days.

Example 12: An ice cream vendor sells 532 ice creams in a day. How many ice creams did he sell in February 2012?

Number of ice creams sold in 1 day = 532

Number of ice creams sold in 29 days = 532×29

$$\begin{array}{r} {}^{2}5\,{}^{1}3\,2 \\ \times\ 2\,9 \\ \hline {}^{1}4\,{}^{1}7\,8\,8 \\ +\,1\,0\,6\,4\,0 \\ \hline 1\,5\,4\,2\,8 \\ \hline \end{array}$$

So, in February 2012, the ice-cream vendor sold 15,428 ice creams.

Exercise 4.4

Solve the following word problems.

1. 1 week is equal to 7 days. How many days are there in 3 weeks?
2. 1 day is equal to 24 hours. How many hours are there in 5 days?
3. 1 minute is equal to 60 seconds. How many seconds are there in 9 minutes?
4. 1 hour is equal to 60 minutes. How many minutes are there in 4 hours?
5. 1 hour is equal to 3600 seconds. How many seconds are there in 3 hours?
6. What is the cost of 232 books if each book costs ₹150?
7. A school has 530 children. Each child makes 20 flags. How many flags have been made in the school?
8. A city has 432 buses. 40 people can sit in one bus. How many people can sit in all the buses at any given time?

Revision Exercise

1 Choose the correct options. Write the answer in the box provided.

a. 24 × 1000 =
i. 24 ii. 240 iii. 2400 iv. 24,000 ☐

b. 56 × 200 =
i. 200 ii. 11,200 iii. 112 iv. 1120 ☐

c. 569 × 7 =
i. 3983 ii. 3987 iii. 5697 iv. 3893 ☐

d. 8959 × 9 =
i. 80,630 ii. 80,631 iii. 80,361 iv. 80,163 ☐

e. 72395 × 5 =
i. 3,61,095 ii. 3,61,555 iii. 3,61,957 iv. 3,61,975 ☐

f. 6239 × 27 =
i. 1,68,435 ii. 1,68,453 iii. 1,68,543 iv. 1,29,645 ☐

g. How many minutes are there in 5 hours?
i. 60 minutes ii. 5 minutes iii. 300 minutes iv. 3600 minutes ☐

h. Each year 2645 children pass out of a school. How many children pass out of the school in 15 years? (Assume that all the children pass out.)
i. 39,625 ii. 39,765 iii. 39,655 iv. 39,675 ☐

i. 250 passengers can sit in one aeroplane. How many passengers can sit in 16 aeroplanes?
i. 2500 ii. 1600 iii. 4000 iv. 2516 ☐

j. The cost of 1 scooter is ₹2100. What will be the cost of 121 scooters?
i. ₹2,54,100 ii. ₹2,45,000 iii. ₹2,10,000 iv. ₹2,00,000 ☐

2 Fill in the blanks (Q2 to Q6).

a. 35 × 0 = ______ b. 0 × 789 = ______

3 a. 1 × 4693 = ______ b. 827 × 1 = ______

4 a. 39 × 10 = ______ b. 39 × 100 = ______
c. 39 × 1000 = ______ d. 39 × 10000 = ______

5 a. 12 × 19 = 19 × ______ b. 439 × 84 = ______ × 439

6 a. 342 × 3000 = ______ b. 293 × 400 = ______
c. 1234 × 500 = ______ d. 699 × 90 = ______

Multiply the following (Q7 to Q8).

7. 7829×35

8. 2568×126

9. In one town, there are 5,20,300 people. How many people are there in 3 such towns?

10. Ravi receives ₹350 per day as wage. How much does he receive in

    a. February 2003?
    b. February 2004?

11. A shopkeeper sells one mobile for ₹23,500. If he sells 320 mobiles in one month, how much money does he receive?

12. A bakery sells 253 loaves of bread every day. How many loaves of bread does it sell in the month of

    a. July?
    b. September?

13. 732 passengers can sit in one train. How many passengers can sit in 250 such trains?

14. Mr Ahmad has to pay ₹5720 a month to every person who works for him. What is the total he will have to pay in a month if 120 people work for him?

15. A cycle costs ₹13,490. What is the cost of 295 cycles?

16. Mr Khan earns ₹5600 a month. How much does he earn in a year?

17. An airline charges ₹293 per passenger. How much does the airline receive if there are 495 passengers?

18. One piece of land costs ₹73,250. Rajat wants to buy 173 pieces. How much does he need to pay?

19. For a school party, each child brought ₹150. Find the total amount collected if there were 290 children.

20. A man earns ₹6500 per month. How much does he earn in 3 years?

21. A movie hall has 43 rows of seats. Each row has 35 seats. How many seats are there in all?

Worksheet

1. **Fill in the blanks.**

a. i. $1679 \times 1 =$ ______ ii. $1679 \times 10 =$ ______

iii. $1679 \times 100 =$ ______ iv. $1679 \times 1000 =$ ______

b. i. $12 \times 56 =$ ______ ii. $120 \times 560 =$ ______

c. i. $24 \times 4 =$ ______ ii. $24 \times 40 =$ ______ iii. $24 \times 400 =$ ______

d. $112 \times 4000 =$ ______

e. $120459 \times 0 =$ ______

2. $0 \times 1679 =$ ____________

3. $1 \times 3251 =$ ____________

4. $73291 \times 0 =$ ____________

5. $84307 \times 1 =$ ____________

6. Class 7 went on a day trip by train to the seaside. 37 children and 5 adults went on the trip. How much did the trip cost in total?

Train Trip to the Seaside	
Adult (return)	₹525
Child(return)	₹225

₹____________

7. $85 \times 10 =$ ____________

8. $1694 \times 1000 =$ ____________

9. $7385 \times 10000 =$ ____________

10. $12 \times 20 =$ ____________

11. $15 \times 300 =$ ____________

12. $112 \times 4000 =$ ____________

13. $2321 \times 8 =$ ____________

14. 7 weeks = ____________ days

For the Curious Mind

For my birthday party, I bought 50 balloons at ₹5 per balloon, 51 streamers at ₹2 per streamer and 35 caps at ₹3 per cap. How much did I spend in all?

Division

5

Dividing 4-digit Numbers by 1-digit Numbers

We have learned to divide 4-digit numbers by 1-digit numbers in Class 3. Let us revise.

Example 1: $7312 \div 3$

Step 1

$$\begin{array}{r} 2 \\ 3\overline{)7312} \\ -6 \\ \hline 1 \end{array}$$

$3 \times 2 = 6$

$3 \times 3 = 9$

We use 6 since 9 is bigger than 7.
$7 - 6 = 1$

Step 2

$$\begin{array}{r} 24 \\ 3\overline{)7312} \\ -6 \\ \hline 13 \\ -12 \\ \hline 1 \end{array}$$

Bring down 3.

Now, we divide 13 by 3.

$3 \times 4 = 12$

$3 \times 5 = 15$

We use 12 since 15 is bigger than 13.
$13 - 12 = 1$

Step 3

$$\begin{array}{r} 243 \\ 3\overline{)7312} \\ -6 \\ \hline 13 \\ -12 \\ \hline 11 \\ -9 \\ \hline 2 \end{array}$$

Bring down 1.

Now, we divide 11 by 3.

$3 \times 3 = 9$

$3 \times 4 = 12$

We use 9 since 12 is bigger than 11.
$11 - 9 = 2$

Step 4

$$\begin{array}{r} 2437 \\ 3\overline{)7312} \\ -6 \\ \hline 13 \\ -12 \\ \hline 11 \\ -9 \\ \hline 22 \\ -21 \\ \hline 01 \end{array}$$

Bring down 2.

Now, we divide 22 by 3.

$3 \times 7 = 21$

$3 \times 8 = 24$

We use 21 since 24 is bigger than 22.

$22 - 21 = 1$

Remainder = 1

Answer: Quotient = 2437, Remainder = 1

Division when there is Zero in the Quotient

Now let us learn to divide numbers for which we need to put a 0 in the quotient. Look at the following example.

Example 2: 7515 ÷ 5

Step 1

$$\begin{array}{r} 1 \\ 5\overline{)7515} \\ -5 \\ \hline 2 \end{array}$$

$5 \times 1 = 5$

$5 \times 2 = 10$

We use 5 since 10 is bigger than 7.

$7 - 5 = 2$

Step 2

$$\begin{array}{r} 15 \\ 5\overline{)7515} \\ -5\downarrow \\ \hline 25 \\ -25 \\ \hline 00 \end{array}$$

Bring down 5.

$5 \times 5 = 25$

$25 - 25 = 0$

Step 3

$$\begin{array}{r} 150 \\ 5\overline{)7515} \\ -5\downarrow \\ \hline 25 \\ -25\downarrow \\ \hline 001 \end{array}$$

Bring down 1.

Since 1 is smaller than the divisor 5, we write a 0 next to 5 in the quotient.

Step 4

$$\begin{array}{r} 1503 \\ 5\overline{)7515} \\ -5\downarrow \\ \hline 25 \\ -25\downarrow\downarrow \\ \hline 0015 \\ -15 \\ \hline 0 \end{array}$$

Bring down 5.

$5 \times 3 = 15$

$15 - 15 = 0$

Remainder = 0

Answer = 1503

Division when the Dividend contains Zero

Let us learn to divide numbers which contain 0. Look at the following example.

Example 3: 2240 ÷ 4

Step 1

$$4\overline{)2240}$$

Since the first digit is too small to be divided by 4, we take 22 and divide it by 4.

Step 2

```
  05
4)2240
 -20
  2
```

$4 \times 5 = 20$

$4 \times 6 = 24$

We use 20 since 24 is bigger than 22.

$22 - 20 = 2$

Step 3

```
  056
4)2240
 -20↓
   24
  -24
   00
```

Bring down 4.

$4 \times 6 = 24$

$24 - 24 = 0$

Remember

When the number to be divided is smaller than the divisor, we write 0 in the quotient. In the final answer, the quotient is given as 560; not as 0560.

Step 4

```
  0560
4)2240
 -20↓
   24
  -24↓
   000
```

Bring down the next digit, that is, 0.

Since 000 is smaller than the divisor 4, we write 0 in the quotient next to 6.

Answer = 560

Exercise 5.1

1 Solve the following.

a. $6348 \div 2$ b. $2562 \div 3$ c. $2496 \div 8$ d. $2975 \div 7$

e. $2517 \div 4$ f. $9312 \div 5$ g. $7395 \div 2$ h. $1952 \div 6$

i. $5535 \div 5$ j. $4816 \div 4$ k. $1230 \div 6$ l. $1008 \div 2$

2 Solve the following.

a. $3056 \div 2$ b. $2502 \div 3$ c. $1407 \div 7$ d. $3074 \div 9$

e. $1705 \div 4$ f. $6840 \div 6$ g. $1680 \div 8$ h. $7200 \div 9$

i. $2000 \div 4$ j. $4002 \div 2$ k. $2506 \div 5$ l. $3009 \div 3$

Dividing 5-digit Numbers by 1-digit Numbers

Example 4: $68945 \div 5$

Step 1

```
  1
5)68945
 -5
  1
```

$5 \times 1 = 5$

$5 \times 2 = 10$

We use 5 since 10 is bigger than 6.

$6 - 5 = 1$

Step 2

```
    13
  ______
5)68945
 -5↓
  ---
  18
 -15
  ---
   3
```

Bring down 8.

$5 \times 3 = 15$

$5 \times 4 = 20$

We use 15 since 20 is bigger than 18.

$18 - 15 = 3$

Step 3

```
   137
  ______
5)68945
 -5↓ |
  ---|
  18 |
 -15 ↓
  ----
   39
  -35
   ---
    4
```

Bring down 9.

$5 \times 7 = 35$

$5 \times 8 = 40$

We use 35 since 40 is bigger than 39.

$39 - 35 = 4$

Step 4

```
   1378
  ______
5)68945
 -5↓ | |
  ---| |
  18 | |
 -15 ↓ |
  ---- |
   39  |
  -35  ↓
   -----
    44
    40
    ---
     4
```

Bring down 4.

$5 \times 8 = 40$

$5 \times 9 = 45$

We use 40 since 45 is bigger than 44.

$44 - 40 = 4$

Step 5

```
   13789
  ______
5)68945
 -5↓ | | |
  ---| | |
  18 | | |
 -15 ↓ | |
  ---- | |
   39  | |
  -35  ↓ |
   ----- |
    44   |
    40   ↓
    ------
     45
    -45
     ---
     00
```

Bring down 5.

$5 \times 9 = 45$

$45 - 45 = 0$

Remainder = 0

Answer = 13,789

Example 5: 34098 ÷ 7

Step 1

```
   0 4
 7)3 4 0 9 8
  -2 8
  ----
     6
```

Since 3 is smaller than 7, we divide 34 by 7.

$7 \times 4 = 28$

$7 \times 5 = 35$

We use 28 since 35 is bigger than 34.

$34 - 28 = 6$

Step 2

```
   0 4 8
 7)3 4 0 9 8
  -2 8↓
  ------
     6 0
    -5 6
    ----
       4
```

Bring down 0.

$7 \times 8 = 56$

$7 \times 9 = 63$

We use 56 since 63 is bigger than 60.

$60 - 56 = 4$

Step 3

```
   0 4 8 7
 7)3 4 0 9 8
  -2 8↓ |
  ------|
     6 0|
    -5 6↓
    ------
       4 9
      -4 9
      ----
       0 0
```

Bring down 9.

$7 \times 7 = 49$

$49 - 49 = 0$

Step 4

```
   0 4 8 7 1
 7)3 4 0 9 8
  -2 8↓ | |
  ------| |
     6 0| |
    -5 6↓ |
    ------|
       4 9|
      -4 9↓
      ------
       0 0 8
          -7
          --
           1
```

Bring down 8.

$7 \times 1 = 7$

$7 \times 2 = 14$

We use 7 since 14 is bigger than 8.

Remainder = 1

Answer: Quotient = 4871, Remainder = 1

Example 6: 10029 ÷ 4

Step 1

```
   0 2
 4)1 0 0 2 9
   -8
   --
    2
```

Since 1 is smaller than 4, we divide 10 by 4.

$4 \times 2 = 8$

$4 \times 3 = 12$

We use 8 since 12 is bigger than 10.

$10 - 8 = 2$

Step 2

```
   025
4)10029
  -8↓
  ----
   20
  -20
  ----
   00
```

Bring down 0.

$4 \times 5 = 20$

$20 - 20 = 0$

Step 3

```
   0250
4)10029
  -8↓ ||
  ----||
   20 ||
  -20 ↓↓
  ------
   0029
```

Bring down 2.

2 is smaller than the divisor 4. So, we write 0 next to 5 in the quotient and bring down 9.

Step 4

```
   02507
4)10029
  -8↓ ||
  ----||
   20 ||
  -20 ↓↓
  ------
   0029
    -28
    ---
      1
```

Now, we divide 29 by 4.

$4 \times 7 = 28$

$4 \times 8 = 32$

We use 28 since 32 is bigger than 29.

$29 - 28 = 1$

Remainder = 1

Answer: Quotient = 2507, Remainder = 1

Exercise 5.2

Solve the following.

1. $48628 \div 2$
2. $34234 \div 3$
3. $45345 \div 4$
4. $71600 \div 5$
5. $14940 \div 6$
6. $17925 \div 7$
7. $14724 \div 3$
8. $14058 \div 2$
9. $41532 \div 5$
10. $57649 \div 6$
11. $24892 \div 2$
12. $12186 \div 6$
13. $10006 \div 5$
14. $11225 \div 9$
15. $45678 \div 4$
16. $74936 \div 7$

Dividing 3-digit and 4-digit Numbers by Multiples of 10

Now let us learn to divide 3-digit and 4-digit numbers by 2-digit numbers ending with 0. Look at the following examples.

Note

Short Method

$10\,\big|\,4\,7\,\big|\,0$

Draw a line after 1 digit from the right side since 10 has only 1 zero. The number on the left of the line, that is, 47 is the quotient and that on the right, that is, 0 is the remainder.

Example 7: 470 ÷ 10

Long Method

$$\begin{array}{r} 47 \\ 10\overline{)470} \\ -40\downarrow \\ \hline 070 \\ 70 \\ \hline 00 \end{array}$$

Answer = Quotient = 47, Remainder = 0

Note

Short Method

$10\,\big|\,5\,8\,\big|\,3$

Example 8: 583 ÷ 10

Long Method

$$\begin{array}{r} 58 \\ 10\overline{)583} \\ -50\downarrow \\ \hline 83 \\ -80 \\ \hline 3 \end{array}$$

Answer = Quotient = 58, Remainder = 3

Example 9: 560 ÷ 70

$$\begin{array}{r} 008 \\ 70\overline{)560} \\ -560 \\ \hline 000 \end{array}$$

Since 5 and 56 are smaller than 70, we divide 560 by 70.

$$\begin{array}{r} 70 \\ \times 5 \\ \hline 350 \\ \hline \end{array} \qquad \begin{array}{r} 70 \\ \times 6 \\ \hline 420 \\ \hline \end{array} \qquad \begin{array}{r} 70 \\ \times 7 \\ \hline 490 \\ \hline \end{array} \qquad \begin{array}{r} 70 \\ \times 8 \\ \hline 560 \\ \hline \end{array}$$

Answer = 8

Example 10: 9730 ÷ 50

$$\begin{array}{r} 01 \\ 50\overline{)9730} \\ -50 \\ \hline 47 \end{array}$$

Since 9 is smaller than 50, we divide 97 by 50.

$$\begin{array}{r} 50 \\ \times 5 \\ \hline 250 \\ \hline \end{array} \qquad \begin{array}{r} 50 \\ \times 4 \\ \hline 200 \\ \hline \end{array} \qquad \begin{array}{r} 50 \\ \times 3 \\ \hline 150 \\ \hline \end{array} \qquad \begin{array}{r} 50 \\ \times 2 \\ \hline 100 \\ \hline \end{array} \qquad \begin{array}{r} 50 \\ \times 1 \\ \hline 50 \\ \hline \end{array}$$

Since 100 is bigger than 97, we use 50.
97 – 50 = 47

$$\begin{array}{r} 1 \\ 50\overline{)9730} \\ -50\downarrow \\ \hline 473 \end{array}$$

Bring down 3.
Since 473 is bigger than 50 × 5 = 250,
we try 50 × 6.

19
50)9730
−50
473
−450
23

$50 \times 6 = 300$

$50 \times 7 = 350$

$50 \times 8 = 400$

$50 \times 9 = 450$

$50 \times 10 = 500$

Since 500 is bigger than 473, we use $50 \times 9 = 450$.

$473 - 450 = 23$

Remainder = 23

194
50)9730
−50
473
450
230
200
30

Bring down 0

Since 250 is bigger than 230, we use $50 \times 4 = 200$.

$230 - 200 = 30$

Remainder = 30

Answer = Quotient = 154, Remainder = 30

Exercise 5.3

Divide the following.

a. without remainders.

i. $90 \div 10$	ii. $270 \div 10$	iii. $270 \div 30$	iv. $320 \div 40$
v. $640 \div 80$	vi. $810 \div 90$	vii. $6000 \div 30$	viii. $8000 \div 20$

b. with remainders.

i. $35 \div 10$	ii. $389 \div 10$	iii. $479 \div 40$	iv. $379 \div 20$
v. $1296 \div 50$	vi. $2057 \div 20$	vii. $3091 \div 30$	viii. $4078 \div 40$

Dividing 3-digit and 4-digit Numbers by 2-digit Numbers

When we divide a number by a 2-digit number whose table we do not know, we may have to multiply to get the answers.

Example 11: $483 \div 23$

23)483

4 is smaller than 23. So we will take 48 to divide by 23.

First multiply 23 by 5.

$^{1}23$
$\times 5$
115

$$\begin{array}{r} 0\,2 \\ 23\overline{)4\,8\,3} \\ -4\,6 \\ \hline 2 \end{array}$$

115 is bigger than 48, so we have to multiply 23 with a number smaller than 5.

$$\begin{array}{r} ^{1}2\,3 \\ \times 4 \\ \hline 9\,2 \\ \hline \end{array} \qquad \begin{array}{r} 2\,3 \\ \times 3 \\ \hline 6\,9 \\ \hline \end{array} \qquad \begin{array}{r} 2\,3 \\ \times 2 \\ \hline 4\,6 \\ \hline \end{array}$$

We use $23 \times 2 = 46$ since $23 \times 3 = 69$ is bigger than 48.

$48 - 46 = 2$

$$\begin{array}{r} 0\,2\,1 \\ 23\overline{)4\,8\,3} \\ -4\,6\downarrow \\ \hline 2\,3 \\ -2\,3 \\ \hline 0\,0 \end{array}$$

Bring down 3.

$23 \times 1 = 23$

$23 - 23 = 0$

Remainder = 0

Answer = 21

Example 12: 920 ÷ 46

$$\begin{array}{r} 0 \\ 46\overline{)9\,2\,0} \end{array}$$

9 is smaller than 46, so we take 92 to divide by 46.

$$\begin{array}{r} ^{3}4\,6 \\ \times 5 \\ \hline 2\,3\,0 \\ \hline \end{array}$$

230 is bigger than 92, so we multiply 46 with numbers smaller than 5.

$$\begin{array}{r} 0\,2 \\ 46\overline{)9\,2\,0} \\ 9\,2\downarrow \\ \hline 0\,0 \end{array}$$

$$\begin{array}{r} ^{2}4\,6 \\ \times 4 \\ \hline 1\,8\,4 \\ \hline \end{array} \qquad \begin{array}{r} ^{1}4\,6 \\ \times 3 \\ \hline 1\,3\,8 \\ \hline \end{array} \qquad \begin{array}{r} ^{1}4\,6 \\ \times 2 \\ \hline 9\,2 \\ \hline \end{array}$$

$$\begin{array}{r} 0\,2\,0 \\ 46\overline{)9\,2\,0} \\ 9\,2\downarrow \\ \hline 0\,0\,0 \end{array}$$

Bring down 0.

Since 000 is smaller than 46, we write 0 in the quotient next to 2.

Remainder = 0

Answer = 20

Example 13: 9828 ÷ 52

$$\begin{array}{r} 0\,1 \\ 52\overline{)9\,8\,2\,8} \\ -5\,2 \\ \hline 4\,6 \end{array}$$

Since 9 is smaller than 52, we divide 98 by 52.

$$\begin{array}{r} ^{1}5\,2 \\ \times 5 \\ \hline 2\,6\,0 \\ \hline \end{array} \qquad \begin{array}{r} 5\,2 \\ \times 4 \\ \hline 2\,0\,8 \\ \hline \end{array} \qquad \begin{array}{r} 5\,2 \\ \times 3 \\ \hline 1\,5\,6 \\ \hline \end{array} \qquad \begin{array}{r} 5\,2 \\ \times 2 \\ \hline 1\,0\,4 \\ \hline \end{array} \qquad \begin{array}{r} 5\,2 \\ \times 1 \\ \hline 5\,2 \\ \hline \end{array}$$

$$\begin{array}{r} 0\,1 \\ 52\overline{)9\,8\,2\,8} \\ -5\,2\downarrow \\ \hline 4\,6\,2 \end{array}$$

We use 52.

$98 - 52 = 46$

$$\begin{array}{r} 018 \\ 52\overline{)9828} \\ -52\downarrow \\ \hline 462 \\ 416 \\ \hline 46 \end{array}$$

Bring down 2.

$\begin{array}{r} {}^{1}52 \\ \times 6 \\ \hline 312 \\ \hline \end{array}$ $\begin{array}{r} {}^{1}52 \\ \times 7 \\ \hline 364 \\ \hline \end{array}$ $\begin{array}{r} {}^{1}52 \\ \times 8 \\ \hline 416 \\ \hline \end{array}$ $\begin{array}{r} {}^{1}52 \\ \times 9 \\ \hline 468 \\ \hline \end{array}$

We use 416.

462 – 416 = 46

$$\begin{array}{r} 0189 \\ 52\overline{)9828} \\ -52\downarrow\,\, \\ \hline 462\,\, \\ 416\downarrow \\ \hline 468 \\ 468 \\ \hline 000 \end{array}$$

Bring down 8.

Now, we use 468.

468 – 468 = 0

Remainder = 0

Answer = 189

Example 14: 5481 ÷ 27

$$27\overline{)5481}$$

$\begin{array}{r} {}^{3}27 \\ \times 5 \\ \hline 135 \\ \hline \end{array}$ $\begin{array}{r} {}^{2}27 \\ \times 4 \\ \hline 108 \\ \hline \end{array}$ $\begin{array}{r} {}^{2}27 \\ \times 3 \\ \hline 81 \\ \hline \end{array}$ $\begin{array}{r} {}^{1}27 \\ \times 2 \\ \hline 54 \\ \hline \end{array}$

$$\begin{array}{r} 02\,\,\,\, \\ 27\overline{)5481} \\ -54\,\,\,\, \\ \hline 00\,\,\,\, \end{array}$$

We use 27 × 2 = 54.

54 – 54 = 0

$$\begin{array}{r} 02\,\,\,\, \\ 27\overline{)5481} \\ -54\downarrow\,\, \\ \hline 008\,\, \end{array}$$

Bring down 8.

$$\begin{array}{r} 020\,\, \\ 27\overline{)5481} \\ -54\downarrow\downarrow \\ \hline 0081 \end{array}$$

Since 8 is smaller than 27, we write 0 in the quotient next to 2 and bring down 1.

$$\begin{array}{r} 0203 \\ 27\overline{)5481} \\ -54\downarrow\downarrow \\ \hline 0081 \\ -81 \\ \hline 00 \end{array}$$

Now, we use 81.

81 – 81 = 0

Remainder = 0

Answer = 203

Exercise 5.4

Divide the following.

1. Without remainders.

a. 432 by 12	b. 368 by 16	c. 888 by 24	d. 700 by 25
e. 1728 by 36	f. 2520 by 72	g. 1545 by 15	h. 5436 by 18
i. 6741 by 63	j. 8820 by 84	k. 4284 by 42	l. 2613 by 13

2. With remainders.

a. 739 by 16	b. 569 by 24	c. 834 by 32	d. 459 by 75
e. 1400 by 42	f. 1327 by 53	g. 1280 by 15	h. 3719 by 64
i. 1939 by 19	j. 7109 by 35	k. 6982 by 12	l. 4009 by 45

Word Problems on Division

Word problems on division are solved in the same manner as studied in the previous class except, now, the numbers are larger.

Remember

1. When the value of many items is given and we have to find the value of 1 item, we divide.
2. Whenever we distribute something, we divide.
3. The value of the item which we have to find must always be on the right side.
4. It is important to write short statements.
5. The answer to word problems must always be written in the statement form.

Example 15: 6 books cost ₹4680. What is the cost of 1 book?

Note

In this question, we have to find the cost. So, the cost should be on the right side in our statements.

Cost of 6 books = ₹4680

Cost of 1 book = 4680 ÷ 6

```
    780
 6)4680
   42↓
    48
    48↓
     00
```

The cost of 1 book is ₹780.

Example 16: 827 chocolates are to be distributed equally among 15 children. How many chocolates will each child get? And, how many chocolates will be left?

Number of chocolates = 827

Number of children = 15

Number of chocolates each child will get = 827 ÷ 15

```
     55 ⟶ This is what each child will get.
15)827
  −75↓
    77
    75
     2 ⟶ The remainder is always what is left.
```

Each child will get 55 chocolates and 2 chocolates will be left.

Example 17: ₹6750 are to be distributed equally among 25 families. How much will each family get?

Amount to be distributed = ₹6750

Number of families = 25

Amount each family will get = 6750 ÷ 25

```
     270
25)6750
  −50↓
    175
    175
   0000
```

Each family will get ₹270.

Example 18: What is the least number of packets required if we have to pack 242 potatoes if each packet can contain 10 potatoes?

Number of potatoes = 242

Number of potatoes in 1 packet = 10

Number of packets required = 242 ÷ 10

```
     24
10)242
  −20↓
    42
   −40
     2
```

The above division shows that we need 24 packets. But there are still 2 potatoes (remainder) left.

Since the question wants the least number of packets required, we will add 1 more packet (for the remaining 2 potatoes) to the 24 packets.

24 + 1 = 25

So, the least number of packets required is 25.

Hints and Tips

In such questions, remember to give the answers properly. Writing the answer just as quotient and remainder will not be enough.

Exercise 5.5

1. 648 mango saplings are to be planted with 36 saplings in each row. How many rows would be planted?

2. 1288 sweets were to be distributed equally among 23 children. How many sweets did each child get?

3. A bus can accommodate 42 people. How many buses do we need for 2730 people?

4. Rose has ₹241. She buys books at ₹53 each. How many books does she buy and how much money is left with her?

5. 2349 gallons of water was filled in buckets. Each bucket contained 52 gallons of water. How many buckets were filled and how much water was left?

6. What is the least number of bags required to store 1695 kg rice if each bag can store 25 kg rice?

7. What is the least number of houses needed to accommodate 2345 people if 7 people can be accommodated in each house?

8. A box weighs 50 g. How many such boxes would weigh 1600 g?

9. A school is arranging to screen a show of Walt Disney characters. If the school wants to raise an amount of ₹1,500 from 50 students, how much should each ticket cost?

10. Based on the above question, if the number of students is the same in each class, how much money will be collected from 10 classes?

Revision Exercise

1. **Choose the correct options.**

   a. 0 ÷ 95 =

   i. 95 ii. 1 iii. 0 iv. 950 ☐

   b. 638 ÷ 1 =

   i. 1 ii. 638 iii. 0 iv. 6381 ☐

   c. 1368 ÷ 3 =

   i. 456 ii. 3 iii. 1368 iv. 1386 ☐

   d. 16994 ÷ 2 =

   i. 8497 ii. 8400 iii. 8456 iv. 8499 ☐

   e. 8240 ÷ 35

   i. Q = 25, R = 18 ii. Q = 23, R = 10 iii. Q = 235, R = 15 iv. Q = 25, R = 0 ☐

   f. 6749 ÷ 10

   i. Q = 6749, R = 9 ii. Q = 674, R = 9 iii. Q = 6 , R = 0 iv. Q = 67, R = 9 ☐

   g. 3908 ÷ 36

   i. Q = 18, R =20 ii. Q = 180, R = 0 iii. Q = 108, R = 20 iv. Q = 108, R = 18 ☐

   h. 5683 ÷ 20

   i. Q = 284, R = 8 ii. Q = 28, R = 7 iii. Q = 284, R = 0 iv. Q = 284, R = 3 ☐

2. 5200 books were distributed among 40 children. How many books did each child get?

3. 523 litres of juice is to be distributed equally among 92 children. How many litres of juice will each child get and how many litres will be left?

4. What is the least number of boxes required to keep 1684 pencils if each box can contain 35 pencils?

5. What is the least number of bags required to store 105 kg of wheat if each bag contains 10 kg?

Worksheet

1 Fill in the blanks.

a. The sign for division is ______________.

b. In the given division,

$$\begin{array}{r} 5 \\ 2\overline{)10} \\ -10 \\ \hline 0 \end{array}$$

the dividend = ______________

the divisor = ______________

the quotient = ______________

the remainder = ______________

c. Divisor × Quotient + Remainder = ______________.

2 a. $0 \div 35$ b. $187 \div 1$

3 If $15 \times 29 = 435$,

then $435 \div 15 =$ ______________ and $435 \div 29 =$ ______________.

4 a. When the value of many items is given and we have to find the value of ______________ item, we divide.

b. Whenever we distribute something, we ______________.

For the Curious Mind

Divide 1000 sweets among 4 boxes.

Each box will contain ______ sweets.

Divide each box into 5 packets.

Each packet will contain ______ sweets.

Divide each packet among 4 children.

Each child will get ______ sweets and ______ sweets will be left over.

Factors and Multiples 6

Divisibility

When we divide one number by another and the remainder is zero, we say that the first number is divisible by the second number.

There are certain rules to find out whether a number is completely divisible by another number or not. Let us study these rules.

Divisibility by 2

A number is divisible by 2 if its last digit is 0, 2, 4, 6 or 8.

The number 29,46,892 is divisible by 2 because the last digit is 2.

The number 8,32,948 is divisible by 2 because the last digit is 8.

Similarly, 5,94,397 is not divisible by 2 because the last digit is 7.

Divisibility by 5

A number is divisible by 5 if its last digit is 0 or 5.

The number 32,94,685 is divisible by 5 because the last digit is 5.

The number 32,94,680 is divisible by 5 because the last digit is 0.

Similarly, 32,94,684 is not divisible by 5 because the last digit is neither 0 nor 5.

Note

A number divisible by 10 will always be divisible by 2 and 5.

Divisibility by 10

A number is divisible by 10 if its last digit is 0.

The number 53,29,480 is divisible by 10 because the last digit is 0.

The number 53,29,481 is not divisible by 10 because the last digit is not 0.

Try These!

Is the number 13790 divisible by 2, 5 and 10?

By 2: __________

By 5: __________

By 10: __________

Exercise 6.1

1. **Find out if the following numbers are divisible by 2 or not.**

   a. 432 b. 9683 c. 5,94,320 d. 6,84,967

   e. 1,88,931 f. 6,84,986 g. 2,49,695 h. 3,49,684

2. **Find out if the following numbers are divisible by 5 or not.**

   a. 6,94,380 b. 9,32,985 c. 1,69,248 d. 7,32,986

   e. 9,96,890 f. 3,39,345 g. 18,830 h. 68,394

3. **Find out if the following numbers are divisible by 10 or not.**

   a. 63,294 b. 18,250 c. 66,345 d. 93,250

   e. 78,945 f. 3,24,905 g. 2,93,400 h. 7880

Divisibility by 3

A number is divisible by 3 if the sum of its digits is divisible by 3.

3,49,218 → 3 + 4 + 9 + 2 + 1 + 8 = 27

Since 27 is divisible by 3, the number is divisible by 3.

3,49,219 → 3 + 4 + 9 + 2 + 1 + 9 = 28

Since 28 is not divisible by 3, the number is not divisible by 3.

Divisibility by 9

A number is divisible by 9 if the sum of its digits is divisible by 9.

2,34,927 → 2 + 3 + 4 + 9 + 2 + 7 = 27

2,34,927 is divisible by 9 because the sum of its digits is divisible by 9.

2,34,928 → 2 + 3 + 4 + 9 + 2 + 8 = 28

2,34,928 is not divisible by 9 because the sum of its digits is not divisible by 9.

Note

A number divisible by 9 will always be divisible by 3.

Divisibility by 4

A number is divisible by 4 if the number formed by its last two digits is divisible by 4.

62,94,348 is divisible by 4 because 48, that is, the number formed by the last two digits is divisible by 4.

62,94,346 is not divisible by 4 because 46, that is, the number formed by the last two digits is not divisible by 4.

Note

A number divisible by 4 will always be divisible by 2.

Divisibility by 8

A number is divisible by 8 if the number formed by its last three digits is divisible by 8.

Example 1: Is 4,32,168 divisible by 8?

```
   21
8)168
 -16
 ---
   08
  - 8
 ---
    0
```

Since the number formed by the last three digits of 4,32,168, that is, 168 is divisible by 8, the number is also divisible by 8.

Note

A number divisible by 8 will always be divisible by 4 and 2.

Example 2: Is 4,32,518 divisible by 8?

```
   64
8)518
 -48
 ---
   38
  -32
 ---
    4
```

Since the last three digits of 4,32,518, that is, 518 is not divisible by 8, the number is also not divisible by 8.

Divisibility by 6

A number is divisible by 6 if it is divisible by both 2 and 3. So, we check its divisibility first by 2 and then by 3.

Example 3: Is 43,296 divisible by 6?

Checking divisibility by 2: it is divisible by 2 because the last digit is 6.

Checking divisibility by 3: 4 + 3 + 2 + 9 + 6 = 24

It is divisible by 3 because the sum of its digits is 24 which is divisible by 3.

Note

A number divisible by 6 will always be divisible by 2 and 3.

So, 43,296 is divisible by 6.

Example 4: Is 43,298 divisible by 6?

Checking divisibility by 2: it is divisible by 2 because the last digit is 8.

Checking divisibility by 3: 4 + 3 + 2 + 9 + 8 = 26

It is not divisible by 3 because the sum of the digits, that is, 26 is not divisible by 3.

So, 43,298 is not divisible by 6 because it is divisible by 2 but not by 3.

Example 5: Is 43,297 divisible by 6?

Checking divisibility by 2: It is not divisible by 2 because the last digit is 7.

Since it is not divisible by 2, we need not check its divisibility by 3 because to be divisible by 6, the number should be divisible by both 2 and 3.

So, 43,297 is not divisible by 6.

Exercise 6.2

1. **Find out if the following numbers are divisible by 3 or not (show the working).**

a. 3,94,296	b. 5,32,961	c. 6,82,468	d. 5,39,217
e. 7,89,231	f. 52,938	g. 68,934	h. 23,492

2. **Find out if the following numbers are divisible by 9 or not (show the working).**

a. 23,482	b. 53,298	c. 13,248	d. 43,296
e. 16,293	f. 62,943	g. 11,133	h. 29,345

3. **Find out if the following numbers are divisible by 4 or not.**

a. 6,29,426	b. 5,39,244	c. 1,62,349	d. 6,89,384
e. 9,39,467	f. 1,68,396	g. 3,52,955	h. 6,89,304

4. **Find out if the following numbers are divisible by 8 or not.**

a. 6,39,816	b. 2,94,244	c. 18,896	d. 23,493
e. 83,29,888	f. 1,62,982	g. 9,32,444	h. 52,938

5. **Find out if the following numbers are divisible by 6 or not (show the working).**

a. 68,439	b. 68,436	c. 18,349	d. 34,572
e. 1,69,813	f. 6,392	g. 16,934	h. 64,296

Even Numbers and Odd Numbers

An even number is a number that is completely divisible by 2. Even numbers will always have 2,4,6,8 or 0 in their ones place.

A number that is not completely divisible by 2 is an odd number. Odd numbers will always have 1,3,5, 7 or 9 in their ones place.

To find out if a number is even or odd, we can check its divisibility by 2.

Given below is a list of some even and odd numbers.

Even numbers	Odd numbers
0	1
2	3
4	5
6	7
8	9
10	11

Example 6: Is 14 an even number?

Since 14 is divisible by 2, it is an even number.

Example 7: Is 93,487 an even or an odd number?

Checking its divisibility by 2, we find that 93,487 is not completely divisible by 2 (since the last digit is 7).

Thus, 93,487 is an odd number.

Factors

A number *a* is said to be a factor of another number *b* if it divides the number *b* completely. If 'b' is completely divisible by 'a', then we say 'a' is a factor of 'b' or 'a' divides 'b'.

For example, 3 is a factor of 12 as it divides 12 completely. But, 3 is not a factor of 11 as it does not divide 11 completely.

Example 8: Is 3 a factor of 18?

$$\begin{array}{r} 6 \\ 3\overline{)18} \\ -18 \\ \hline 0 \end{array}$$

3 divides 18 completely as the remainder is 0.

So, 3 is a factor of 18.

Finding Factors of a Number

Factors of 18

To find the factors of 18, we will follow the steps given below.

1×18
2×9
3×6 → Pair of statements
6×3 ← We stop here.
9×2
18×1

Step 1: Start writing the multiplication facts for the given number as shown.

Step 2: Stop at that point when the factors are the same, but in the reverse order, that is, $3 \times 6 = 18$ and $6 \times 3 = 18$.

Step 3: For all the remaining statements, reverse the order of the factors above this pair of factors and write them.

Factors of 24

$1 \times 24 = 24$
$2 \times 12 = 24$
$3 \times 8 = 24$
$4 \times 6 = 24$
$6 \times 4 = 24$ ← We stop here as the factors are same as the above statement but in reverse order
$8 \times 3 = 24$
$12 \times 2 = 24$
$24 \times 1 = 24$

The factors of 24 are 1, 2, 3, 4, 6, 8, 12 and 24.

Factors of 9

$1 \times 9 = 9$ $\quad$ $3 \times 3 = 9$

Since 3 is written twice at this point, we treat it as the point where the digits are interchanged. So, we will write the statements below this point by reversing the digits.

Note

1 is a factor of every number because every number can be divided by 1.

Thus, this will be written as:

$$1 \times 9 = 9$$
$$3 \times 3 = 9$$
$$9 \times 1 = 9$$

The factors of 9 are 1, 3 and 9.

Exercise 6.3

1. **In the following numbers, circle the even numbers and tick the odd numbers.**
   0, 9, 14, 290, 147, 635, 6752, 9384, 139, 2340, 6843
2. **Use the divisibility rules, wherever you can, to solve the questions.**
   a. Is 9 a factor of 504? b. Is 6 a factor of 237?
   c. Is 12 a factor of 240? d. Is 35 a factor of 560?
   e. Is 2 a factor of 63,290? f. Is 5 a factor of 23,490?
   g. Is 8 a factor of 53,244?
3. **Write all the factors of the following numbers.**
   a. 12 b. 18 c. 24 d. 28 e. 30 f. 32 g. 42 h. 48
   i. 60 j. 9 k. 16 l. 25 m. 36 n. 3 o. 17 p. 13

Prime Numbers and Composite Numbers

Prime Numbers

Prime numbers are numbers that have only two factors – 1 and the number itself.

Prime numbers cannot be completely divided by numbers smaller than themselves except 1.

Examples: 2, 3, 5, 7, 11, 13, 17, 19, 23 and so on.

Notice that none of these numbers can be completely divided by a number smaller than itself except 1.

Composite Numbers

Composite numbers are numbers that have more than two factors. It has factors other than 1 and the number itself.

Given below is a chart of some prime numbers and composite numbers.

Prime numbers	Composite numbers
2	4
3	6
5	8
7	9
11	10
13	12
17	14
19	15
23	16
29	18

Examples: 4 can be divided by 2; 6 can be divided by 2 and 3; 8 can be divided by 2 and 4. Therefore, 4, 6 and 8 are composite numbers.

Except 1, the numbers that are not prime numbers are composite numbers.

Note

1 is neither a prime number nor a composite number. 1 is a unique number.

Exercise 6.4

1. **Write the prime numbers and the composite numbers from 1 to 30.**
2. **State whether the following statements are true or false.**
   a. 1 is a prime number.
   b. 1 is a composite number.
   c. 1 is a unique number.
   d. 23 is a prime number.
   e. 42 is a composite number.
   f. 12 is a prime number.
   g. 37 is a composite number.
3. a. Write prime numbers from 30 to 50.
   b. Write composite numbers from 30 to 50.

Prime Factors

The factors that are prime numbers are known as prime factors.

For example, factors of 24 are 1, 2, 3, 4, 6, 12 and 24. Among these, 2 and 3 are prime factors.

Prime Factorisation

Prime factorisation refers to the method of expressing numbers as a product of prime numbers.

For example, $24 = 2 \times 2 \times 2 \times 3$. Here, all the factors are prime numbers. Mentioned below are two methods of prime factorisation.

Division Method

In division method, we start by dividing the number by the smallest prime number, that is, 2. If the number is not divisible by 2, then we divide it by the next prime number, that is, 3 and so on. We go on like this until the dividend becomes 1.

Example 9: Find the prime factors of 24.

Step 1: Divide 24 by 2. Write the quotient under the dividend.

2	24
	12

Step 2: 12 is the new dividend. Divide it by 2 again.

2	24
2	12
	6

Step 3: Divide 6 by 2.

2	24
2	12
2	6
	3

Step 4: 3 is not completely divisible by 2. So, divide it by the next prime number, that is, 3.

2	24
2	12
2	6
3	3
	1

We stop after step 4 as the new dividend is 1.

Therefore, prime factorisation of 24 = $2 \times 2 \times 2 \times 3$.

Example 10: Find the prime factors of 12 using the division method.

2	12
2	6
3	3
	1

So, prime factorisation of 12 = $2 \times 2 \times 3$.

Factor Tree Method

In this method, factorisation is represented pictorially, which resembles the shape of an inverted tree.

Let us learn about it through an example. Follow the steps given below to find the prime factors of 24 using the factor tree method.

Step 1: Write 24 as a product of any two numbers, say, 24 = 4×6.

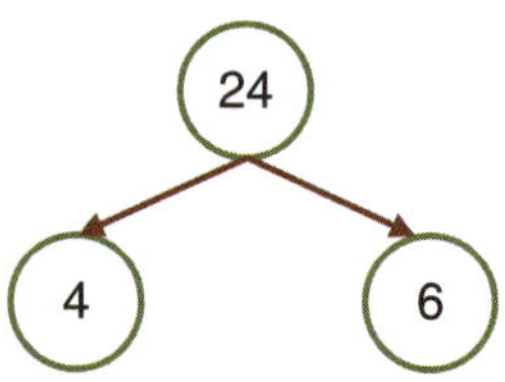

Step 2: Now, take one of the numbers, say, 4, and factorise it further.

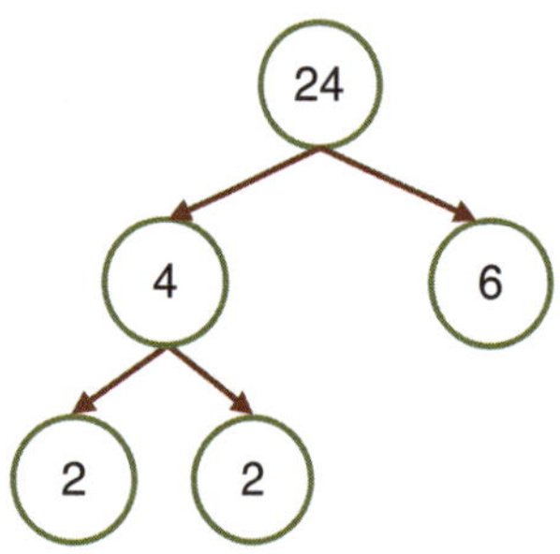

Step 3: Now, factorise 6.

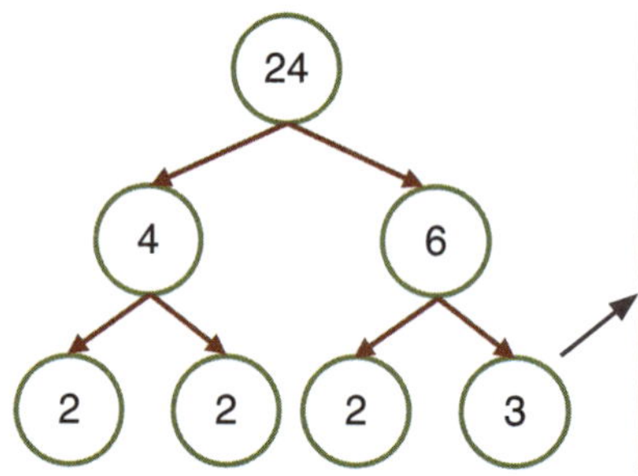

We stop at the point where all the factors are prime numbers.

These numbers are the prime factors of 24.

Therefore, prime factorisation of 24 = $2 \times 2 \times 2 \times 3$.

Exercise 6.5

Find the prime factors and write the prime factorisation of the following numbers.

1. 6
2. 10
3. 12
4. 18
5. 20
6. 24
7. 30
8. 36
9. 42
10. 48
11. 52
12. 60

Multiples

Radha puts some balloons along a wall for her birthday party. She makes sure that every second balloon is a red balloon. Given below are the balloons she puts.

Every second balloon is a red balloon and from the left side, they are the 2nd, 4th, 6th, 8th and 10th balloons, which are the multiples of 2.

A number *c* is said to be a multiple of another number *d* if *d* divides *c* completely. For example, 12 is a multiple of 2 as 2 divides 12 exactly.

We get the multiples of 2 by multiplying it by 1, 2, 3, 4, 5 and so on.

		×1	×2	×3	×4	×5	×6
Hence, the multiples of 2	=	2,	4,	6,	8,	10,	12, ...

In the same way, we can find the multiples of 3.

		×1	×2	×3	×4	×5	×6
Multiples of 3	=	3,	6,	9,	12,	15,	18, ...

Using this method, we can find multiples of any number.

		×1	×2	×3	×4	×5	×6
Multiples of 1	=	1 ,	2 ,	3 ,	4 ,	5 ,	6, ...
Multiples of 2	=	2 ,	4 ,	6 ,	8 ,	10 ,	12, ...
Multiples of 3	=	3 ,	6 ,	9 ,	12 ,	15 ,	18, ...
Multiples of 4	=	4 ,	8 ,	12 ,	16 ,	20 ,	24, ...
Multiples of 5	=	5 ,	10 ,	15 ,	20 ,	25 ,	30, ...
Multiples of 6	=	6 ,	12 ,	18 ,	24 ,	30 ,	36, ...

Note

1. Multiples are the products in the table of every number.
2. Every number is a multiple of itself.
3. Every number is a multiple of 1.
4. Multiples carry on endlessly.

Multiples on the Number Line

The multiples of 2 are shown on the number line below.

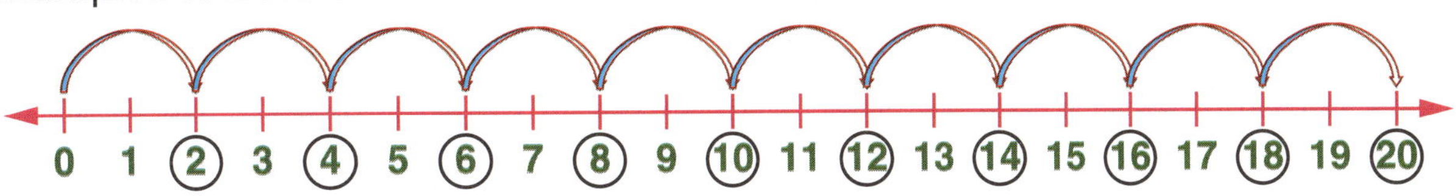

The multiples of 3 are shown on the number line below.

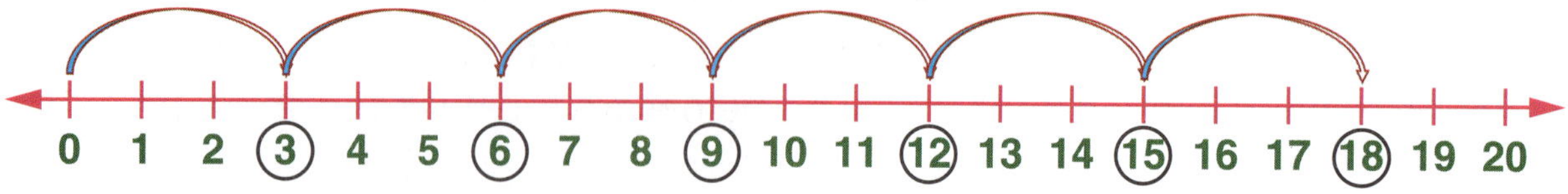

We find that the multiple of a number is always the product of factors in the table of that number.

Example 11:

$2 \times 3 = 6$

2 → factor, 3 → factor, 6 → multiple

6 is a multiple of 2 and 3.

2 is a factor of 6.

3 is a factor of 6.

Example 12:

$4 \times 5 = 20$

4 → factor, 5 → factor, 20 → multiple

20 is a multiple of 4 and 5.

4 is a factor of 20.

5 is a factor of 20.

If on dividing a bigger number by a smaller number the remainder is 0, then

- the bigger number is a multiple of the smaller number and
- the smaller number is a factor of the bigger number.

Example 13:

a. Is 27 a multiple of 9?

```
   3
9)27
 -27
 ---
   0
```

On dividing 27 by 9, the remainder is zero. Therefore, 27 is a multiple of 9.

b. Is 41 a multiple of 3?

```
  13
3)41
 -3↓
 ---
  11
 - 9
 ---
   2
```

On dividing 41 by 3, the remainder is not zero. Therefore, 41 is not a multiple of 3.

Example 14:

a. Write the first 3 multiples of 4.

Answer = 4, 8 and 12

b. Write the first 5 multiples of 6.

Answer = 6, 12, 18, 24 and 30

c. Write the multiples of 2 less than 10.

Answer = 2, 4, 6 and 8

d. Write 2 multiples of 8 greater than 16.

Answer = 24 and 32

(**Note:** The answer can be any two multiples of 8 greater than 16.)

Exercise 6.6

1. 

   Write the position of pink stars. The first position is written below.

   __3__ , ______ , ______ , ______

   These numbers are the multiples of ______.

2. a. Circle the multiples of 6 in the given numbers.

1	2	3	4	5	6	7	8	9	10
11	12	13	14	15	16	17	18	19	20
21	22	23	24	25	26	27	28	29	30

   b. Circle the multiples of 7 in the given numbers.

1	2	3	4	5	6	7	8	9	10
11	12	13	14	15	16	17	18	19	20
21	22	23	24	25	26	27	28	29	30

3. **Write the first 3 multiples of the following.**

   a. 2 b. 5 c. 7 d. 9

4. **Write the first 4 multiples of the following.**

   a. 3 b. 4 c. 6 d. 10

5. **Fill in the blanks.**

   a. 1 is a ______ of every number.

   b. Every ______ is a multiple of itself.

6. a. Mark the multiples of 2 on the number line given below.

   b. Mark the multiples of 5 on the number line given below.

7. In $3 \times 7 = 21$,

   a. ______ and ______ are factors of ______.

   b. ______ is the multiple of ______ and ______.

8. Write the multiples of 6 that are less than 25.

9. Write 3 multiples of 5 that are greater than 15.

10. Write the multiples of 7 between 10 and 40.

Common Multiples

Common multiples are the multiples that are common to two or more numbers.

Examples: Write the common multiples of 2 and 3 that are less than 20.

First write all the multiples of 2 that are less than 20. Then, write all the multiples of 3 that are less than 20.

After that, circle the multiples that are common to both. Those will be the common multiples.

Multiples of 2 that are less than 20

2, 4, (6), 8, 10, (12), 14, 16, (18)

Multiples of 3 that are less than 20

3, (6), 9, (12), 15, (18)

So, 6, 12 and 18 are the common multiples of 2 and 3 that are less than 20.

The same can be shown on a number line.

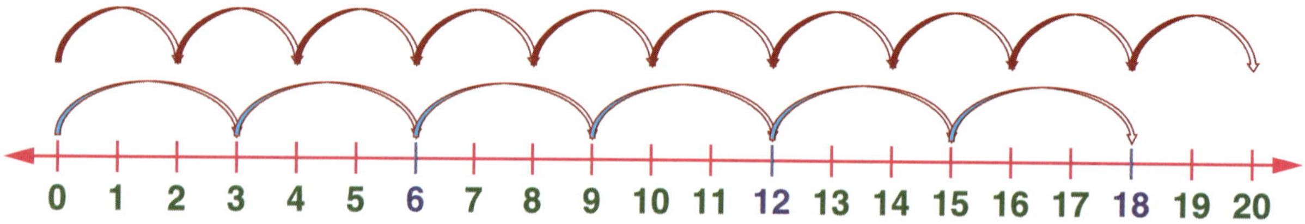

Exercise 6.7

1. a. Write the common multiples of 2 and 4 from 1 to 30.
   b. Show the above on the number line.
2. a. Write the common multiples of 4 and 6 from 1 to 30.
   b. Show the above on the number line.
3. Write the first common multiple of 3 and 6.
4. Write the first common multiple of 2 and 7.
5. Circle the multiples of 3 and tick the multiples of 5 in the numbers given below. Find out the first common multiple of 3 and 5.

1	2	3	4	5	6	7	8	9	10
11	12	13	14	15	16	17	18	19	20
21	22	23	24	25	26	27	28	29	30

Mental Maths

1. Write the first 5 multiples of 5: ____________
2. Write the first 3 multiples of 10: ____________
3. From the above, write the common multiples: ____________

Revision Exercise

1 **Choose the correct options.**

a. Which of the following numbers is divisible by 9?
   i. 4,009 ii. 4,104 iii. 4,902 iv. 4,999 ☐

b. Which of the following numbers is divisible by 5 but not by 10?
   i. 4,320 ii. 7,250 iii. 6,140 iv. 9,785 ☐

c. Which of the following options has all the factors of 12?
   i. 2, 3, 4, 6, 12 ii. 1, 2, 3, 4, 6, 12 iii. 2, 3 iv. 1, 12 ☐

d. Which of the following numbers is a factor of all numbers?
   i. 0 ii. 1 iii. 10 iv. 9 ☐

e. A number which has only 2 factors is called a
   i. composite number ii. unique number iii. prime number ☐

f. Which of the following is the unique number?
   i. 0 ii. 1 iii. 100 iv. 101 ☐

g. The prime factors of 6 are
   i. 1, 2, 3, 6 ii. 0, 1, 2, 3, 6 iii. 6 iv. 2, 3 ☐

h. The prime factorisation of 15 is
   i. 1, 3, 5, 15 ii. 3, 5, 15 iii. $1 \times 3 \times 5 \times 15$ iv. 3×5 ☐

i. The multiples of 3 from 3 to 20 are
   i. 3, 9, 15 ii. 1, 2, 4, 5, 10, 20 iii. 3, 6, 9, 12, 15, 18 iv. 6, 9, 12, 15, 18 ☐

j. The multiples of 5 between 6 and 22 are
   i. 5, 10, 15, 20 ii. 10, 15, 20, 25 iii. 10, 15, 20 iv. 5, 10, 15, 20 ☐

2 Use divisibility rules to find out if 59,684 is divisible by 4 or not. Give reasons.

3 Use divisibility rules to find out if 5,594 is divisible by 6 or not. Give reasons.

4 Which of the following numbers are odd numbers?

568, 439, 1398, 2405, 19,846, 47,389

5 Pick out the prime numbers and the composite numbers from the following.

2, 5, 7, 11, 13, 15, 18, 21, 25, 27, 31, 35, 36, 39

6 Find all the factors of 48.

7 Write two factors of 12 whose sum is 7.

8 Write the prime factorisation of 60 and hence write the prime factors of it.

9 Write two odd multiples of 3 that are less than 10.

10 Write three even multiplies of 4 that are less than 15.

Worksheet

1. **Fill in the blanks.**

   a. A number that has exactly two factors is called a ________.

   b. A number that has more than two factors is called a ________.

   c. The number ________ is a factor of every number.

   d. Every prime number except ________ is an odd number.

2. **Look at the numbers given below and answer the questions that follow.**

   4 8 5 12

   a. Which number is multiple of 3? ________

   b. Which number is not a factor of 60? ________

   c. Which number is a factor of 52? ________

   d. Which number is a prime number? ________

3. **Circle the correct answer for each of these.**

   a. A common multiple of 3 and 5 is:

   35 45 55

   b. A common multiple of 2 and 3 is:

   28 38 48

4. **Write the missing pair of factors for 18.**

   (1,18) (2,9) (_____ , _____)

5. **Write the missing factor of 36.**

   1, 2, 3, 4, _____, 9, 12, 18, 36

6. **Circle the number that is prime as well as even.**

   3 1 5 2 7

7. **Circle the number that is not a prime number.**

   23 43 13 33

8. **Circle the number that is a common multiple of 5 and 3.**

   40 70 60

For the Curious Mind

1. Find two factors of 96 whose sum is 35.
2. Find two prime numbers whose sum is 73.

Mixed Review 2

1. A dealer bought 693 kg rice at ₹2 per kg, 462 kg sugar at ₹3 per kg and 195 kg tea at ₹4 per kg. How much money did he spend altogether?
2. A factory manufactures 4000 cars every day. How many cars does it manufacture in
   a. one week?
   b. one week if every Sunday is a holiday?
   c. three weeks if every Sunday is a holiday?
3. If you distribute 171 sweets equally among 19 boys, how many sweets will each boy get?
4. 575 chocolates were distributed equally among 23 children. How many chocolates did each child get?
5. Manish bought 4 sofas at ₹1,21,250 each. What is the total amount he spent in buying the sofas?
6. Mary has ₹533. She buys a few pairs of earrings at ₹64 each. How many pairs of earrings can she buy with the amount she has and how much money will be left with her?
7. An office employs 165 people. Each person is paid ₹7500 a month. How much does the factory pay in
   a. a month?
   b. a year?
8. What is the least number of bags required to store 1632 kg of rice if each bag can store 35 kg?
9. A set of books is available for ₹145. What will be the cost of 25 such sets?
10. Using the divisibility rules, find out which of the following numbers are divisible by 3 but not by 6.
    21, 24, 486, 351, 732, 9,336
11. Which of the following are odd numbers?
    0, 4, 15, 20, 21, 48, 99
12. Find out two factors of 42 whose sum is 23.
13. Circle the prime numbers in the numbers given below.
    9, 12, 15, 17, 23, 25, 29.
14. Write the prime factorisation and prime factors of 48.
15. Write the multiples of 3 that lie between 10 and 25.

LCM and HCF

7

We have learned about factors and multiples. Let us study LCM and HCF.

Lowest Common Multiple (LCM)

LCM of two or more numbers is the smallest multiple which is common to these numbers. There are two methods to find LCM.

Method 1 Listing Method

List out the multiples of the numbers and then choose the smallest common multiple.

Example 1: Find the LCM of 2 and 6.

2 = 2, 4, (6), 8, 10, (12), 14, 16, (18), 20

6 = (6), (12), (18), 24, 30

6, 12 and 18 are the common multiples. Among them, 6 is the smallest multiple which is common to 2 and 6. So, 6 is the LCM of 2 and 6.

Method 2 Prime Factorization Method

In this method of finding LCM we take the numbers and factorise them by dividing with the smallest possible prime factor. If any number gets divided completely, we divide it. If a number does not get divided, we keep it as it is; and in the next step, divide it by the next possible prime factor till all the quotients become 1. In the end, we multiply all the prime factors (divisors) to get the LCM.

Example 2: Find the LCM of 2 and 6.

2	2, 6
3	1, 3
	1, 1

$\text{LCM} = 2 \times 3$

$= 6$

Example 3: Find the LCM of 12, 24 and 36.

2	12, 24, 36
2	6, 12, 18
2	3, 6, 9
3	3, 3, 9
3	1, 1, 3
	1, 1, 1

$\text{LCM} = 2 \times 2 \times 2 \times 3 \times 3$

$= 72$

Highest Common Factor (HCF)

HCF of two numbers means the highest factor which is common to the given numbers, that is, the greatest number that divides the given numbers completely. There are three methods to find HCF.

Method 1 Listing Method

List all the factors of the given numbers and then choose the highest common factor out of them.

Example 4: Find the HCF of 6 and 12.

$$6 = 1,\ 2,\ 3,\ \textcircled{6}$$

$$12 = 1,\ 2,\ 3,\ 4,\ \textcircled{6},\ 12$$

The highest factor among the common factors is 6. Hence, the HCF is 6.

Method 2 Prime Factorization Method

Factorise each number separately. List out the prime factors of each number. Circle the common prime factors and multiply them to get the HCF. This is called the **prime factorisation** method.

Example 5: Find the HCF of 6 and 12.

$$\begin{array}{c|c} 2 & 6 \\ \hline 3 & 3 \\ \hline & 1 \end{array} \qquad \begin{array}{c|c} 2 & 12 \\ \hline 2 & 6 \\ \hline 3 & 3 \\ \hline & 1 \end{array}$$

$$6 = \textcircled{2} \times \textcircled{3}$$

$$12 = \textcircled{2} \times 2 \times \textcircled{3}$$

$\text{HCF} = 2 \times 3 = 6$

Hence, the HCF is 6.

Example 6: Find the HCF of 12, 24 and 36.

$$\begin{array}{c|c} 2 & 12 \\ \hline 2 & 6 \\ \hline 3 & 3 \\ \hline & 1 \end{array} \qquad \begin{array}{c|c} 2 & 24 \\ \hline 2 & 12 \\ \hline 2 & 6 \\ \hline 3 & 3 \\ \hline & 1 \end{array} \qquad \begin{array}{c|c} 2 & 36 \\ \hline 2 & 18 \\ \hline 3 & 9 \\ \hline 3 & 3 \\ \hline & 1 \end{array}$$

$$12 = \textcircled{2} \times \textcircled{2} \times \textcircled{3}$$

$$24 = \textcircled{2} \times \textcircled{2} \times 2 \times \textcircled{3}$$

$$36 = \textcircled{2} \times \textcircled{2} \times \textcircled{3} \times 3$$

$\text{HCF} = 2 \times 2 \times 3 = 12$

Method 3 Division Method

If there are two numbers, we divide the bigger number by the smaller number. We use the remainder to divide the previous divisor. We continue this method till the remainder becomes zero. When the remainder becomes zero, the last divisor is the HCF.

Example 7: Find the HCF of 12 and 40.

```
       3
12 ) 40          Previous divisor
    -36    3
     4 ) 12
         -12
           0
```

We know that the last divisor is the HCF. Thus, HCF is 4.

If there are three numbers, then we use this method for the first two numbers. After that, we divide the third number by the last divisor of the first two numbers. The last divisor we get after dividing the third number will be the HCF. This is called the **division** method.

Example 8: Find the HCF of 12, 18 and 26.

First divide 18 by 12.

```
       1
12 ) 18
    -12    2
     6 ) 12
         -12
           0
```

The last divisor is 6. Now, divide the third number 26 by 6.

```
      4
6 ) 26
   -24   3
    2 ) 6
        6
        0
```

Here, the last divisor is 2.

Hence, the HCF of 12, 18 and 26 is 2.

Exercise 7.1

1. Find the LCM of the following.

a. 3, 9 b. 4, 3 c. 5, 7 d. 6, 8
e. 2, 3, 5 f. 4, 8, 16 g. 5, 10, 20 h. 8, 16, 20
i. 12, 20, 24 j. 6, 9, 15 k. 12, 15, 30 l. 10, 15, 25

2. Find the HCF of the following.

a. 4, 12 b. 3, 12 c. 6, 15 d. 12, 18
e. 10, 12, 14 f. 12, 15, 18 g. 8, 16, 20 h. 18, 27, 36
i. 15, 20, 25 j. 36, 48, 72 k. 60, 72, 84 l. 36, 99, 126

Revision Exercise

1 Find the LCM of the following.

a. 12, 24, 48 b. 12, 15, 30 c. 8, 10, 12 d. 9, 18, 15, 20
e. 7, 21, 35 f. 8, 48, 52 g. 13, 17, 26 h. 15, 90, 125
i. 24, 36, 84 j. 80, 144, 64 k. 12, 32, 48, 24 l. 24, 36, 60, 75

2 Find the HCF of the following.

a. 4, 12, 40 b. 60, 72, 84 c. 15, 30, 45 d. 81, 108, 126
e. 48, 99, 112 f. 63, 105, 147 g. 81, 108, 126 h. 68, 34, 102
i. 140, 175, 315 j. 12, 32, 44 k. 24, 60, 48 l. 13, 39, 52

3 State whether the following are true or false.

a. The HCF of 4, 8 and 12 is 24. ________
b. The LCM of 12 and 24 is 12. ________
c. The HCF of 3, 4 and 5 is 15. ________
d. The LCM of 10, 20 and 30 is 60. ________

4 What is the LCM for each of these?

a. 6 and 8 ________
b. 9 and 5 ________
c. 2, 3 and 5 ________
d. 4, 9 and 6 ________

5 What is the HCF for each of these?

a. 30 and 42 ________
b. 27 and 45 ________
c. 36 and 42 ________
d. 27, 42 and 48 ________

Mental Maths

The LCM of 2 and 4 is ________.
The HCF of 2 and 4 is ________.

Fractions

8

A fraction represents a part of the whole. An example of a fraction is $\frac{1}{4}$, which means 1 part out of 4 equal parts. This can also be represented in figures as given below.

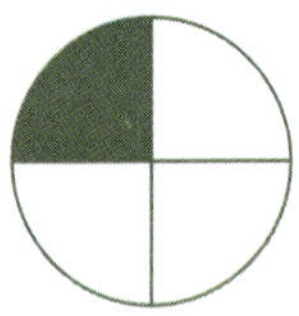

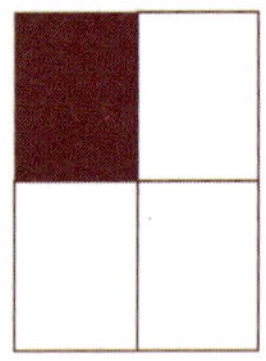

In each of the above figures, the shaded part represents the fraction $\frac{1}{4}$ and the unshaded parts represent the fraction $\frac{3}{4}$.

In a fraction, the number on top is called the **numerator** and the number below is called the **denominator**.

Note

In a fraction, the denominator always represents the total. Therefore, in $\frac{3}{4}$, 4 is the total number of parts.

So, in $\frac{3}{4}$, 3 is the numerator and 4 is the denominator.

If, out of 8 sweets, I eat 2 sweets, then the fraction of the sweets that I eat is $\frac{2}{8}$ and the fraction of the sweets that I do not eat is $\frac{6}{8}$.

6 ⟶ Number of sweets I do not eat
8 ⟶ Total number of sweets

If out of 5 birds 2 fly away, then the fraction of the birds that fly away is $\frac{2}{5}$ and the fraction of the birds that did not fly is $\frac{3}{5}$.

In the given figure,

fraction of the lined part = $\frac{1}{4}$

fraction of the unlined part = $\frac{3}{4}$

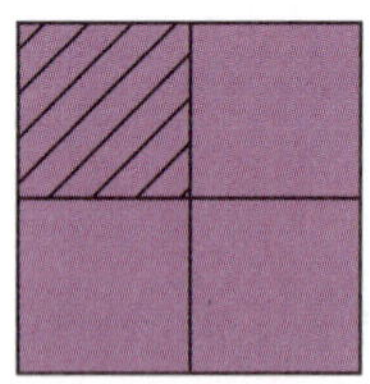

In this figure,

Fraction of the lined part = $\frac{5}{10}$

Fraction of the unlined part = $\frac{5}{10}$

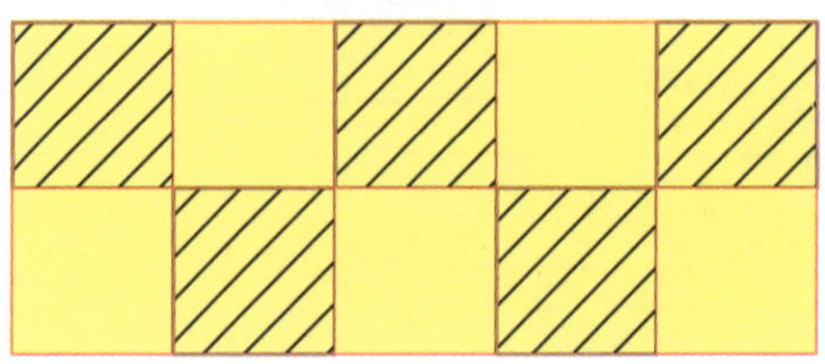

Kinds of Fractions

Unit Fractions

Fractions which have 1 as their numerator are called unit fractions.

Examples: $\frac{1}{3}, \frac{1}{19}, \frac{1}{45}, \frac{1}{193}$

Proper Fractions

Fractions where the numerator is smaller than the denominator are called proper fractions.

Examples: $\frac{2}{3}, \frac{5}{9}, \frac{7}{19}, \frac{93}{214}$

Improper Fractions

Fractions where the numerator is greater than or equal to the denominator are called improper fractions.

Examples: $\frac{7}{3}, \frac{8}{5}, \frac{25}{4}, \frac{193}{12}, \frac{5}{5}, \frac{89}{89}, \frac{135}{135}$

Mixed Fractions

A mixed fraction is a combination of a whole number and a proper fraction.

Examples: $2\frac{6}{8}, 3\frac{2}{5}, 5\frac{3}{15}, 9\frac{4}{12}$

Simplest Form of a Fraction

A fraction is said to be in the simplest form if its numerator and denominator have no common factor except 1.

Consider the fraction $\frac{9}{27}$.

How do you convert it into the simplest form?

Is the given fraction in the simplest form? No.

Find the HCF of the numerator and the denominator. Divide the numerator and the denominator by this HCF.

That is, $\frac{9 \div 9}{27 \div 9} = \frac{1}{3}$

Now, 1 and 3 have no common factor except 1. Hence, $\frac{1}{3}$ is in the simplest form.

Converting Improper Fractions to Mixed Fractions

Improper fractions can be converted into mixed fractions. Since in an improper fraction the numerator is bigger than the denominator, the numerator can be divided by the denominator. Thus, to change an improper fraction into a mixed fraction, we divide the numerator by the denominator. The quotient becomes the whole number and the remainder becomes the new numerator. The denominator remains unchanged.

Example 1:

a. Convert $\frac{7}{3}$ into a mixed fraction.

$$\begin{array}{r} 2 \\ 3\overline{)\ 7} \\ -\ 6 \\ \hline 1 \end{array}$$

Answer = $2\frac{1}{3}$

b. Convert $\frac{8}{5}$ into a mixed fraction.

$$\frac{8}{5} = \begin{array}{r} 1 \\ 5\overline{)\ 8} \\ -\ 5 \\ \hline 3 \end{array}$$

Answer = $1\frac{3}{5}$

Note

An improper fraction should always be converted into a mixed fraction.

Method 1

To make a mixed fraction out of an improper fraction that is not in its lowest term, first reduce the fraction to its lowest term and then make a mixed fraction.

Example 2: Convert $\frac{130}{12}$ into a mixed fraction.

First reduce $\frac{130}{12}$ to its lowest term.

$$\frac{130}{12} = \frac{\cancel{130}^{65}}{\cancel{12}_{6}} = \frac{65}{6}$$

Now, make a mixed fraction.

$$\begin{array}{r} 10 \\ 6\overline{)\ 65} \\ -\ 6 \\ \hline 05 \end{array}$$

Answer = $10\frac{5}{6}$

Method 2

In case you forget to first simplify the fraction to its lowest term, then you first make the mixed fraction and then simplify the fraction part to its lowest term.

Remember

It is always better to use the first method, that is, to first simplify the improper fraction to its lowest term and then make the mixed fraction.

Example 3: Convert $\frac{130}{12}$ into a mixed fraction.

$$\begin{array}{r} 10 \\ 12\overline{)\ 130} \\ -12 \\ \hline 10 \end{array}$$

$$\frac{130}{12} = 10\frac{10}{12} = 10\frac{\cancel{10}^{5}}{\cancel{12}_{6}}$$

Answer = $10\frac{5}{6}$

Converting Mixed Fractions to Improper Fractions

To convert a mixed fraction to an improper fraction, multiply the denominator of the fraction with its whole number and then add the numerator to the product. Write the sum over the denominator. The denominator remains unchanged.

Example 4: Convert $2\frac{1}{3}$ to an improper fraction.

$$2\frac{1}{3} = 2\frac{^{+}1}{_{\times}3} = \frac{(2\times 3)+1}{3} = \frac{6+1}{3} = \frac{7}{3}$$

Answer $= \frac{7}{3}$

Example 5: Convert $1\frac{3}{5}$ to an improper fraction.

$$1\frac{3}{5} = 1\frac{^{+}3}{_{\times}5} = \frac{(1\times 5)+3}{5} = \frac{5+3}{5} = \frac{8}{5}$$

Answer $= \frac{8}{5}$

Equivalent Fractions

Look at the three circles given here. Can you see that all the three circles have their half portion shaded? But, as fractions, they are different. The first one represents $\frac{1}{2}$, the second represents $\frac{2}{4}$ and the third one represents $\frac{4}{8}$. Since all the three fractions represent the same amount of shaded portion, we can say that $\frac{1}{2}$, $\frac{2}{4}$ and $\frac{4}{8}$ are equivalent fractions.

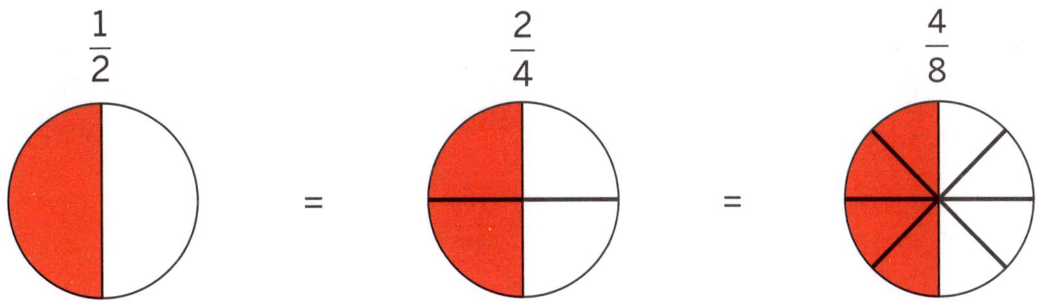

To find an equivalent fraction, we multiply the numerator and the denominator by the same number.

Example 6: Write two equivalent fractions for $\frac{2}{4}$.

Multiplying the numerator and the denominator by 2 and 3, we get.

$$\frac{2}{4} = \frac{2\times 2}{4\times 2} = \frac{4}{8};\ \frac{2}{4} = \frac{2\times 3}{4\times 3} = \frac{6}{12}$$

Therefore, two equivalent fractions for $\frac{2}{4}$ are $\frac{4}{8}$ and $\frac{6}{12}$.

Example 7: Write the first four equivalent fractions of $\frac{2}{5}$.

$$\frac{2}{5} = \frac{4}{10}^{\times 2} = \frac{6}{15}^{\times 3} = \frac{8}{20}^{\times 4} = \frac{10}{25}^{\times 5}$$

Example 8: Write a fraction equivalent to $\frac{7}{8}$ with 16 as the denominator.

$\frac{7}{8} = \frac{?}{16}$

We have to find the numerator of the second fraction.

Now, we find out the number by which the smaller denominator (8) is to be multiplied to get the bigger denominator (16). In this case, we should multiply 8 by 2 to get 16. Since we multiply 8 by 2, we multiply the numerator (7) also by 2.
$7 \times 2 = 14$

So, the numerator above 16 should be 14. $\therefore \frac{7}{8} = \frac{14}{16}$

The same method is used if we have to find the denominator when the numerator is given.

Example 9: Write a fraction equivalent to $\frac{2}{9}$ with 10 as the numerator.

$\frac{2}{9} = \frac{10}{?}$

The values of the numerators are given. Out of them, 2 is smaller. 2 should be multiplied by 5 to get 10. So, we multiply the denominator also by 5 and get 45.

$$\therefore \frac{2}{9} = \frac{10}{45}$$

Exercise 8.1

1 Reduce the following to the simplest form.

a. $\frac{12}{16}$ b. $\frac{20}{32}$ c. $\frac{12}{18}$ d. $\frac{122}{240}$

2 Circle the unit fractions out of all the fractions given below.

a. $\frac{2}{3}$ b. $\frac{1}{9}$ c. $\frac{7}{8}$ d. $\frac{1}{17}$

3 **Fill in the numerators of the following fractions to make them proper fractions.**

a. $\frac{\square}{8}$ b. $\frac{\square}{29}$ c. $\frac{\square}{101}$ d. $\frac{\square}{93}$

4 **Fill in the numerators of the following fractions to make them improper fractions.**

a. $\frac{\square}{5}$ b. $\frac{\square}{7}$ c. $\frac{\square}{23}$ d. $\frac{\square}{52}$

5 **Convert the following improper fractions into mixed fractions.**

a. $\frac{5}{2}$ b. $\frac{17}{3}$ c. $\frac{52}{7}$ d. $\frac{94}{5}$

e. $\frac{101}{4}$ f. $\frac{139}{6}$ g. $\frac{129}{5}$ h. $\frac{192}{7}$

6 **Convert the following mixed fractions into improper fractions.**

a. $2\frac{1}{6}$ b. $3\frac{1}{5}$ c. $19\frac{2}{3}$ d. $7\frac{5}{7}$

e. $14\frac{2}{9}$ f. $3\frac{12}{53}$ g. $11\frac{3}{7}$ h. $9\frac{2}{11}$

7 **Write a fraction for the shaded part and the unshaded part in the following figures.**

a.

Shaded part ______

Unshaded part ______

b.

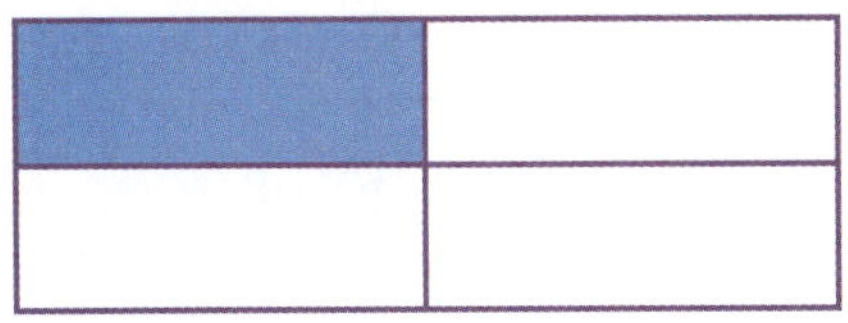

Shaded part ______

Unshaded part ______

c.

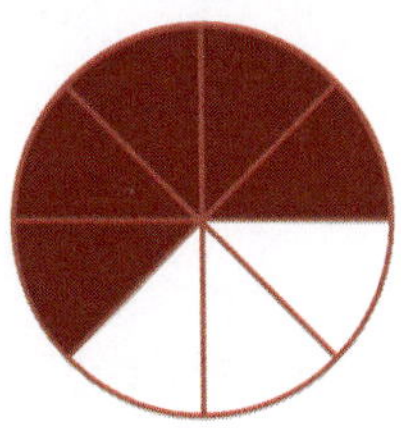

Shaded part ______

Unshaded part ______

d.

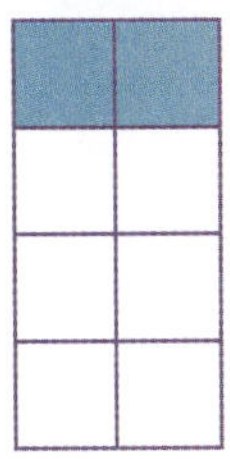

Shaded part ______

Unshaded part ______

8 **Colour the figures for the fractions given.**

a. $\frac{1}{2}$ 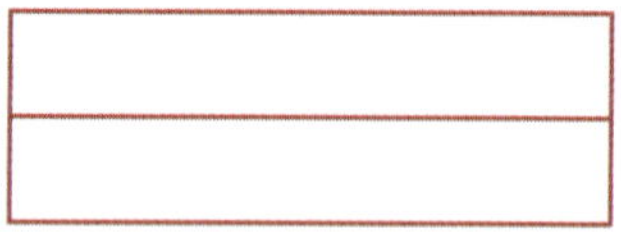

b. $\frac{2}{3}$ 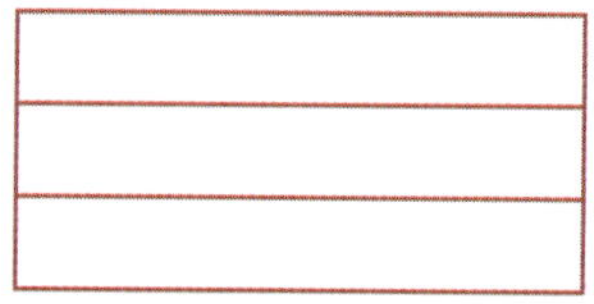

c. $\frac{5}{6}$ 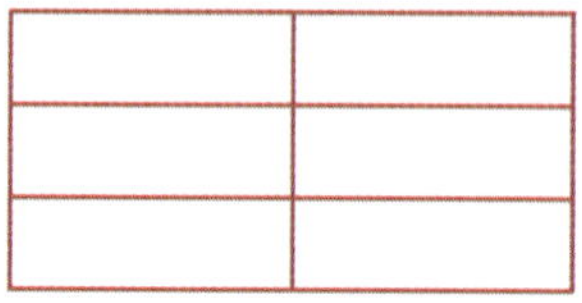

d. $\frac{4}{5}$ 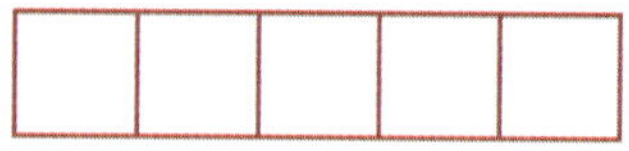

9 Out of 10 apples, 2 apples are rotten. What is the fraction of rotten apples?

10 Out of 12 boys, 9 boys cannot swim. What fraction of the boys

a. can swim?

b. can't swim?

11 Out of 15 girls, 8 girls wore pink dresses. What fraction of the girls

a. wore pink dresses?

b. did not wear pink dresses?

12 **Write the numerator and the denominator of the following fractions.**

Fraction	$\frac{4}{9}$	$\frac{2}{3}$	$\frac{1}{8}$	$\frac{3}{7}$	$\frac{2}{5}$	$\frac{1}{3}$	$\frac{7}{9}$
Numerator							
Denominator							

13 **Write the first five equivalent fractions of the following.**

a. $\frac{2}{3}$

b. $\frac{1}{5}$

c. $\frac{3}{7}$

d. $\frac{2}{7}$

14 **Write a fraction equivalent to**

a. $\frac{2}{3}$ with denominator 12.

b. $\frac{1}{5}$ with numerator 5.

c. $\frac{3}{7}$ with denominator 49.

d. $\frac{2}{5}$ with numerator 16.

Comparing Fractions

Comparing Like Fractions

If the denominators of both the fractions are the same, then we compare the numerators of the fractions; the fraction with the bigger numerator is the bigger fraction.

Example 10: Which of the following is smaller $\frac{4}{8}$ or $\frac{5}{8}$?

Since both the fractions have the same denominator, we compare the numerators.

$4 < 5$. Therefore, $\frac{4}{8} < \frac{5}{8}$.

Comparing Unlike Fractions

Unlike Fractions With the Same Numerator

If the numerators of both the fractions are the same, then the fraction with the smaller denominator is the bigger fraction.

Example 11: Which of the following is greater: $\frac{5}{2}$ or $\frac{5}{8}$?

Since both the fractions have the same numerator, we compare the denominators.

$8 > 2$. Therefore, $\frac{5}{2} > \frac{5}{8}$.

Unlike Fractions With Different Numerators

If the numerators of both the fractions are different, then to find the greater fraction, we write both the fractions and cross-multiply. For example, to find the greater fraction between $\frac{2}{3}$ and $\frac{5}{7}$, we cross multiply as given below.

15 is bigger than 14 and 15 is on the right side, so the fraction on the right side, which is $\frac{5}{7}$, is bigger. So, $\frac{5}{7} > \frac{2}{3}$.

Comparing Mixed Fractions

To compare mixed fractions, we check the whole numbers.

Example 12: Compare $4\frac{1}{3}$ and $5\frac{3}{7}$.

Checking the whole numbers, we find that, $4 < 5$.

So, $4\frac{1}{3} < 5\frac{3}{7}$.

Note

Compare $4\frac{2}{3}$ and $4\frac{5}{7}$.
Here, the whole number is same, but $\frac{2}{3} < \frac{5}{7}$ as shown in the previous example.
So, $4\frac{2}{3} < 4\frac{5}{7}$

Ascending Order and Descending Order

Arranging Fractions in Ascending Order

Example 13: Write the fractions in ascending order: $\frac{2}{3}, \frac{1}{6}, \frac{4}{12}$

To arrange fractions in ascending order, we first take out the LCM of all the denominators.

2	3, 6, 12
2	3, 3, 6
3	3, 3, 3
	1, 1, 1

LCM = $2 \times 2 \times 3$

= 12

LCM of all denominators = 12

$$\frac{\frac{2}{3}, \frac{1}{6}, \frac{4}{12}}{12}$$

In the first fraction $\frac{2}{3}$, the denominator 3 should be multiplied by 4 to get the LCM 12. Therefore, we multiply the numerator 2 by 4.

In the second fraction $\frac{1}{6}$, the denominator 6 should be multiplied by 2 to get the LCM 12. Therefore, we multiply the numerator 1 by 2.

In the third fraction $\frac{4}{12}$, the denominator 12 should be multiplied by 1 to get the LCM 12. Therefore, we multiply its numerator, that is, 4 by 1. Or, we can say that the denominator is already equal to the LCM, so leave that fraction as it is.

So we get,

$\overset{\times 4}{\frac{2}{3}}, \overset{\times 2}{\frac{1}{6}}, \overset{\times 1}{\frac{4}{12}}$ ⟶ We multiply the numerators with their respective numbers.

$\frac{8, \quad 2, \quad 4}{12}$ ⟵ The product obtained is written like this.

Now, we arrange the products from the smallest to the biggest.

$\frac{\overset{③}{8}, \quad \overset{①}{2}, \quad \overset{②}{4}}{12}$

2 is the smallest and it corresponds to $\frac{1}{6}$. So, $\frac{1}{6}$ is the smallest fraction.

4 is the next number in ascending order and it corresponds to $\frac{4}{12}$. So, $\frac{4}{12}$ is the next fraction.

8 is the biggest number and it corresponds to $\frac{2}{3}$. So, $\frac{2}{3}$ is the biggest fraction.

The answer is then written in the fraction form (as given in the question.)

Therefore, the fractions in ascending order are $\frac{1}{6}, \frac{4}{12}, \frac{2}{3}$

Arranging Fractions in Descending Order

For descending order, the numbers obtained after taking out the LCM are arranged from the biggest to the smallest. The answer is then written in the fraction form as given in the question.

Example 14: Arrange the fractions in descending order: $\frac{2}{3}, \frac{1}{6}, \frac{4}{12}$

We have already found out that the LCM = 12.

① ③ ②

$$\frac{8, \quad 2, \quad 4}{12}$$

Answer = $\frac{2}{3}, \frac{4}{12}, \frac{1}{6}$

Try These!

Write the following fractions in descending order: $\frac{1}{2}, \frac{1}{5}, \frac{2}{3}$

Exercise 8.2

1 **Fill in the blanks with >, < or =.**

a. $\frac{2}{3}$ ___ $\frac{4}{5}$ b. $\frac{6}{7}$ ___ $\frac{2}{3}$ c. $\frac{4}{5}$ ___ $\frac{9}{16}$ d. $\frac{3}{7}$ ___ $\frac{2}{5}$

2 **Fill in the blanks with >, < or =.**

a. $\frac{2}{7}$ ___ $\frac{1}{7}$ b. $\frac{8}{13}$ ___ $\frac{2}{13}$ c. $\frac{20}{23}$ ___ $\frac{21}{23}$ d. $\frac{2}{15}$ ___ $\frac{3}{15}$ e. $\frac{9}{10}$ ___ $\frac{1}{10}$

3 **Fill in the blanks with >, < or =.**

a. $\frac{2}{3}$ ___ $\frac{2}{4}$ b. $\frac{5}{6}$ ___ $\frac{5}{7}$ c. $\frac{17}{3}$ ___ $\frac{17}{5}$ d. $\frac{12}{9}$ ___ $\frac{12}{7}$ e. $\frac{50}{12}$ ___ $\frac{50}{3}$

4 **Fill in the blanks with >, < or =.**

a. $\frac{2}{15}$ ___ $\frac{3}{15}$ b. $\frac{6}{2}$ ___ $\frac{6}{1}$ c. $\frac{2}{5}$ ___ $\frac{1}{6}$ d. $\frac{5}{12}$ ___ $\frac{3}{12}$ e. $\frac{19}{3}$ ___ $\frac{19}{5}$

f. $\frac{12}{9}$ ___ $\frac{9}{12}$ g. $\frac{6}{3}$ ___ $\frac{9}{12}$ h. $\frac{5}{6}$ ___ $\frac{25}{30}$ i. $\frac{19}{3}$ ___ $\frac{19}{5}$ j. $\frac{16}{40}$ ___ $\frac{18}{40}$

5. **Arrange the following fractions in ascending order.**

a. $\frac{2}{5}, \frac{1}{2}, \frac{1}{10}$ b. $\frac{5}{6}, \frac{1}{12}, \frac{3}{4}$ c. $\frac{12}{30}, \frac{9}{5}, \frac{2}{6}$

d. $\frac{5}{8}, \frac{2}{12}, \frac{5}{24}$ e. $\frac{3}{4}, \frac{5}{16}, \frac{1}{2}$ f. $\frac{5}{6}, \frac{4}{18}, \frac{5}{9}$

6. **Arrange the following fractions in descending order.**

a. $\frac{5}{8}, \frac{3}{4}, \frac{7}{12}$ b. $\frac{3}{5}, \frac{1}{2}, \frac{7}{10}$ c. $\frac{2}{9}, \frac{5}{6}, \frac{1}{18}$ d. $\frac{3}{5}, \frac{1}{10}, \frac{15}{50}$ e. $\frac{4}{3}, \frac{1}{9}, \frac{5}{18}$

Addition of Fractions

Adding Like Fractions

To add like fractions, we first add the numerators. Then, we place the sum over the common denominator. Finally, we simplify, if required.

Example 15: Add $\frac{2}{8}$ and $\frac{5}{8}$.

$$\frac{2}{8} + \frac{5}{8} = \frac{2+5}{8} = \frac{7}{8}$$

Example 16: Add $\frac{8}{5}$ and $\frac{7}{5}$.

$$\frac{8}{5} + \frac{7}{5} = \frac{8+7}{5} = \frac{\cancel{15}}{\cancel{5}}\ \frac{3}{1} = 3$$

Adding Unlike Fractions

To add unlike fractions, we first find the LCM of the denominators. Then, we convert the fractions into like fractions with the LCM as the common denominator. Finally, we add the like fractions.

Example 17: Add $\frac{2}{8}$ and $\frac{5}{12}$.

2	8, 12
2	4, 6
2	2, 3
3	1, 3
	1, 1

$$\text{LCM} = 2 \times 2 \times 2 \times 3 = 24$$

8 multiplied by 3 is equal to 24; therefore, we multiply the numerator 2 by 3 and get 6. 12 multiplied by 2 is 24; therefore, we multiply the numerator 5 by 2 and get 10.

$$\frac{2}{8}+\frac{5}{12}=\frac{\frac{2}{8}+\frac{5}{12}}{24}=\frac{2}{8}^{\times 3}+\frac{5}{12}^{\times 2}$$

$$=\frac{6+10}{24}$$

Now, we add 6 and 10 and we get $\frac{16}{24}$.

$\frac{16}{24}$ can be further simplified and brought to its simplest form by dividing both 16 and 24 by their HCF of, that is, 8.

$$\frac{\cancel{16}^{2}}{\cancel{24}_{3}}=\frac{2}{3}$$

$$\frac{2}{8}+\frac{5}{12}=\frac{2}{3}$$

Try These!

1. $\frac{1}{3}+\frac{1}{9}=$ ______
2. $\frac{3}{4}+\frac{1}{8}=$ ______
3. $\frac{4}{7}+\frac{1}{21}=$ ______

Example 18: Add $\frac{11}{5}$ and $\frac{16}{15}$.

$$\overset{\times 3}{\frac{11}{5}}+\overset{\times 1}{\frac{16}{15}}=\frac{33+16}{15}=\frac{49}{15}=3\frac{4}{15} \quad \text{(LCM of 5 and 15 is 15.)}$$

If 3 or more fractions are to be added, we follow the same method.

Example 19: Add $\frac{5}{6}, \frac{7}{12}$ and $\frac{1}{4}$.

$$\frac{5}{6}+\frac{7}{12}+\frac{1}{4}=\overset{\times 2}{\frac{5}{6}}+\overset{\times 1}{\frac{7}{12}}+\overset{\times 3}{\frac{1}{4}} \quad \text{(LCM of 6, 12, 4 is 12.)}$$

$$=\frac{10+7+3}{12}=\frac{\cancel{20}^{\cancel{10}\,5}}{\cancel{12}_{\cancel{6}\,3}}=\frac{5}{3}=1\frac{2}{3}$$

Exercise 8.3

Solve the following. Keep the answers in the simplest form.

1. $\frac{3}{5}+\frac{6}{5}$
2. $\frac{2}{3}+\frac{10}{3}$
3. $\frac{2}{7}+\frac{6}{7}$
4. $\frac{3}{8}+\frac{1}{8}$
5. $\frac{1}{3}+\frac{1}{6}$
6. $\frac{2}{7}+\frac{3}{4}$
7. $\frac{1}{9}+\frac{2}{7}$
8. $\frac{3}{5}+\frac{17}{20}$
9. $\frac{7}{12}+\frac{11}{24}+\frac{5}{6}$
10. $\frac{2}{3}+\frac{5}{6}+\frac{1}{9}$
11. $\frac{1}{7}+\frac{4}{11}$
12. $\frac{4}{5}+\frac{1}{10}+\frac{2}{15}$
13. $\frac{5}{11}+\frac{1}{7}$
14. $\frac{9}{13}+\frac{5}{26}+\frac{3}{13}$
15. $\frac{9}{11}+\frac{5}{22}+\frac{7}{11}$

Adding Mixed Fractions

Method 1

Convert the mixed fractions to improper fractions and then add the way we learned earlier.

Example 20: Add $2\frac{1}{5}$ and $3\frac{2}{5}$.

When we convert the above fractions to improper fractions, we get

$$2\frac{1}{5} + 3\frac{2}{5} = \frac{11}{5} + \frac{17}{5}$$

Now, follow the addition procedure by taking out the LCM of the denominators.

LCM of 5 and 5 is 5.

$$\frac{11}{5} + \frac{17}{5} = \frac{11+17}{5} = \frac{28}{5} = 5\frac{3}{5}$$

Method 2

To add by this method, we first add the whole numbers and keep that sum aside. Then, we add the fractions. To write the answer, we first write the whole number and on its right, we write the sum of the fractions.

Example 21: Add $2\frac{1}{5}$ and $3\frac{2}{5}$.

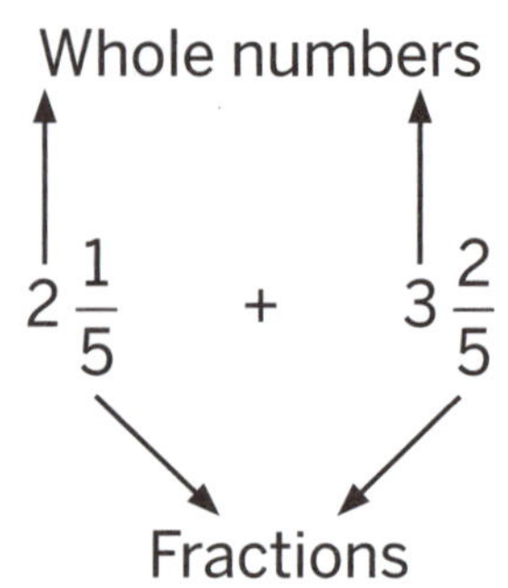

First we add the whole numbers, that is, 2 + 3 = 5 and keep it aside on the left.

Then, add the fractions $\frac{1}{5}$ and $\frac{2}{5}$.

We get $5\left(\frac{1}{5} + \frac{2}{5}\right) = 5\frac{1+2}{5} = 5\frac{3}{5}$

In the answer $5\frac{3}{5}$, 5 is the whole number and $\frac{3}{5}$ is the fraction part.

In this case, the fraction part of the answer $\frac{3}{5}$ is a proper fraction in its lowest term.

But if the fraction is not in its lowest form, then we must convert it to its lowest term.

If the fraction part of the answer is an improper fraction, then we must bring it to its lowest term and then convert it to a mixed fraction. At the end, we must add our first whole number to the whole number of this mixed fraction to write the answer.

Example 22: Add $2\frac{3}{5}$ and $3\frac{9}{10}$.

First, add the whole number, that is, 2 + 3 = 5.

Then, add the fractions.

$$\text{So, } 2\frac{3}{5}+3\frac{9}{10} = 5\left(\overset{\times 2}{\frac{3}{5}} + \overset{\times 1}{\frac{9}{10}}\right) \quad \text{(LCM of 5 and 10 is 10.)}$$

$$= 5\,\frac{6+9}{10}$$

$= 5\boxed{\frac{15}{10}}$ ⟶ This is an improper fraction and not in its lowest term. So, we will bring it to its lowest term.

$$= 5\,\frac{\cancel{15}^{3}}{\cancel{10}_{2}}$$

$= 5\boxed{\frac{3}{2}}$ ⟶ Now, it is in its lowest term, but it is still an improper fraction.

So, we convert this improper fraction $\frac{3}{2}$ into a mixed fraction.

$$\begin{array}{r|l} & 1 \\ 2\,) & 3 \\ - & 2 \\ \hline & 1 \end{array} \quad = 1\frac{1}{2}$$

Now, $5\frac{3}{2}$ can be written as $5 + 1\frac{1}{2}$.

So, $5 + 1\frac{1}{2}$ becomes $6\frac{1}{2}$.

So, the required answer = $6\frac{1}{2}$

Try This!

Find $9\frac{2}{5} + 2\frac{3}{5}$

Adding Three Mixed Fractions

We follow the same method as above for adding three fractions.

Example 23: Add $2\frac{1}{3}$, $5\frac{3}{5}$ and $7\frac{3}{10}$.

$$2\frac{1}{3}+5\frac{3}{5}+7\frac{3}{10} = 14\left(\overset{\times 10}{\frac{1}{3}} + \overset{\times 6}{\frac{3}{5}} + \overset{\times 3}{\frac{3}{10}}\right) \quad \text{(LCM of 3, 5, 10 is 30.)}$$

$$= 14\,\frac{10+18+9}{30} = 14\,\frac{37}{30}$$

$\frac{37}{30}$ as a mixed fraction is $1\frac{7}{30}$.

So, the answer is $14 + 1\frac{7}{30} = 15\frac{7}{30}$.

So, the sum of the fractions = $15\frac{7}{30}$

Exercise 8.4

Solve the following.

1. $2\frac{1}{4} + 3\frac{2}{4}$
2. $5\frac{1}{6} + 2\frac{4}{6}$
3. $4\frac{3}{7} + 2\frac{4}{7}$
4. $10\frac{1}{3} + 2\frac{2}{3}$
5. $4\frac{2}{9} + 10\frac{1}{9}$
6. $9\frac{5}{3} + 1\frac{1}{12}$
7. $3\frac{2}{7} + 1\frac{6}{7}$
8. $10\frac{2}{5} + 2\frac{4}{5}$
9. $5\frac{2}{3} + 4\frac{1}{6}$
10. $9\frac{2}{7} + 5\frac{1}{2}$
11. $2\frac{2}{6} + 3\frac{2}{5}$
12. $3\frac{3}{10} + 9\frac{1}{6}$
13. $10\frac{2}{9} + 5\frac{4}{3}$
14. $2\frac{3}{4} + 5\frac{1}{8} + 2\frac{1}{16}$
15. $5\frac{2}{9} + 4\frac{7}{8} + 1\frac{1}{12}$

Subtraction of Fractions

Subtracting Like Fractions

To subtract like fractions, we first subtract the numerators. Then, we place the answer over the common denominator. Then, we simplify, if required.

Subtraction of fractions follows exactly the same method as addition, the only difference is that we subtract instead of adding.

Example 24: Subtract $\frac{1}{4}$ from $\frac{5}{4}$.

$$\frac{5}{4} - \frac{1}{4} = \frac{5-1}{4} = \frac{\cancel{4}^{1}}{\cancel{4}_{1}} = 1$$

Subtracting Unlike Fractions

To subtract unlike fractions, we first take the LCM of the denominators. Then, we convert the fractions into like fractions with the LCM as common denominator. Finally, we subtract the like fractions.

Example 25: Subtract $\frac{1}{4}$ from $\frac{5}{8}$.

$$\frac{5}{8} - \frac{1}{4} = \frac{\overset{\times 1}{5}}{8} - \frac{\overset{\times 2}{1}}{4} \quad \text{(LCM of 8 and 4 is 8.)}$$

$$= \frac{5-2}{8} = \frac{3}{8}$$

Subtracting Mixed Fractions

Example 26: Subtract $1\frac{1}{4}$ from $2\frac{3}{5}$.

This can be solved in two ways.

Method 1

Convert all mixed fractions into improper fractions and then subtract by taking out the LCM.

$$2\frac{3}{5} - 1\frac{1}{4}$$

$$= \frac{\overset{\times 4}{13}}{5} - \frac{\overset{\times 5}{5}}{4} \quad \text{(LCM of 5 and 4 is 20.)}$$

$$= \frac{52-25}{20} = \frac{27}{20}$$

$$= 1\frac{7}{20}$$

Mental Maths

Find the following:

1. $1\frac{3}{5} - \frac{3}{5} =$ ______

2. $2\frac{1}{4} - \frac{1}{2} =$ ______

Method 2

Example 27: First subtract the whole numbers and then the fractions.

$$2\frac{3}{5} - 1\frac{1}{4}$$

First subtract the whole number 1 from 2. We get 1 and then we subtract the fraction by finding the LCM.

$$1\left(\frac{\overset{\times 4}{3}}{5} - \frac{\overset{\times 5}{1}}{4}\right) = 1\frac{12-5}{20} = 1\frac{7}{20}$$

Example 28: Subtract $1\frac{3}{5}$ from $2\frac{1}{4}$.

Using Method 2 for $2\frac{1}{4} - 1\frac{3}{5}$, we subtract the whole numbers.

That is, $2 - 1 = 1$

$$1\left(\overset{\times 5}{\frac{1}{4}} - \overset{\times 4}{\frac{3}{5}}\right) = 1\,\frac{5-12}{20}$$

We cannot subtract 12 from 5, so we borrow the whole number 1. When we do that, we add 20 (which is the denominator) to 5 and then we are left with no whole number as $1 - 1 = 0$.

Now, we get

$$\frac{\overset{+20}{5} - 12}{20} = \frac{25-12}{2} = \frac{13}{20}$$

Example 29: Subtract $2\frac{3}{4}$ from $5\frac{1}{3}$.

$$5\frac{1}{3} - 2\frac{3}{4}$$

$$= 3\left(\overset{\times 4}{\frac{1}{3}} - \overset{\times 3}{\frac{3}{4}}\right)$$

$$= 3\,\frac{4-9}{12} \quad = \overset{-1}{3}\,\frac{\overset{+12}{4}-9}{12}$$

$$= 2\,\frac{16-9}{12} = 2\frac{7}{12}$$

Subtraction from 1

Note

Any number with no denominator has the denominator 1.

Method 1

Example 30: Subtract $\frac{9}{10}$ from 1.

We have to find $1 - \frac{9}{10}$

Since 1 does not have a denominator, we write its denominator as 1.

So, we can write the same question as:

$$\frac{1}{1} - \frac{9}{10}$$

Now, we solve it like any other fraction. The LCM of 1 and 10 is 10.

$$\frac{1}{1} - \frac{9}{10} = \frac{10-9}{10} = \frac{1}{10}$$

Method 2

Find $1 - \frac{9}{10}$

We subtract the numerator of the second fraction from the denominator of the second fraction, that is, $10 - 9 = 1$. The answer is the number we get after subtraction, that is, 1 upon the denominator of the second fraction, that is, 10.

So, $1 - \frac{9}{10} = \frac{1}{10}$

Subtracting a Fraction from a Whole Number

Method 1

Find $8 - \frac{2}{5}$

Since 8 does not have a denominator, we write its denominator as 1.

So, we can write the same question as $\frac{8}{1} - \frac{2}{5}$.

Now, we solve it like any other fraction.

The LCM of 1 and 5 is 5.

$$\frac{8}{1} - \frac{2}{5} = \frac{40-2}{5} = \frac{38}{5} = 7\frac{3}{5}$$

Method 2

Find $8 - \frac{2}{5}$

In this case, we can write 8 as 7 $\left(\text{one less than 8 with } \frac{1}{1} \text{ next to it, which is } 7\frac{1}{1}\right)$.

$$\text{So, } 8 - \frac{2}{5} = 7\frac{1}{1} - \frac{2}{5}$$

$$= 7\frac{5-2}{5}$$

$$= 7\frac{3}{5}$$

Exercise 8.5

Solve the following.

1. $\frac{6}{7}-\frac{1}{2}$
2. $\frac{5}{3}-\frac{2}{9}$
3. $\frac{9}{4}-\frac{1}{4}$
4. $\frac{7}{8}-\frac{3}{5}$
5. $\frac{8}{7}-\frac{1}{5}$
6. $\frac{9}{5}-\frac{2}{7}$
7. $\frac{9}{2}-\frac{1}{4}$
8. $\frac{12}{35}-\frac{3}{14}$
9. $3-\frac{1}{2}$
10. $5-\frac{3}{4}$
11. $9-\frac{2}{7}$
12. $5-\frac{1}{9}$
13. $8-\frac{2}{5}$
14. $7-\frac{3}{8}$
15. $1-\frac{4}{9}$
16. $1-\frac{3}{7}$
17. $1-\frac{7}{11}$
18. $1-\frac{4}{5}$
19. $1-\frac{3}{8}$
20. $1-\frac{3}{9}$
21. $1-\frac{2}{3}$
22. $1-\frac{4}{15}$
23. $1-\frac{9}{11}$
24. $1-\frac{2}{13}$
25. $5\frac{2}{3}-4\frac{3}{8}$
26. $9\frac{7}{11}-2\frac{3}{11}$
27. $8\frac{2}{9}-5\frac{1}{9}$
28. $7\frac{2}{5}-2\frac{1}{5}$
29. $5\frac{2}{3}-5\frac{1}{9}$
30. $7\frac{3}{5}-7\frac{1}{5}$

Word Problems on Fractions

Example 31: Ram spent $\frac{1}{5}$ of his money on food and $\frac{3}{8}$ of his money on rent. What fraction of his money did he spend on food and rent?

2	5, 8
2	5, 4
2	5, 2
5	5, 1
	1, 1

Fraction of money spent on rent and food = $\frac{1}{5}+\frac{3}{8}$

LCM = $2\times2\times2\times5=40$

$$\frac{1}{5}\overset{\times 8}{}+\frac{3}{8}\overset{\times 5}{}=\frac{8+15}{40}=\frac{23}{40}$$

Ram spends $\frac{23}{40}$ of his money on rent and food.

Example 32: Naina's mother gave her $\frac{3}{7}$ m ribbon. Naina gave $\frac{1}{6}$ m ribbon to her friend. How much ribbon is left with Naina?

Total length of ribbon = $\frac{3}{7}$

Length of ribbon Naina gave = $\frac{1}{6}$

Length of ribbon left with Naina = $\frac{3}{7} - \frac{1}{6} = \overset{\times 6}{\frac{3}{7}} - \overset{\times 7}{\frac{1}{6}} = \frac{18 - 7}{42} = \frac{11}{42}$

Naina has $\frac{11}{42}$ m ribbon left with her.

Exercise 8.6

1. A glass holds $\frac{2}{5}$ litres of water. Another glass holds $\frac{3}{7}$ litres of water. How many litres of water do the glasses hold together?
2. Anita ate $\frac{3}{7}$ of the total chocolates on Monday and $\frac{1}{2}$ of the total chocolates on Tuesday. What fraction of the chocolates did Anita eat on Monday and Tuesday?
3. From a wire $6\frac{1}{2}$ metres long, $2\frac{1}{3}$ metres is cut off. What length of the wire is left?
4. Out of a distance of $2\frac{1}{4}$ km, Amit has covered $1\frac{2}{5}$ km. How much distance is still left?
5. Out of all Josh's pets, $\frac{3}{5}$ are dogs and $\frac{1}{4}$ are cats. What fraction of Josh's pets are cats and dogs?
6. Out of $4\frac{1}{2}$ pieces of cake, Sam ate $1\frac{1}{2}$ pieces. How many pieces were left?

Revision Exercise

1 Choose the correct options.

a. $\frac{5}{3}, \frac{2}{3}, \frac{1}{3}, \frac{4}{3}$ written in ascending order is

i. $\frac{5}{3}, \frac{4}{3}, \frac{2}{3}, \frac{1}{3}$ ii. $\frac{1}{3}, \frac{2}{3}, \frac{4}{3}, \frac{5}{3}$ iii. $\frac{2}{3}, \frac{1}{3}, \frac{4}{3}, \frac{5}{3}$ iv. $\frac{4}{3}, \frac{2}{3}, \frac{5}{3}, \frac{1}{3}$ ☐

b. The simplest form of $\frac{128}{48}$ is

i. $\frac{64}{24}$ ii. $\frac{32}{12}$ iii. $\frac{16}{6}$ iv. $\frac{8}{3}$ ☐

c. $\frac{3}{5} + \frac{19}{2} + \frac{7}{10} + \frac{9}{20} =$

i. $13\frac{1}{4}$ ii. $\frac{43}{4}$ iii. $11\frac{1}{4}$ iv. $\frac{49}{4}$ ☐

d. $13\frac{4}{9} + 2\frac{1}{9} =$

i. $13\frac{5}{9}$ ii. $13\frac{2}{9}$ iii. $15\frac{5}{9}$ iv. $15\frac{2}{9}$ ☐

e. $19\frac{2}{5} - 11\frac{3}{5} =$

i. $7\frac{2}{5}$ ii. $8\frac{2}{5}$ iii. $8\frac{4}{5}$ iv. $7\frac{4}{5}$ ☐

f. Out of $6\frac{1}{2}$ kg of potatoes, $2\frac{3}{4}$ kg were cooked for lunch. How many kilograms of potatoes were left?

i. $3\frac{3}{4}$ ii. $6\frac{1}{2}$ iii. $2\frac{3}{4}$ iv. $3\frac{1}{2}$ ☐

g. If Radha read $\frac{3}{5}$ of the book on Monday and $\frac{1}{4}$ of it on Tuesday, what fraction of the book was left to read?

i. $\frac{17}{20}$ ii. $\frac{7}{20}$ iii. $\frac{3}{5}$ iv. $\frac{1}{4}$ ☐

2 a. Write a fraction equivalent to $\frac{7}{9}$ with 36 as the denominator.

b. If $\frac{8}{11} = \frac{24}{x}$, find x.

3. **Fill in the blanks with >, < or =.**

a. $\frac{3}{5}$ ___ $\frac{2}{5}$ b. $\frac{9}{3}$ ___ $\frac{9}{8}$ c. $\frac{4}{5}$ ___ $\frac{2}{9}$ d. $1\frac{2}{3}$ ___ $5\frac{1}{2}$

4. **Write the following fractions in descending order.**

$\frac{1}{4}, \frac{9}{20}, \frac{3}{5}, \frac{7}{10}$

5. **Write the following fractions in their simplest forms.**

a. $\frac{14}{70}$ b. $\frac{180}{200}$ c. $19\frac{25}{40}$

6. **Convert as directed.**

a. $\frac{29}{5}$ into a mixed fraction   b. $17\frac{3}{4}$ into an improper fraction

7. **Write P for proper fraction, I for improper fraction, M for mixed fraction and U for unit fraction.**

a. $\frac{19}{3}$ ______   b. $\frac{1}{9}$ ______   c. $13\frac{2}{7}$ ______   d. $\frac{15}{17}$ ______

8. **Add the following.**

a. $\frac{5}{6}+\frac{2}{3}+\frac{11}{12}+\frac{1}{4}$ b. $19\frac{2}{5}+2\frac{3}{10}$ c. $\frac{7}{10}+\frac{1}{4}+\frac{3}{4}$ d. $\frac{4}{5}+\frac{1}{3}+\frac{2}{5}$

9. **Subtract the following.**

a. $1-\frac{7}{15}$ b. $19\frac{2}{5}-1\frac{1}{2}$ c. $\frac{11}{12}-\frac{2}{3}$ d. $\frac{7}{10}-\frac{1}{5}$

10. If a milkman sold $19\frac{1}{2}$ litres of milk out of a total of $35\frac{3}{4}$ litres, how many litres of milk was left with him?

11. In a school, $\frac{3}{5}$ of the children are in the primary section and $\frac{1}{5}$ of the children are in the middle school section. What fraction of the children are in the primary and middle section?

12. Copy and complete the following:

a. $\frac{1}{3}+\frac{3}{5}=\frac{\_\_}{15}+\frac{\_\_}{15}=$ ____

b. $\frac{3}{4}-\frac{5}{12}=\frac{\_\_}{12}-\frac{5}{12}=$ ____

Worksheet

1. **Out of 20 girls, 11 girls went for a picnic. Find the fraction of girls who went for the picnic and the fraction of girls who did not go for the picnic.**

2. **Identify the numerator and the denominator of the fraction $\frac{17}{85}$.**

3. **In $\frac{2}{7} = \frac{10}{x}$, find x.**

4. **In $\frac{3}{8} = \frac{x}{16}$, find x.**

5. **Fill in the blanks with >, < or = .**

   a. $\frac{2}{3}$ ______ $\frac{4}{3}$ b. $\frac{9}{2}$ ______ $\frac{9}{1}$ c. $\frac{1}{3}$ ______ $\frac{2}{5}$ d. $\frac{4}{7}$ ______ $\frac{4}{7}$

6. **Write the following fractions in ascending order.**

   $\frac{4}{5}$, $\frac{3}{5}$, $\frac{2}{5}$

7. **Write the following fractions in descending order.**

   $\frac{7}{3}$, $\frac{7}{2}$, $\frac{7}{1}$

8. **Fill in the blanks.**

   a. A unit fraction always has ______ as its numerator.

   b. In a proper fraction, the ______ is always smaller than the ______.

   c. In an improper fraction, the ______ is always bigger than or equal to the ______.

   d. $7\frac{1}{3}$ as an improper fraction is ______.

   e. $\frac{2}{5} + \frac{1}{5} =$ ______

   f. $\frac{7}{9} - \frac{2}{9} =$ ______

   g. $\frac{3}{7} - \frac{3}{7} =$ ______

   h. $3\frac{1}{5} + 1\frac{2}{5} =$ ______

   i. $5\frac{2}{3} - 2\frac{1}{3} =$ ______

   j. A number which has no denominator has the denominator ______.

   k. $1 - \frac{2}{3} =$ ______

Decimals

9

Let's Get Started

When one whole part of a quantity is broken into parts, those parts can be expressed either in fractions or in decimals. When the parts are expressed in terms of 10 or 100 or 1000, we get decimal numbers. Decimal point (.) separates the whole number part from the decimal number part.

For example, in fraction, we express half as $\frac{1}{2}$ and in decimal, we express half as 0.5.

Similarly, one and half is expressed as $1\frac{1}{2}$ in terms of fraction and in decimal, we express it as 1.5. The point between 1 and 5 is known as the decimal point.

Decimal Place Values

Tenths

Till now we have dealt with fractions with denominator 10. These fractions are termed as tenths.

$\frac{2}{10}$ is called two tenth. $\frac{3}{10}$ is called three tenth. $\frac{9}{10}$ is called nine tenth.

Hundredths

If the same numerators have 100 as their denominator, then those fractions would be termed as hundredths.

$\frac{2}{100}$ is called two hundredth. $\frac{3}{100}$ is called three hundredth.

$\frac{9}{100}$ is called nine hundredth.

Thousandths

If the same numerators have 1000 as their denominator, then those fractions would be termed as thousandths.

$\frac{2}{1000}$ is called two thousandth. $\frac{3}{1000}$ is called three thousandth.

$\frac{9}{1000}$ is called nine thousandth.

Converting Fractions into Decimals

Examples:

If a decimal is not written in a number, then it is considered that it is on the extreme right of the number.

9 = 9.0 and 5 = 5.0

Example 1: Convert the fraction $\frac{9}{10}$ to a decimal.

Note that the decimal point is on the right of 9, that is, $\frac{9.0}{10}$

When we divide a number by 10 or 100 or 1000, the decimal point moves to the left. It will move to the left as many times as there are zeros in the denominators. Therefore, in this case, the decimal point will move **once** to the left because the denominator 10 has only one zero.

$\therefore \frac{9.}{10} = .9$ or 0.9.

Example 2: Convert $\frac{2}{100}$ into a decimal.

The decimal point is after 2. When we divide by 100, the decimal moves **two** places to the left because 100 has two zeros.

$\frac{2.}{100}$ One move brings the decimal point before 2 and the next time it moves towards the left one more time. Since there is no number, we put a 0 there preceded by the decimal point.

$\therefore \frac{2}{100} = .02$

Example 3: Convert $\frac{12}{100}$ into a decimal.

$\frac{12.}{100} = .12$

Example 4: Convert $\frac{512}{100}$ into a decimal.

$\frac{5\ 1\ 2.}{100} = 5.12$

Example 5: Convert $\frac{2}{1000}$ into a decimal.

The decimal point is after 2. When we divide by 1000, it will move three places to the left because 1000 has three zeros. The first time the decimal point moves over 2 and then when it moves two more times to the left, there are no numbers and so we add two zeros.

$\therefore \frac{2.}{1000} = .002$

Example 6: Convert $\frac{12}{1000}$ into a decimal number.

$\frac{12.}{1000} = .012$

Example 7: Convert $\frac{243}{1000}$ into a decimal number.

$\frac{243.}{1000} = .243$

Example 8: Convert $\frac{1689}{1000}$ into a decimal number.

$\frac{1689.}{1000} = 1.689$

Converting Mixed Fractions into Decimal Numbers

If we have a mixed fraction and we have to convert it to a decimal, then we first copy the whole number from the mixed fraction and on its right, we write the fraction part converted to a decimal.

Example 9: Convert $2\frac{1}{10}$ into a decimal number.

$2\frac{1.}{10} = 2.1$

Example 10: Convert $2\frac{1}{100}$ into a decimal number.

$2\frac{1.}{100} = 2.01$

Example 11: Convert $2\frac{1}{1000}$ into a decimal number.

$2\frac{1.}{1000} = 2.001$

Example 12: Convert $2\frac{23}{10}$ into a decimal number.

$2\frac{23.}{10} = 2 + 2.3 = 4.3$

Exercise 9.1

1 Convert the following into decimals.

a. $\frac{6}{10}$ b. $\frac{4}{100}$ c. $\frac{9}{1000}$ d. $\frac{9}{10}$ e. $\frac{7}{100}$

f. $\frac{3}{1000}$ g. $\frac{15}{10}$ h. $\frac{15}{100}$ i. $\frac{36}{1000}$ j. $\frac{659}{10}$

k. $\frac{293}{100}$ l. $\frac{189}{1000}$ m. $\frac{982}{100}$ n. $\frac{302}{1000}$ o. $\frac{16}{10}$

2 Convert the following mixed fractions into decimals.

a. $1\frac{7}{10}$ b. $3\frac{5}{100}$ c. $5\frac{16}{10}$ d. $5\frac{16}{100}$ e. $5\frac{16}{1000}$

f. $6\frac{9}{10}$ g. $8\frac{5}{100}$ h. $4\frac{67}{100}$ i. $9\frac{7}{1000}$ j. $2\frac{789}{1000}$

Converting Decimal Numbers into Fractions

Example 13: Convert 0.9 into a fraction.

In 0.9, we have one digit after the decimal point. Therefore, in the denominator, we write 1 with **one** zero, that is, 10.

$$0.9 = \frac{9}{10}$$

Note

A fraction is always written in its lowest form.

Example 14: Convert 0.25 into a fraction in its lowest term.

In 0.25, we have 2 digits after the decimal point. Therefore, in the denominator, we write 1 with **two** zeros, that is 100

$$0.25 = \frac{\not{25}^{\not{5}^{1}}}{\not{100}_{\not{20}_{4}}} = \frac{1}{4}$$

$$\therefore 0.25 = \frac{1}{4}$$

Example 15: Convert 0.005 into a fraction.

In 0.005, we have 3 digits after the decimal point. Therefore, in the denominator, we write 1 with **three** zeros, that is, 1000.

$$0.005 = \frac{{}^{1}\not{5}}{\not{1000}_{200}} = \frac{1}{200}$$

Converting Decimals into Mixed Fractions

If the whole number part of the decimal number is other than 0,then we write the whole number part as it is and convert the decimal number part into fraction.

Mental Maths

Convert the following decimals into fractions.

a. 0.8 = ________

b. 1.9 = ________

c. 0.123 = ________

d. 3.75 = ________

Example 16: Convert 2.1 into a fraction.

After the decimal point there is one digit; therefore, the denominator will be 1 with one 0, which is, 10.

$$2.1 = 2\frac{1}{10}$$

Example 17: Convert 2.53 into a fraction.

In this case, after the decimal point, there are 2 digits. Therefore, when we convert it into a fraction, the denominator will be 100

$$\therefore 2.53 = 2\frac{53}{100}$$

Example 18: Convert 5.937 into a fraction.

The denominator here will be 1000.

$$5.937 = 5\,\frac{937}{1000}$$

Exercise 9.2

1 **Convert the following decimals into fractions in their lowest terms.**

a. 0.7 b. 0.45 c. 0.765 d. 0.9

e. 0.82 f. 0.416 g. 0.03 h. 0.005

2 **Convert the following decimal numbers into fractions. Keep the fractions in the their lowest terms.**

a. 5.2 b. 2.18 c. 1.825 d. 5.1

e. 18.2 f. 134.9 g. 7.16 h. 9.23

i. 10.05 j. 5.212 k. 9.683 l. 14.104

Place Value

The value of the digits of a decimal number are explained below. Before the decimal point, they are as we have learned before, that is, units, tens, hundreds, etc. and after the decimal point, they start with tenth.

Thousands	Hundreds	Tens	Units		Tenths	Hundreds	Thousandths	Ten Thousandths
2	9	3	4	.	1	8	5	7

The place value of the above digits is also written accordingly.

The place value of

2 = 2000 $\qquad$ 1 = $\frac{1}{10}$ (one tenth)

9 = 900 $\qquad$ 8 = $\frac{8}{100}$ (eight hundredth)

3 = 30 $\qquad$ 5 = $\frac{5}{1000}$ (five thousandth)

4 = 4 $\qquad$ 7 = $\frac{7}{10000}$ (seven ten thousandth)

Expanded Form

We know that the expanded form of 893 is 800 + 90 + 3.

Note

We need not write $\frac{0}{100}$ since the numerator is zero.

The expanded form of

a. 893.4751 is $800 + 90 + 3 + \frac{4}{10} + \frac{7}{100} + \frac{5}{1000} + \frac{1}{10000}$

b. 598.6027 is $500 + 90 + 8 + \frac{6}{10} + \frac{0}{100} + \frac{2}{1000} + \frac{7}{10000}$

This can be also written as $500 + 90 + 8 + \frac{6}{10} + \frac{2}{1000} + \frac{2}{1000}$

Writing Numbers from Expanded Forms

The expanded form of 293.457 is $200 + 90 + 3 + \frac{4}{10} + \frac{5}{100} + \frac{7}{1000}$.

If the expanded form is given, then we can write the number as shown below.

$200 + 90 + 3 + \frac{4}{10} + \frac{5}{100} + \frac{7}{1000} = 293.457$

If the expanded form is $600 + 20 + 7 + \frac{1}{10} + \frac{9}{1000}$, then the number is 627.109.

We put zero between 1 and 9 since there is no hundredth term in the expanded form.

Reading Decimal Numbers

There are two ways of expressing number names of decimal numbers.

Method 1

We read the numbers before the decimal point as they are but we read the numbers after the decimal point separately. The decimal itself is referred to as 'point'. For example,

432.17 = Four hundred thirty-two point one seven [not seventeen]

9384.510 = Nine thousand three hundred eighty-four point five one zero [not five hundred ten]

Method 2

The second way of expressing the number names is given below.

2.7 = Two and seven tenth [because 7 falls in the tenth position]

5.12 = Five and twelve hundredth [because 12 together falls in the hundredth position]

432.17 = Four hundred thirty-two and seventeen hundredth

9384.510 = Nine thousand three hundred eighty-four and five hundred ten thousandth

Equivalent Decimals

Equivalent decimals are the decimal numbers which have the same value.

0.3 is a decimal number where the place value of 0 is units and the place value of 3 is tenth.

To rename 0.3 as hundredths, we need to add zeros till the hundredth position. So, 0.3 as hundredth is 0.30.

To rename 0.3 as thousandth, we need to add zeros till the thousandth position. So, 0.3 as thousandth is 0.300.

Here, 0.3, 0.30 and 0.300 are equivalent decimals

Exercise 9.3

1. Write the place value of each digit in 5296.7318.
2. **Write the place value of the digit 7 in each of the following numbers.**
   a. 5379 b. 729.5 c. 685.71
   d. 872.18 e. 539.673 f. 23.8271
3. **Write the expanded form of the following numbers.**
   a. 934 b. 934.6 c. 934.68 d. 934.681
   e. 2.483 f. 15.19 g. 1395.738 h. 529.1357
4. **Write the numbers from the following expanded forms.**
   a. $300 + 40 + 9$
   b. $300 + 40 + 9 + \frac{2}{10}$
   c. $300 + 40 + 9 + \frac{2}{10} + \frac{7}{100}$
   d. $300 + 40 + 9 + \frac{2}{10} + \frac{7}{100} + \frac{1}{1000}$
   e. $500 + 30 + 4 + \frac{1}{10} + \frac{6}{10} + \frac{2}{1000}$
   f. $200 + 6 + \frac{3}{10} + \frac{9}{100} + \frac{1}{1000}$
   g. $200 + 90 + 6 + \frac{9}{100} + \frac{1}{1000}$
   h. $200 + 90 + 6 + \frac{3}{10} + \frac{1}{1000}$
5. **Write the number names of the following decimal numbers in both the methods.**
   a. 2.7 b. 2.79 c. 2.795 d. 32.9
   e. 32.95 f. 32.957 g. 159.2 h. 159.27
   i. 159.275 j. 5726.3 k. 5726.34 l. 5726.341
6. Rename 0.9 as
   a. hundredth b. thousandth
7. **Rename the following numbers as hundredth.**
   a. 2.6 b. 5.2 c. 1.6
8. **Rename the following numbers as thousandth.**
   a. 7.8 b. 2.16 c. 19.3

Like Decimals and Unlike Decimals

Like decimals numbers are numbers that have the same number of decimal places. (Decimal places are the number of digits after the decimal point.)

Examples:

a. 98.9, 5.8, 112.6

These are decimal numbers with one decimal place. Therefore, these are like decimal numbers.

b. 29.57, 9.91, 108.15

These are numbers with 2 decimal places. Therefore, these are like decimal numbers.

c. 5.865, 76.899, 45.346

These are numbers with three decimal places. Therefore, these are like decimal numbers.

Unlike decimals are numbers that have different numbers of decimal places.

Examples: 79.1, 1.798, 19.8991

Converting Unlike Decimals into Like Decimals

To convert unlike decimals into like decimals, we check which number has the greatest number of decimal places and complete all the other numbers to the same number of decimal places by adding zeros.

Example: Convert the following unlike decimal numbers to like decimal numbers.

2.3, 1.684, 561.91

We find that the second number has the greatest number of decimal places, that is, 3. So, we complete the other two numbers too to three places of decimals by adding zeros.

We get 2.300, 1.684, 561.910, which are like fractions.

Equal, Greater Than and Less Than

In a decimal number, if there are zeros at the end then those zeros have no meaning. We can remove them.

In 5.930000, we can remove the last four zeros.

$\therefore$ 5.93000 = 5.93

To check which decimal number is greater, we first check the number before the decimal point. The one with the greater digit or number is greater.

Example 19: Which of the following numbers is greater?

429.642 or 393.999

429 is greater than 393.

$\therefore$ 429.642 > 393.999

If the number before the decimal point is the same, then we check the digits after the decimal point, one at a time. The number which has the bigger digit is the bigger number.

Example 20: Which of the following numbers is greater?

593.342 or 593.442

Before the decimal point, both the numbers are the same, that is, 593. After the decimal point, the tenth digit of the first number is 3 and while it is 4 in the second number. So, the second number is greater than the first one.

$593.\underline{3}42 < 593.\underline{4}42$

Similarly,

39.9 > 39.00099

In the above case, the number before the decimal points are the same, that is, 39. After the decimal point, the digit in the tenth position in the first number is 9 and in the second number, it is 0. Since 9 is bigger than 0, 39.90000 > 39.00099.

Mental Maths

Fill in the blanks with >, < or =

a. 3.200 ☐ 3.20

b. 6. 78 ☐ 7.68

c. 78.902 ☐ 78.908

d. 345.891 ☐ 345.819

Example 21: Write the following numbers in ascending order.

1.35, 1.451, 1.456, 2.65, 1.055

To arrange the numbers in ascending order, we need to arrange the numbers from the smallest to the largest.

The given numbers arranged in ascending order are 1.055, 1.35, 1.451, 1.456, 2.65

Example 22: Write the following numbers in descending order.

3.45, 2.45, 3.456, 4.65, 3.455

To arrange the numbers in descending order, we need to arrange the numbers from the largest to the smallest.

The given numbers arranged in descending order are 4.65, 3.456, 3.455, 3.45, 2.45

Exercise 9.4

1 Which of the following questions have like decimals?

a. 18.74, 6.92, 679.19   b. 9.124, 17.9, 386.89

c. 73.451, 13.519, 4019.953   d. 4.57, 7.89, 9.8

2 Convert the following unlike decimals into like decimals.

a. 1.834, 564.6, 13.82   b. 829.56, 775.7, 2.5

3 Write > , < or =.

a. 29.5 ☐ 729.7   b. 982.3 ☐ 161.8

c. 56.10000 ☐ 56.1   d. 134.97 ☐ 134.87

e. 843.8 ☐ 843.1699   f. 73.03 ☐ 73.30

g. 912.45 $\square$ 912.54 h. 19.071 $\square$ 190.71

i. 4328.7 $\square$ 4328.7 j. 359.800 $\square$ 359.80

4. **Which number is different from the rest in each of the following?**

a. 4.8	4.90	4.900	4.9000
b. 0.42	0.24	0.420	0.4200

5. **Find the largest number in each of the following.**

a. 5.3	5.93	5.39	5.450000
b. 2.893	2.3999	2.1899	2.7999
c. 2.8	2.00008	2.3	2.24

6. **Write the following in ascending order.**

a. 18.34	2.9	5.934	4.0	16.2
b. 634.793	634.799	634.798	634.797	

7. **Write the following in descending order.**

a. 35.13	35.9	35.25	35.89	35.03
b. 139.043	139.041	139.049	139.047	139.042

Converting Fractions Which do not have 10, 100, 1000, etc. as Denominators into Decimals

Till now the fractions that we have converted into decimals, had 10, 100, 1000, etc, as denominators. If the denominators are not multiples of 10, then we try to convert the denominators to 10, 100, 1000, etc.

Example 23: Convert $\frac{2}{5}$ into a decimal.

The denominator 5 can be multiplied by 2 to make it 10. If we multiply the denominator by 2, then we must multiply the numerator also by 2.

$$\frac{2\times2}{5\times2} = \frac{4}{10}$$

This becomes $\frac{4}{10}$, which is equal to 0.4 as a decimal.

So, $\frac{2}{5} = \frac{2\times2}{5\times2} = \frac{4}{10} = 0.4$

Example 24: Convert $\frac{1}{2}$ into a decimal.

2 can be multiplied by 5 to make 10.

So, $\frac{1\times5}{2\times5} = \frac{4}{10} = 0.4$

Example 25: Convert $\frac{11}{20}$ into a decimal.

The denominator 20 cannot be made 10 since 10 is smaller than 20. But 20 can be made 100 by multiplying it by 5.

So, $\frac{11 \times 5}{20 \times 5} = \frac{55}{100} = 0.55$

Remember

$1 \times 100 = 100$	$20 \times 5 = 100$
$2 \times 50 = 100$	$25 \times 4 = 100$
$4 \times 25 = 100$	$50 \times 2 = 100$
$5 \times 20 = 100$	$100 \times 1 = 100$
$10 \times 10 = 100$	

Exercise 9.5

1. **Convert the following into decimals.**

   a. $\frac{3}{5}$ b. $\frac{1}{2}$ c. $\frac{4}{5}$ d. $\frac{9}{10}$

2. **Convert the following into decimals.**

   a. $\frac{1}{2}$ b. $\frac{3}{4}$ c. $\frac{4}{5}$ d. $\frac{9}{10}$

   e. $\frac{13}{20}$ f. $\frac{17}{25}$ g. $\frac{11}{50}$ h. $\frac{7}{20}$

Adding Decimal Numbers

We add decimals numbers in the same way we add other numbers. After adding, the decimal is placed in the answer in the same position as placed in the question.

Example 26: Add 2.34 and 1.32.

$$\begin{array}{r} 2.34 \\ +1.32 \\ \hline \\ \hline \end{array}$$

We place the numbers in columns as shown, making sure that the decimal points are placed one below the other. The digits to the left and right of the decimal points are placed exactly as they are in the question. If there are any blank spaces, we fill them with zeros.

$$\begin{array}{r} 2.34 \\ +1.32 \\ \hline 3.66 \\ \hline \end{array}$$

We then add the numbers and place the decimal point in our answer below the other decimal points.

Example 27: Add 53.98 and 71.56

$$\begin{array}{r} {}^{1}\ \ {}^{1}\ \ \ \\ 53.98 \\ +71.56 \\ \hline 125.54 \\ \hline \end{array}$$

Example 28: Add 234.76, 12.093, 1.3 and 142.5.

We arrange them like this.

```
  234.76
   12.093
    1.3
+ 142.5
________

________
```

Then, we fill the blank spaces with zero like this.

```
  234.760
  012.093
  001.300
+ 142.500
_________

_________
```

Next, we add the numbers and write the answer.

```
  234.760
  012.093
  001.300
+ 142.500
_________
  390.653
_________
```

Answer = 390.653

Note

If there is no decimal point in a number, then the decimal point is put at the end of the number on the right.

Try These!

Work out the answers to these calculations.

a. 3.8 + 2.92 + 4.65 = ____

b. 4.9 + 6.03 + 1.098 = ____

Example 29: Add 2.935, 400 and 68.1.

```
    2.935
  400.000
+  68.100
_________
  471.035
_________
```

Answer = 471.035

Try These!

Solve the following :

a. 6.07 + 3 = ____

b. 3.5 + 9.41 = ____

c. 12.44 + 6 = ____

d. 23.897 + 8.65 = ____

Exercise 9.6

1 Solve the following.

a.	b.	c.	d.
2.3 + 1.6 = ____	3.5 + 2.2 = ____	5.8 + 2.0 = ____	6.3 + 2.6 = ____

e.	f.	g.	h.
7.2 + 3.5 = ____	3.1 + 4.6 = ____	2.6 + 3.7 = ____	4.9 + 3.9 = ____

i.	j.	k.	l.
6.8 + 3.9 = ____	7.9 + 8.2 = ____	9.6 + 7.8 = ____	4.8 + 7.3 = ____

2 **Arrange the following in columns and then add.**

a. 29.3 + 11.8 + 93.7

b. 729.35 + 183.94 + 200.16

c. 1873.9 + 729.8 + 23.1

d. 729.84 + 1983.73 + 2000.86

e. 5268.94 + 293.05 + 9.8

f. 4.9 + 183.05 + 24.009

Subtracting Decimal Numbers

We subtract decimal numbers exactly as we subtract other numbers. We should remember to place the decimals one below the other.

Example 30:

a.

$$\begin{array}{r} 9.3 \\ -\ 2.1 \\ \hline 7.2 \\ \hline \end{array}$$

This is an example of simple subtraction.

b.

$$\begin{array}{r} \overset{7}{\cancel{8}}.\overset{13}{\cancel{3}} \\ -\ 2.9 \\ \hline 5.4 \\ \hline \end{array}$$

This is an example of subtraction with borrowing.

Example 31: Subtract 12.23 from 93.42.

$$\begin{array}{r} 93.\overset{3}{\cancel{4}}\overset{12}{\cancel{2}} \\ -12.23 \\ \hline 81.19 \\ \hline \end{array}$$

Answer = 81.19

Example 32: Subtract 4.13 from 49.9.

When we place the numbers vertically, we should remember to place the decimal points one below the other. The digits to the left and right of the decimal points are placed exactly as they are in the question. If there are any blank spaces, we fill them with zeros.

$$\begin{array}{r} 49.9 \\ -\ \ 4.13 \\ \hline \\ \hline \end{array}$$

Now, fill the blanks with zeros and then subtract.

$$\begin{array}{r} 49.\overset{8}{\cancel{9}}\overset{10}{\cancel{0}} \\ -04.13 \\ \hline 45.77 \\ \hline \end{array}$$

Answer = 45.77

Exercise 9.7

1 Solve the following.

a. $\begin{array}{r} 9.6 \\ -2.3 \\ \hline \\ \hline \end{array}$	b. $\begin{array}{r} 8.7 \\ -1.2 \\ \hline \\ \hline \end{array}$	c. $\begin{array}{r} 7.5 \\ -1.3 \\ \hline \\ \hline \end{array}$	d. $\begin{array}{r} 8.2 \\ -3.6 \\ \hline \\ \hline \end{array}$
e. $\begin{array}{r} 7.5 \\ -2.6 \\ \hline \\ \hline \end{array}$	f. $\begin{array}{r} 5.2 \\ -1.9 \\ \hline \\ \hline \end{array}$	g. $\begin{array}{r} 19.5 \\ -12.9 \\ \hline \\ \hline \end{array}$	h. $\begin{array}{r} 93.4 \\ -19.9 \\ \hline \\ \hline \end{array}$
i. $\begin{array}{r} 45.2 \\ -19.7 \\ \hline \\ \hline \end{array}$	j. $\begin{array}{r} 593.6 \\ -\ \ 14.8 \\ \hline \\ \hline \end{array}$	k. $\begin{array}{r} 749.3 \\ -188.8 \\ \hline \\ \hline \end{array}$	l. $\begin{array}{r} 2468.135 \\ -\ \ 123.946 \\ \hline \\ \hline \end{array}$

2 Arrange in columns and subtract.

a. 389.6 – 125.3 b. 1253.2 – 943.6 c. 730 – 666.6

d. 1830 – 99.9 e. 5934.225 – 1803.87 f. 5000 – 493.842

Word Problems on Decimals

Word problems on decimals are solved in the same way as other word problems. The only difference is that we have to place the decimal points in the numbers at the correct places.

Example 33: I walked 2.5 km, cycled 3.75 km and travelled by bus for 15.9 km. What was the total distance I travelled?

		km
Distance I walked	=	02.50
Distance I cycled	=	03.75
Distance I travelled by bus	=	+ 15.90
Total distance travelled	=	22.15

The total distance I travelled was 22.15 km.

Example 34: Seema bought 5.75 metres of cloth. Radha bought 2.95 metres of cloth. Who bought more cloth and how much more?

		m
Length of cloth bought by Seema	=	$\overset{4}{\cancel{5}}.\overset{17}{\cancel{7}}5$
Length of cloth bought by Radha	=	–2.95
Difference in the length	=	2.80

Seema bought 2.80 metres more than Radha.

Exercise 9.8

1. Ram's height is 5.4 feet and Shyam's height is 6.1 feet.
   a. What is the sum of both their heights?
   b. What is the difference between their heights?
2. One bag contained 3.5 kgs of potatoes and 1.5 kgs of onions. Another bag contained 2.5 kgs of potatoes and 2.4 kgs of onions.
   a. What was the total weight of both the bags?
   b. Which bag had more weight and by how much?
3. I have ₹4320.91 in the bank. I put ₹193.05 more in it. How much money do I have in it now?
4. I have ₹349.50 in the bank. If i withdraw ₹259.30, how much money would be left in the bank?
5. A sack has 3.4 kg of potatoes and 1.65 kg of onions. If 2.03 kg of cucumber is added to it, what will be the total weight of the sack?
6. A sack has 4.9 kg of potatoes, 5 kg of onions and 2.03 kg of cucumber. If 1.05 kg of potatoes are removed from the sack, what will be the weight of the vegetables left in it?
7. Rita wants to buy shoes for ₹435.60. She gives the shopkeeper ₹500. How much money does the shopkeeper return to her?
8. Seema has ₹2395.40. She gives ₹1035.20 to Arun and ₹395 to Vijay. How much money is she left with?
9. Sujata had ₹4382. Tara gave her ₹360.05. Out of all the money she had, Sujata gave ₹1005.50 to Anil. How much money was left with Sujata?
10. Out of a journey of 253.50 km, I have covered 183.20 km. How much more do I have to travel?

Mental Maths

1. Write the following as decimals:

   a. $\frac{4}{5}$ = ______ b. $\frac{2}{5}$ = ______

2. Write the following as fractions. Simplify them if possible.

   a. 0.09 = ______ b. 0.24 = ______

3. Change the following into decimal numbers.

   a. $2\frac{3}{5}$ = ______ b. $4\frac{1}{5}$ = ______

4. Change these to tenths or hundredths and write them as decimal numbers.

   a. $1\frac{9}{50}$ = ______ = ______ b. $3\frac{11}{20}$ = ______ = ______

5. Put a circle around the largest decimal below:

   8.02 8.002 8.2 8.022 8.020

Revision Exercise

1 **Choose the correct options.**

a. $15\frac{2}{10}$ as a decimal is

i. 15.12 ii. 15.10 iii. 15.2 iv. 5.2 ☐

b. $\frac{3987}{100}$ as a decimal is

i. 3.987 ii. 39.87 iii. 398.7 iv. 3987 ☐

c. $15\frac{9}{1000}$ as a decimal is

i. 15.9 ii. 15.90 iii. 15.09 iv. 15.009 ☐

d. 2.24 as a fraction in its lowest term is

i. $\frac{224}{100}$ ii. $\frac{112}{50}$ iii. $\frac{56}{25}$ iv. $\frac{2.24}{100}$ ☐

e. 673.29 can be read as

i. six hundred seventy-three and twenty-nine
ii. six hundred seventy-three and twenty-nine hundredth
iii. six hundred seventy-three and twenty-nine thousandth
iv. six hundred seventy-three and twenty-nine hundred ☐

f. $300 + 90 + 1 + \frac{2}{10} + \frac{7}{1000}$ written in number form is

i. 391.207 ii. 391.27 iii. 391.270 iv. 390.207 ☐

g. 2.2, 222, 22.222, 22.000 in ascending order is

i. 222, 22.222, 22.000, 2.2 ii. 22.000, 2.2, 22.222, 222
iii. 2.2, 22.000, 22.222, 222 iv. 22.222, 2.2, 222, 22.000 ☐

h. $\frac{9}{20}$ as a decimal is

i. 0.45 ii. 0.09 iii. 0.20 iv. 9.20 ☐

i. 5.8 + 600 + 39.25 is equal to

i. 639.25 ii. 605.8 iii. 645.05 iv. 645.825 ☐

j. Out of a total of 13 kg of vegetables, if the cook cooks 5.35 kg, then how many kilograms of vegetables will be left?

i. 7.65 kg ii. 13 kg iii. 5.35 kg iv. 18.35 kg ☐

2. **Convert the following fractions into decimals.**

a. $\frac{7}{10}$ b. $\frac{58}{10}$ c. $35\frac{3}{10}$ d. $\frac{2}{100}$

e. $\frac{1}{1000}$ f. $\frac{53}{1000}$ g. $15\frac{7}{100}$ h. $93\frac{11}{100}$

3. **Convert the following decimals into fractions in their lowest form.**

a. 0.3 b. 0.73 c. 5.4 d. 13.2

4. **What is the numeral for the following.**

a. Nine thousand nine and fifty-one hundredth

b. Seven hundred forty-eight point two seven three

5. Write the place value of 7 in 983.715.

6. Write the expanded form of the following.

$500000 + 90 + 6 + \frac{9}{10} + \frac{7}{1000}$

7. Write the following numbers in descending order.

9.9, 9.999, 99.9, 999, 9.009

8. **Convert the following fractions into decimals.**

a. $\frac{2}{5}$ b. $\frac{1}{20}$ c. $\frac{9}{25}$ d. $\frac{11}{100}$

9. Add the following.

3.4, 900, 123.21, 12.9

10. Solve 73 – 2.95.

11. Rani walked 165.95 m in one hour and Robin walked 188.02 m in one hour. Who walked more and by how many metres?

12. Seema bought a pen for ₹7.25 and a notebook for ₹4.50. She gave the shopkeeper ₹20. How much money did the shopkeeper give back to her?

13. **I walked around a field shaped like a triangle where each side was equal to 18.25 metres. How much distance did I travel when I went around the field**

a. once? b. two times?

Worksheet

1. **Convert the following fractions into decimals.**

   a. $\frac{9}{10}$ b. $\frac{23}{10}$ c. $\frac{386}{100}$

   d. $\frac{592}{1000}$ e. $3\frac{3}{100}$ f. $19\frac{2}{1000}$

2. **Convert the following decimals into fractions.**

   a. 0.7   b. 2.5   c. 13.1

   d. 3643.293   e. 95.032   f. 5.2005

3. **Write in words the value of the digit 5 in each number:**

   a. 14.05 ______________________

   b. 14.5 ______________________

   c. 14.005 ______________________

4. **Work out the answers to these calculations.**

   a. 18.09 −4.2 = __________   b. 23.6 + 14.23 = __________

5. **Below is listed the weights of 6 friends. Work out how much they weigh altogether.**

   25.4 kg   28.72 kg   21.8 kg   30.02kg   33.19 kg   24.5 kg

   Total weight = __________

6. Radha bought 1.5 kg oranges and Meeta bought 1.25 kg of oranges. Who bought more oranges and by how much?

For the Curious Mind

Sunita moves 10.2 m straight. Then, she moves 11.5 m straight back.

What is the distance between her original place and where she is standing now?

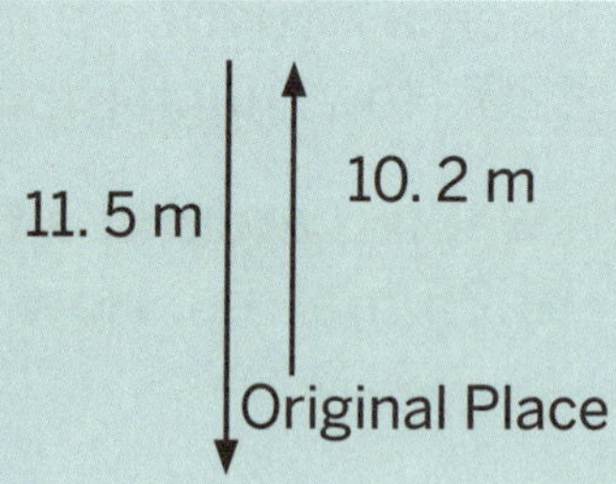

Unitary Method

10

Let's Get Started

Hints and Tips

If the answer is expected to be 'more', then we multiply. If the answer is expected to be 'less', then we divide.

Unit means one item of a certain quantity.

In unitary method, we first find the value of one item of the quantity being discussed and then we find the value of many.

For example, if the value of one unit is given and the value of many units of the same kind is to be calculated, then we multiply the number of units by the value of one unit. We do this because the value of many units is expected to be more than the value of one unit.

Similarly, if the value of many units is given and the value of one unit is to be calculated, then we divide the value of many units by the number of units. We do this because the value of one unit is expected to be less than the value of many units.

Example 1: 5 pens cost ₹80. What is the cost of 3 pens?

Here, the two quantities being discussed are pens and their value in rupees. Since the question requires us to find the value of the pens in rupees we write the statement in such a way that the cost is written on the right side and the number of pens is written on the left side of the page. The first statement will be 'Cost of 5 pens = ₹80'.

Now, we write 1 pen under 5 pens to find its cost. Since 1 pen will cost less than 5 pens, we divide 80 by 5. The working up to this point is given below.

Cost of 5 pens = ₹80

Cost of 1 pen = 80 ÷ 5 = ₹16

Now, we have to find the cost price of 3 pens. So, under 1 pen, we write 3 pens. Since 3 pens cost more than 1 pen, we multiply by 3 to get the answer.

Cost of 5 pens = ₹80

Cost of 1 pen = ₹16

Cost of 3 pens = 3 × 16 = ₹48

So, 3 pens cost ₹48.

cost ₹80.

will cost ₹16.

will cost ₹46.

Example 2: 3 boxes weigh 36 kg. What will be the cost of 10 boxes?

Weight of 3 boxes = 36 kg

Weight of 1 box = 36 ÷ 3 = 12 kg

Weight of 10 boxes = 10 × 12 = 120 kg

Thus, 10 boxes will weigh 120 kg.

Example 3: In 20 minutes, I run 500 metres. In how much time will I run 2000 metres?

Time needed to run 500 metres = 20 minutes

Time needed to run 1 metre = $20 \div 500 = \frac{1}{25}$ minutes

Time needed to run 2000 metres = $2000 \times \frac{1}{25}$

= 80 minutes

= 1 hour 20 minutes

Thus, to run 2000 metres, I will need 1 hour 20 minutes.

Example 4: 6 ice creams cost ₹72. What is the cost of 1 ice cream?

Cost of 6 ice creams = ₹72

Cost of 1 ice cream = $\frac{72}{6}$ = ₹12

So, the cost of 1 ice cream is ₹12.

Exercise 10.1

1. 2 baskets of mangoes weigh 36 kg. What is the weight of 8 baskets of mangoes?

2. 8 sweets cost ₹56. All of them have the same cost. What is the cost of 5 sweets?
3. The cost of 4 buns is ₹12. What is the cost of 9 buns?
4. In 3 hours, I walk 6 km. How much do I walk in 7 hours?
5. In 3 days, a train covers 3900 km. How much does it cover in 10 days?

6. 1 kg tomatoes cost ₹84. What is the cost of 5 kg tomatoes?
7. 9 toy cars cost ₹1215. What is the cost of 5 toy cars?

Revision Exercise

1 Choose the correct options.

a. 5 chocolates cost ₹75. What will be the cost of 9 chocolates?

i. ₹45 ii. ₹135 iii. ₹675 iv. ₹90

b. In 3 hours, I run 12 km. How many km do I run in 5 hours ?

i. 20 km ii. 12 km iii. 5 km iv. 15 km

c. In 2 hours, Meena paints 14 flowers. How many flowers does she paint in 5 hours?

i. 14 ii. 10 iii. 70 iv. 35

d. 6 pens cost ₹252. What is the cost of 8 pens?

i. ₹336 ii. ₹48 iii. ₹42 iv. ₹32

e. In 2 hours, Rajat can eat 4 apples. How many apples can he eat in 6 hours?

i. 24 ii. 4 iii. 12 iv. 2

2 9 T-shirts cost ₹810. How many T-shirts can I buy for ₹1080?

3 5 litres of petrol cost ₹375. What is the cost of 3 litres of petrol?

4 2 pieces of pastry cost ₹30. How many pieces of pastry can I buy for ₹90?

5 8 metres of cloth cost ₹560. How many metres of cloth can I buy for ₹420?

6 A car uses 13 litres of petrol to cover a distance of 143 km. How many litres of petrol will it use to cover 132 km?

7 In 10 weeks, a man earns ₹980. In how many weeks will he earn ₹1372?

Mental Maths

1. If 1 pen costs ₹10, what will be the cost of 5 pens?
2. If 4 books cost ₹200, what will be the cost of 3 books?
3. If 6 books costs ₹300, what will be the cost of 10 books?

Measurement

11

We have different measurements for measuring length, mass and capacity. In India, we use the metric system, which is an internationally used system of measurement.

Measurement of Length

Kilometre, hectometre, decametre, metre, decimetre, centimetre and millimetre are various units of measurement of length. Among them, the most commonly used are **kilometre**, **metre**, **centimetre** and **millimetre**.

If you stretch your left arm, the length from the finger tip of your left arm to the shoulder of your right arm is 1 metre approximately.

Centimetre and millimetre are smaller units of measurements, and are shown on rulers.

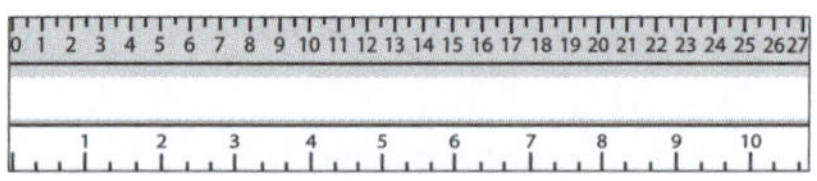

The following chart shows the different units of measurement of length in the metric system.

Name	Kilometre	Hectometre	Decametre	Metre	Decimetre	Centimetre	Millimetre
Abbreviation	km	hm	dam	m	dm	cm	mm

For converting a bigger unit to a smaller unit, multiply the bigger unit by 10 or multiples of 10, depending upon the units involved. Similarly, for converting a smaller unit to a bigger unit, divide the smaller unit by 10 or multiples of 10, depending upon the units involved.

Bigger to smaller: multiply

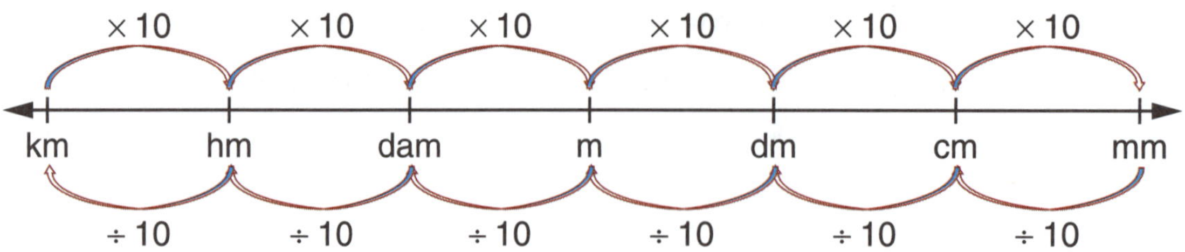

Smaller to bigger: divide

Real-life Examples

The length of a pen is approximately 14 centimetres.

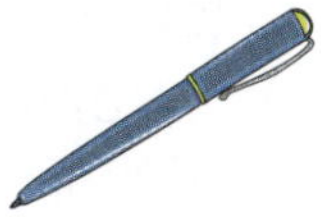

The length of a car is approximately 4 metres.

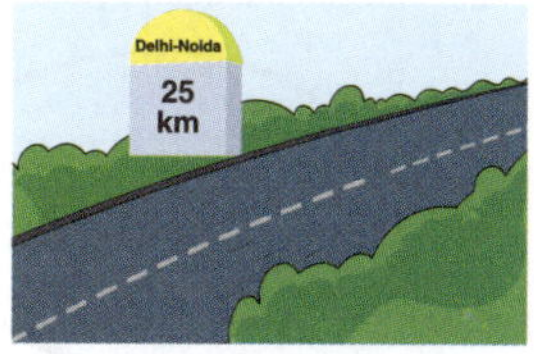

We measure the distance between any two towns in kilometres.

Example 1: Convert 5 dam to dm.

On the chart, between dam and dm, there are two multiplications by 10—dam to m and m to dm. So, we multiply with $10 \times 10 = 100$.

$\therefore$ 5 dam $= 5 \times 100 = 500$ dm

Example 2: Find $\frac{1}{4}$ of 9 m in cm.

1 m $= 10 \times 10$ cm $= 100$ cm

$$\frac{1}{4} \times 9 \text{ m} = \frac{1}{\cancel{4}_{\cancel{2}_{1}}} \times 9 \times \cancel{100}^{\cancel{50}^{25}} = 225 \text{ cm}$$

$\therefore \frac{1}{4}$ of 9 m $= 225$ cm

Example 3: 9 km 6 hm 3 dam 8 m = ________ m

9 km	$= 9 \times 1000$	$= 9000$ m	9000 m
6 hm	$= 6 \times 100$	$= 600$ m	600 m
3 dam	$= 3 \times 10$	$= 30$ m	30 m
8 m	$= 8 \times 1$	$= 8$ m	8 m

$\therefore$ 9 km 6 hm 3 dam 8 m = <u>9638</u> m

Measurement of Mass

Kilogram, hectogram, decagram, gram, decigram, centigram and milligram are various units of measurement used to weigh objects. The commonly used ones are **kilogram**, **gram** and **milligram**.

The following chart shows the different units of measurement of mass.

Name	Kilogram	Hectogram	Decagram	Gram	Decigram	Centigram	Milligram
Abbreviation	kg	hg	dag	g	dg	cg	mg

When we convert a bigger unit into a smaller unit (that is, when we move from the left to the right on the chart), we multiply.

When we convert a smaller unit into a bigger unit (that is, when we move from the right to the left on the chart), we divide.

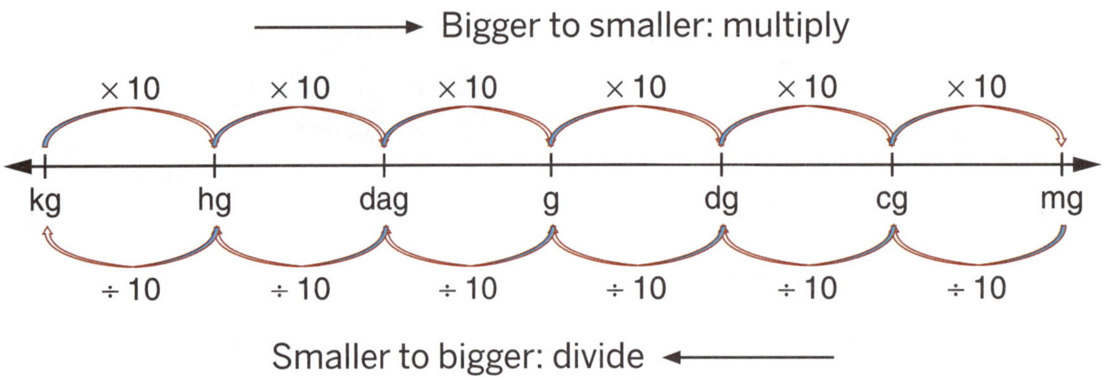

Real-life Examples

The spices used in the kitchen are usually measured in milligrams or grams.

Fruit and vegetables are normally measured in grams or kilograms.

A teaspoon of salt is around 5 mg.

A tablespoon of salt is around 15 g.

The weight of a Class 4 boy would be around 30 kg.

Example 4: Convert 9 kg to g.

We have to convert from a bigger unit to a smaller unit. So, we multiply. On the chart, between kg and g, there are three multiplications by 10. So, we multiply with $10 \times 10 \times 10 = 1000$.

So, 1 kg = 1000 g

$\therefore$ 9 kg = $9 \times 1000 = 9000$ g

Example 5: Find $\frac{2}{5}$ of 6 kg in g.

$\frac{2}{5}$ of 6×1000 (To convert kg to g, we multiply by 1000.)

$= \frac{2}{\cancel{5}} \times 6 \times \overset{200}{\cancel{1000}} = 2400$ g (6 kg = 6×1000 g)

$\therefore \frac{2}{5}$ of 6 kg = 2400 g

Example 6: Solve 18 g 3 cg = ________ cg

$$\begin{array}{r} 18 \text{ g} = 18 \times 100 = \quad 1800 \text{ cg} \\ + \quad 3 \text{ cg} \\ \hline 1803 \text{ cg} \end{array}$$

So, 18 g 3 cg = 1803 cg

Measurement of Capacity

Kilolitre, hectolitre, decalitre, litre, decilitre, centilitre and millilitre are various units of measuring capacity. The commonly used ones are **kilolitre**, **litre** and **millilitre**.

We follow the chart given below to convert the units of measurement of capacity.

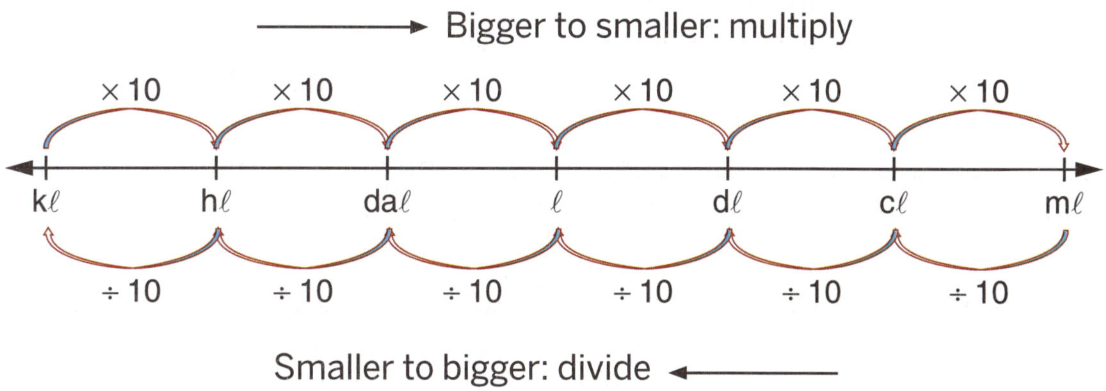

Example 7: Convert 7 ℓ to mℓ

On the chart for the units of capacity, to move from ℓ to mℓ, we need to multiply by 10 thrice. So, we multiply with 1000.

1 ℓ = 1000 mℓ

7 ℓ = 7 × 1000 = 7000 ℓ

Example 8: Convert 3.459 hℓ to ℓ.

To convert hℓ to ℓ, we multiply with 100, the decimal point moves two places to the right.

3.459 × 100 = 345.9 ℓ

∴ 3.459 hℓ = 345.9 ℓ

Example 9: Convert 6 kℓ 300 ℓ into litre.

First convert 6 kℓ to ℓ.

6 kℓ = 6 × 1000 = 6000 ℓ

Since 300 is already in litre, so we add the two quantities.

6 kℓ 300 ℓ = 6000 ℓ
+ 300 ℓ
6300 ℓ

∴ 6 kℓ 300 ℓ = 6300 ℓ

Example 10: Convert 5321 mℓ into ℓ.

In this case, we convert from smaller to bigger unit. To move from mℓ to ℓ, we need to divide by 10 thrice. Therefore, we divide by 1000.

$\frac{5321}{1000} = 5.321$ [We move the decimal point three times to the left.]

$\therefore$ 5321 mℓ = 5.321 ℓ

Example 11: Convert 5321 mℓ into ℓ and mℓ.

To convert mℓ to ℓ, we divide by 1000.

$\frac{5321}{1000} = 5.321$ [We move the decimal point three times to the left.]

$\therefore$ 5321 mℓ = 5 ℓ 321 mℓ [On the left of the decimal point is ℓ and on the right is mℓ.]

Exercise 11.1

1 Fill in the blanks with appropriate units.

a. A bucket can hold 5 ________ of water.

b. Mother added 5 ________ of sugar in a glass of milk.

c. The bed is 2 ________ long.

d. Ajay's house is just 200 ________ away from mine.

e. Mother cooked half ________ potatoes for lunch.

2 Calculate the following.

a. 5 kg = ________ g

b. 9 km = ________ m

c. 16 kℓ = ________ ℓ

d. $\frac{1}{2}$ of 5 kℓ = ________ ℓ

e. $\frac{1}{3}$ of 6 m = ________ cm

f. $\frac{1}{3}$ of 9 kg = ________ g

g. $\frac{1}{5}$ of 1 m = ________ cm

h. $\frac{1}{3}$ of 3 hℓ = ________ mℓ

i. $\frac{1}{3}$ of 9 kℓ = ________ dg

j. $\frac{1}{4}$ of 16 dm = ________ mm

k. $\frac{1}{5}$ of 5 hg = ________ g

l. 2 kg 163 g = ________ g

m. 1 km 55 m = ________ m

n. 9 m 12 cm = ________ cm

o. 5 m 9 cm = ________ cm

p. 2 kg 5 hg 3 dag 9 g = ________ g

q. 1 km 9 dam 5 m = ________ m

r. 6 kℓ 3 hℓ 7ℓ = ________ ℓ

s. 19 kg 2 g = ________ g

t. 6235 g = ________ kg

u. 6235 g = ________ kg ________ g

v. 4309 ℓ = ________ kℓ

Understanding Metric Measures in Decimal Notation

Consider the case where 38.579 kg is to be expressed in kg, hg, dag and g.

The numbers before the decimal, that is, 38 will be kg. The first digit after the decimal, that is, 5 will be hectogram. The next digit 7 will be decagram and the digit 9 will be gram.

Therefore, 38.579 kg = 38 kg 5 hg 7 dag 9 g

Let us look at a few more examples.

Note

The units are in the same order as in the charts.

Example 12: 739.209 km = 739 km 2 hm 0 dam 9m

Example 13: 231. 587 ℓ = 231 ℓ 5 dℓ, 8 cℓ, 7 mℓ

Example 14: 593.82 m = 593 m 8 dm 2 cm 0 mm

[Here, we put 0 for mm because we have to complete three digits after the decimal.]

Now, let us try to convert smaller units to bigger units with the help of decimal notation.

Example 15: Express 162 g 9 dg 6 cg 1 mg in grams.

Following the same pattern we used above, but in the reverse order, we get

162 g 9 dg 6 cg 1 mg = 162.961 g

Example 16: Express 162 ℓ 9 dℓ 1 mℓ in litres.

162 ℓ 9 dℓ 1 mℓ = 162. 901 ℓ

Example 17: Express 13 km 8 hm 5 dam 3m in km

13 km 8 hm 5 dam 3 m = 13. 853 km

Example 18: Express 52 g 7 mg in g

52 g 7 mg = 52.007 g

Mental Maths

1. Express 98 km 4 m in km.

   ____

2. Express 30 g 9 dg 5 mg in grams.

   ____

Exercise 11.2

1. **Express the following in kg, hg, dag and g.**

   a. 49.613 kg b. 8.54 kg c. 279.108 kg

2. **Express the following in km, hm, dam and m.**

   a. 52.268 km b. 179.26 km c. 3.008 km

3. **Express the following in kℓ, hℓ, daℓ and ℓ.**

   a. 27.83 kℓ b. 6.154 kℓ c. 789.402 kℓ

4. 97.16 m = ______ m ______ cm
   = ______ m ______ dm ______ cm ______ mm
5. 288. 30 m = ______ m ______ cm
   = ______ m ______ dm ______ cm ______ mm
6. 46 g 3 dg 9 cg 7 mg = ______ g
7. 5 g 8 dg 1 mg = ______ g
8. 59 ℓ 6 dℓ 8 cℓ 7 mℓ = ______ ℓ
9. 17 ℓ 1 cℓ 2 mℓ = ______ ℓ
10. 73 km 4 hm 2 dam 1 m = ______ km
11. 3 kg 5 hg 6 dag 2 g = ______ kg
12. 8 kℓ 3 dal 9 ℓ = ______ kℓ
13. 7 m 1 dm 4 cm 6 mm = ______ m
14. 2 km 9 hm 3 m = ______ km
15. 4 kg 6 g = ______ kg
16. 9 kℓ 3 hℓ = ______ kℓ
17. 2 m 8 cm 5 mm = ______ m
18. 1 km 6 dam = ______ km
19. 135. 672 ℓ = ______ ℓ ______ dℓ ______ cℓ ______ mℓ
20. 9 dℓ 5 cℓ 2 mℓ = ______ ℓ

Word Problems on Measurements

Example 19: Anuradha bought 2 kg 500 g of papaya, 5 kg 150 g of watermelon, 750 g of grapes and 20 g of mint leaves. What is the total weight of the items that Anuradha bought?

kg		**g**
$^{1}2$	.	$^{1}500$
5	.	150
0	.	750
0	.	020
8	.	420

20 gm will be written like this.

The total weight of the items that Anuradha bought is 8 kg 420 g.

Example 20: Ram travelled 13 km 250 m by car, 5 km by cycle and 750 m by foot. What was the total distance Ram travelled?

5 km will be written like this.

	km	**m**
	$1^{1}3$	$^{1}250$
	0 5	000
+	0 0	750
	19	000

750 m will be written like this.

The total distance Ram travelled was 19 km.

Example 21: Out of 4 ℓ 500 mℓ of water in a bucket, Seema used 1 ℓ 5 mℓ. How much water was left in the bucket?

	ℓ	mℓ
		9
		4 10 10
	4	~~5~~ ~~0~~ ~~0~~
−	1	0 0 5
	3	4 9 5

5 mℓ will be written like this.

3 ℓ and 495 mℓ of water was left in the bucket.

Exercise 11.3

1. The weights of Anil, Sunil and Raman are 45 kg 250 gm, 53 kg 5 gm and 48 kg 10 g respectively.
   a. Who is the heaviest among these three boys?
   b. Who is the lightest among these three boys?
   c. What is the total weight of these boys?
2. Out of a distance of 250 km 305 m, Sanjay has covered 157 km 295 m. How much distance is still left to be covered?
3. A square field has a side of 52 m 75 cm. What is the total length of all the four sides?
4. The weight of two buckets of water is 11 ℓ 450 mℓ. One bucket weighs 5 ℓ 10 mℓ. What is the weight of the second bucket?
5. The weight of an empty box is 2 kg. If it is filled with toys, the weight becomes 11 kg 350 g. What is the weight of the toys?
6. Seema's weight is 65 kg 250 g. Reena's weight is 6 kg 5 g lesser than Seema's. What is Reena's weight?
7. Alok bought 2 kg 150 g apples, 3 kg oranges and 1 kg 20 g bananas. What is the total weight of the fruits Alok bought?
8. The distance from Dehradun to Delhi is 250 km 500 m. The distance from Dehradun to Meerut is 90 km 250 m lesser. What is the distance from Meerut to Delhi?
9. Radhika bought 4ℓ 75 mℓ of orange juice, 5 ℓ 50 mℓ of guava juice and 7 ℓ 25 mℓ of mixed juice. What is the total amount of juice she bought?
10. Renu has 10 kg 600g of rice and Geeta has 12 kg 500 g of rice. Who has more rice and how much more?

Revision Exercise

1 Choose the correct options.

a. 15.93 km = ________

i. 1593 m ii. 15903 m iii. 15930 m iv. 1.593 m ☐

b. $\frac{3}{4}$ of 12 m = ________

i. 900 cm ii. 9000 cm iii. 90 cm iv. 9 cm ☐

c. 7 kg 7 g = ________

i. 7700 g ii. 7007 g iii. 7000 g iv. 7070 g ☐

d. 19 kℓ 5 ℓ = ________

i. 195 ℓ ii. 19005 ℓ iii. 1905 ℓ iv. 1950 ℓ ☐

e. 3 km 2 hm 5 m = ________

i. 3250 m ii. 325 m iii. 3.250 m iv. 3205 m ☐

f. 8156 g = ________

i. 8.156 kg ii. 8156 kg iii. 8156 kg iv. 81.56 kg ☐

g. 15.29 ℓ = ________

i. 1 ℓ 529 mℓ ii. 15 ℓ 290 mℓ iii. 152 ℓ 9 mℓ iv. 1529 ℓ 0 mℓ ☐

h. 46.179 km = ________ km ________ hm ________ dam ________ m

i. 4 km 6 hm 1 dam 7 m ii. 46 km 1 hm 7 dam 9 m ☐

iii. 461 km 7 hm 9 dam 0 m iv. 4 km 6 hm 1 dam 9 m

i. 11 kg 25 g more than 180 kg 5 g = ________

i. 191 kg 300 g ii. 191 kg 25 g iii. 191 kg 030 g iv. 191 kg 5 g ☐

j. Sunita bought 5 kg of apples and 2 kg 290 g of mangoes. How many more kg of apples than mangoes did she buy?

i. 2.710 kg ii. 2.071 kg iii. 27.1 kg iv. 271 kg ☐

2 Fill in the blanks.

a. To convert kg to dag, we multiply by ______.

b. To convert mm to dℓ, we ______ by 100.

c. 1 kℓ = ______ ℓ

d. 1 hg = ______ dg

3 Fill in the blanks with appropriate units.

a. My eyedrops bottle contains 15 ________ of the medicine.

b. My school bag weighs 3 ________.

c. The tailor needed 2 ________ of cloth to make my shirt.

d. My mother needs 1 ________ of potatoes in the kitchen.

e. Radha's house is close to my house. It's about 2 ________ away.

4 **Write the following in ascending order.**

5 kg, 4000 g, 350 hg, 4500 dg

5 19 km = ________ m

6 47. 82 g = ________ dg

7 3.6 cm = ________ mm

8 $\frac{1}{6}$ of 6 hℓ = ________ dℓ

9 59 g 9 dg 7 mg = ________ mg

10 12.345 km = ________ km ________ hm ________ dam ________ m

11 Anita is 2.9 m tall and Beena is 2.45 m tall. Who is taller and by how much?

12 Out of 20.750 kg of potatoes, 5. 750 kg got spoiled. The rest of the potatoes were distributed among three families. How much did each family get?

For the Curious Mind

A blue whale can be as long as 31 m, which is roughly the length of a basketball court, and can weigh up to 160 tons.

The height of the Burj Khalifa in Dubai, the tallest building in the world, is about 830 m.

Mixed Review 3

1. **Find the LCM of the following.**

   a. 12, 15, 30 b. 24, 36, 84

2. **Find the HCF of the following.**

   a. 40, 52, 64 b. 38, 57, 76

3. Write the first four equivalent fractions of $\frac{1}{3}$.

4. Write a fraction equal to $\frac{3}{8}$ with 48 as the denominator.

5. **Fill in the blanks with >, < or =.**

   a. $\frac{2}{7}$ ___ $\frac{30}{105}$ b. $\frac{5}{2}$ ___ $\frac{18}{19}$ c. $\frac{14}{30}$ ___ $\frac{3}{2}$ d. $\frac{9}{13}$ ___ $\frac{8}{13}$ e. $\frac{15}{2}$ ___ $\frac{15}{3}$

6. **Write the following fractions in descending order.**

   $\frac{1}{32}, \frac{3}{2}, \frac{5}{16}, \frac{17}{4}$

7. **Write the following fractions in their lowest terms.**

   a. $\frac{56}{78}$ b. $\frac{140}{7000}$ c. $9\frac{2}{6}$ d. $18\frac{15}{40}$

8. **Which of the following fractions are unit fractions?**

   $\frac{9}{17}, \frac{2}{11}, \frac{1}{6}, \frac{7}{13}, \frac{1}{19}, \frac{1}{46}$

9. **Write P for proper fractions and I for improper fractions.**

   a. $\frac{19}{7}$ ____ b. $\frac{42}{9}$ ____ c. $\frac{3}{4}$ ____ d. $\frac{7}{11}$ ____ e. $\frac{99}{5}$ ____ f. $\frac{8}{7}$ ____

10. $\frac{129}{8}$ as a mixed fractions is __________.

11. **Solve the following.**

    a. $\frac{7}{10} + \frac{3}{20}$ b. $\frac{1}{6} + \frac{5}{12} + \frac{11}{24}$ c. $2\frac{1}{4} + 3\frac{7}{8} + 1\frac{1}{2}$

12. **Solve the following.**

    a. $\frac{7}{9} - \frac{1}{18}$ b. $13 - \frac{5}{8}$ c. $1 - \frac{11}{12}$ d. $7\frac{1}{2} - 2\frac{3}{4}$

13. **Solve the following.**

    a. $\frac{24}{17} \times \frac{51}{8}$ b. $3\frac{1}{5} \times 7\frac{1}{5}$ c. $2\frac{4}{7} \times 1\frac{5}{9} \times 1\frac{2}{3}$ d. $9\frac{1}{2}$ of $4\frac{2}{3}$

14. **Solve the following.**

a. $3\frac{3}{4} \div 2\frac{6}{7}$ b. $\frac{18}{5} \div \frac{36}{35}$

15. In my house, $\frac{2}{5}$ of the books are storybooks, $\frac{1}{4}$ of the books are general knowledge books and the rest are activity books. What is the fraction of activity books in my house?

16. I had ₹6000. I spent three quarters of it. How much money did I spend and how much was left with me?

17. **Convert the following fractions into decimals.**

a. $\frac{9}{10}$ b. $\frac{738}{100}$ c. $\frac{6}{100}$ d. $5\frac{1}{10}$ e. $\frac{18}{1000}$ f. $7\frac{1}{1000}$

18. **Convert the following decimals into fractions.**

a. 0.7 b. 9.5 c. 168.2 d. 34.179 e. 2.56

19. **Write the compact form of the following.**

$500 + 30 + 4 + \frac{9}{10} + \frac{7}{100} + \frac{8}{1000}$

20. **Write the following decimals in ascending order.**

8888, 8.888, 888.8, 88.8, 8, 0.8

21. Radha bought 9.48 kg of apples and sold 2.5 kg out of it. How many kg of apples were left with her?

22. A man travelled 249.5 km by train, 23.95 km by bus and 350 m by car. Find the total distance travelled by him?

23. **Calculate the following.**

a. 7 km = ______ m b. $\frac{1}{4}$ of 2Kg = ______ g

c. 9 m = ______ cm d. 9 km 7 hm = ______ dam

e. 8 kg 1 dam 9 g = ______ g f. 1234 ℓ = ______ kℓ ______ ℓ

24. Express 38.524 kℓ in kℓ, hℓ, daℓ and ℓ.

25. **Fill in the blanks.**

a. 86.25 m = ______ m ______ cm b. 56 g 4 dg 8 cg 9 mg = ______ g

c. 4.926 kg = ______ g

Time

12

To understand time, we must understand the durations of seconds, minutes and hours.

A **second** would normally be the time taken to click our fingers.

A **minute** is equal to 60 seconds. So, a minute would normally be equal to the time taken to click our fingers 60 times. Usually, in schools, one period lasts for about 40 minutes.

An **hour** is equal to 60 minutes.

A clock has 3 hands—the hour hand, the minute hand and the second hand.

The **second hand** is a long hand. It is normally the thinnest and moves the fastest; it moves every second.

The **minute hand** is also a long hand. It moves a little slower; when the second hand moves 60 times, the minute hand moves once. This happens because

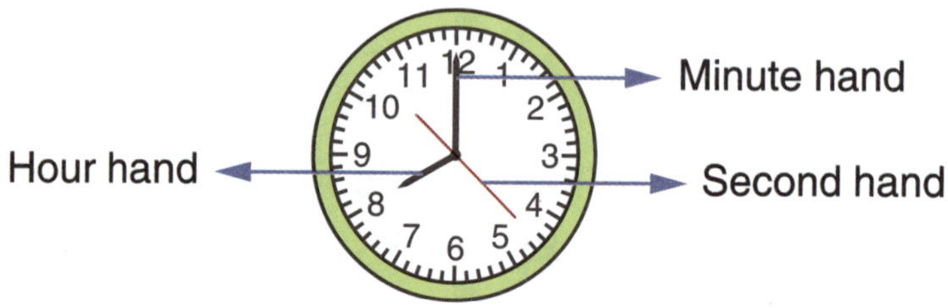

1 minute = 60 seconds.

The **hour hand** is the shortest hand. It moves the slowest; when the minute hand moves 60 times, the hour hand moves from one hour to the next, that is, from one number to the next. This happens because 1 hour = 60 minutes.

Some clocks have numbers written in Roman numerals. They work the same way as other clocks.

We can write the time shown in a clock in two ways, in numbers and in words, as shown below.

Note

When the minute hand is between 12 and 6 on the right side of the clock, we write the time using 'minutes past'.

When the minute hand is between 6 and 12 on the left side of the clock, we write the time using 'minutes to'.

4:05

or

Five minutes past four

7:50

or

Ten minutes to eight

Exercise 12.1

1 **Write the time shown by the clocks given below in both ways.**

a.  ________ or ________

b.  ________ or ________

2 **In the following clocks, the hour hand and the minute hand are missing. Draw the missing hands according to the time given below each clock.**

a. 

1:30

b. 

4:45

c. 

7:10

Conversion of Time

To understand conversion of time, we must learn the following.

1 minute = 60 seconds

1 hour = 60 minutes

1 hour = 3600 seconds

1 day = 24 hours

1 week = 7 days

Remember

When we convert from a bigger unit to a smaller unit, we always multiply.

When we convert from a smaller unit to a bigger unit, we always divide.

Conversion Between Minutes and Seconds

When we convert minutes to seconds, we use the following relationship.

1 minute = 60 seconds

So, to convert minutes to seconds, we multiply by 60.

But to convert seconds to minutes, we divide by 60.

Example 1: 3 min = ______ s

3×60 s = 180 s. Therefore, 3 min = <u>180</u> s

Example 2: 360 seconds = ______ minutes

1 minute = 60 seconds

1 second = $\frac{1}{60}$ minutes

So, 360 seconds = $\frac{\overset{6}{\cancel{360}}}{\cancel{60}}$ = 6 min

360 seconds = <u>6</u> minutes

Note

The same rule applies for all the other conversions like hours to minutes or minutes to hours, days to hours or hours to days, etc.

Conversion Between Hours and Minutes

Example 3: 2 hours = ______ minutes

1 hour = 60 minutes

Therefore, 2 hours = 2 × 60 minutes

= 120 minutes

So, we get 2 hours = <u>120</u> minutes

Example 4: 240 minutes = ______ hours

Since 60 minutes = 1 hour

Therefore, 1 minute = $\frac{1}{60}$

240 minutes = $\frac{\cancel{240}^{4}}{\cancel{60}}$ = 4 hours

So, we get 240 minutes = <u>4</u> hours

Conversion Between Hours and Seconds

Example 5: 3 hours = ______ seconds

Since 1 hour = 3600 seconds

3 hours = 3 × 3600 = 10800 seconds

3 hours = <u>10800</u> seconds

Example 6: 21600 seconds = ______ hours

Since 3600 seconds = 1 hour

Therefore, 1 second = $\frac{1}{3600}$

21600 seconds = $\frac{\cancel{21600}^{\cancel{36}^{6}}}{\cancel{3600}_{\cancel{6}}}$ = 6 hours

So, we get 21600 seconds = <u>6</u> hours

Example 7: 2 hours 12 minutes 30 seconds = ______ seconds

2 hours = 2 × 3600	=	7200 seconds
12 min = 12 × 60	=	720 s
30 s	= +	30 s
		7950 s

2 hours 12 minutes 30 seconds = <u>7950</u> seconds

Example 8: 393 seconds = ______ minutes ______ seconds

We have to first convert seconds to minutes. So, we divide by 60.

```
      6 min   ——→ We must write the quotient in minutes.
60)3 9 3 s    ——→ We must write seconds here because the remainder will be
 - 3 6 0↓         in seconds.
   -------
     3 3 s
```

The remainder will be 33 seconds and the quotient will be 6 minutes.

393 seconds = <u>6</u> minutes <u>33</u> seconds

Example 9: 5389 seconds = _____ hours _____ minutes _____ seconds

We will first divide 5389 seconds by 60.

$$\begin{array}{r} 89\text{ min} \\ 60\overline{)5389\text{ s}} \\ -480\downarrow \\ \hline 589 \\ 540 \\ \hline 49\text{ s} \end{array}$$

The remainder is 49 seconds and the quotient is 89 minutes. But 89 minutes are more than 60 minutes. So, we divide 89 by 60.

$$\begin{array}{r} 1\text{ h} \\ 60\overline{)89\text{ min}} \\ -60\downarrow \\ \hline 29\text{ min} \end{array}$$

We get 1 hour and 29 minutes.

5389 seconds = <u>1</u> hour <u>29</u> minutes <u>49</u> seconds

Exercise 12.2

Fill in the blanks.

1. 2 h 35 min = _____ min
2. 1 h 20 min = _____ min
3. 1 h 20 min = _____ s
4. 1 h 10 min 10 s = _____ s
5. 23 min 8 s = _____ s
6. 1 h 25 min = _____ s
7. 1 day 10 h 20 min = _____ min
8. 5 days 2 h 12 min = _____ min
9. 243 s = _____ min _____ s
10. 597 min = _____ h _____ min
11. 6235 s = _____ h _____ min _____ s
12. 4289 s = _____ h _____ min _____ s

Adding and Subtracting Units of Time

Example 10: Add 45 minutes, 27 minutes and 18 minutes.

$$\begin{array}{r} \text{min} \\ 45 \\ 27 \\ +18 \\ \hline 90 \end{array}$$

Since 90 minutes is more than 60 minutes, we convert 90 minutes to hours by dividing by 60.

$$\begin{array}{r} 1\text{ h} \\ 60\overline{)90\text{ min}} \\ -60\downarrow \\ \hline 30\text{ min} \end{array}$$

Answer = 1 hour 30 minutes

Example 11: Add 27 seconds, 49 seconds and 45 seconds.

s
27
49
+ 45
121

Since 121 seconds is more than 60 seconds, we divide 121 seconds by 60 to convert them to minutes.

$$\begin{array}{r} 2\text{ min} \\ 60\overline{)\,121\text{ s}} \\ -120\downarrow \\ \hline 1\text{ s} \end{array}$$

Answer = 2 minutes 1 second

Try These!

Add the following.

1. 4 h 6 min and 17 h 8 min
2. 5 h 13 min and 3 h 29 min

Example 12: Add 3 h 25 min and 2 h 10 min.

	h	min
	3	25
+	2	10
	5	35

Answer = 5 hours 35 minutes

Example 13: Add the following.

	h	min
	5	59
+	2	42
	7	101

We write full 101 here and not carry it forward to hours.

$$\begin{array}{r} 1\text{ h} \\ 60\overline{)\,101\text{ min}} \\ -60\ \downarrow \\ \hline 41\text{ min} \end{array}$$

101 minutes is more than 60 minutes. Therefore, we divide it by 60 to convert to hours.

101 minutes = 1 hour 41 minutes

h	min
7^{+1}	41

We write our minutes as 41 and the 1 hour gets added to 7 hours and becomes 8 hours.

= 8 hours 41 minutes

Answer = 8 hours 41 minutes

We follow the same method if seconds are more than 60 and also if hours are more than 24.

Example 14: Solve the following.

	day	h	min	s
	3	12	58	55
+	2	32	59	55

	day	h	min	s
	3	12	58	55
+	2	32	59	55
	5	44	117	110

We do not carry forward numbers.

Now, 110 seconds is more than 60 seconds. Therefore, we divide 110 seconds by 60 to convert them to minutes.

$$\begin{array}{r} 1\text{ min} \\ 60\overline{)110\text{ s}} \\ -60\downarrow \\ \hline 50\text{ s} \end{array}$$

We get 50 seconds and 1 minute is added to 117 minutes to get 118 minutes.

Since 118 minutes is more than 60 minutes, we divide 118 minutes by 60 to convert them into hours.

$$\begin{array}{r} 1\text{ h} \\ 60\overline{)118\text{ min}} \\ -60\downarrow \\ \hline 58\text{ min} \end{array}$$

We will get 58 minutes and 1 hour is added to 44 hours.

Since 45 hours is more than 24 hours, we will divide 45 hours by 24 to convert them into days.

$$\begin{array}{r} 1\text{ day} \\ 24\overline{)45\text{ h}} \\ -24\downarrow \\ \hline 21\text{ h} \end{array}$$

We will get 21 hours and 1 day gets carried forward.

5 days + 1 day = 6 days

	day	h	min	s
	3	12	58	55
+	2	32	59	55
	5^{+1}	44^{+1}	117^{+1}	110
	6	21	58	50

Answer = 6 day 21 h 58 min 50 s

Example 15: Solve the following.

h	min	s
9	35	20
− 2	40	35

We cannot subtract 35 seconds from 20 seconds. So, we borrow 1 minute from 35 minutes. When we do that, we are left with 34 minutes. Since 1 minute is equal to 60 seconds, we add 60 seconds to 20 seconds. We get 80 seconds and 80 − 35 = 45 seconds.

In the same way, we cannot subtract 40 minutes from 34 minutes. So, we borrow 1 hour from 9 hours. When we do that we are left with 8 hours and we add 60 minutes to 34 minutes because 1 hour is equal to 60 minutes. We get 94 minutes and 94 – 40 = 54 minutes.

Now, 8 hours – 2 hours = 6 hours

	h	min	s
	8	$^{+60}$34	
	~~9~~	~~35~~	$^{+60}$20
–	2	40	35
	6	54	45

Answer = 6 h 54 min 45 s

Multiplying and Dividing Units of Time

Multiplying Units of Time

Note

If hours become more than 24, then we can divide them by 24 and convert them to days.

Example 16: Multiply the following.

h	min	s
1	15	20
		11
11	165	220

Note: We do not carry forward the numbers.

220 seconds are more than 60 seconds. Therefore, we divide 220 seconds by 60 to convert them to minutes.

220 seconds = 40 seconds and 3 minutes

$$\begin{array}{r} 3\text{ min} \\ 60\overline{)\,220\text{ s}} \\ 180\downarrow \\ \hline 40\text{ s} \end{array}$$

165 minutes + 3 minutes = 168 minutes

168 minutes are more than 60 minutes. Therefore, we divide 168 minutes by 60 to convert them to hours.

168 min = 48 min and 2 h

$$\begin{array}{r} 2\text{ h} \\ 60\overline{)\,168\text{ min}} \\ 120\downarrow \\ \hline 48\text{ min} \end{array}$$

11 hours + 2 hours = 13 hours

h	min	s
1	15	20
		11
11^{+2}	165^{+3}	220
13	48	40

Answer = 13 hours 48 minutes 40 seconds

Dividing Units of Time

There are two methods to divide units of time. Let us study them with the help of the following examples.

Example 17: Divide 2 h 12 min 30 s by 20.

First convert 2 h 12 min 30 s to seconds.

$2\text{ h} = 2 \times 3600 = 7200\text{ s}$

$12\text{ min} = 12 \times 60 = 720\text{ s}$

$20\text{ s} = 20\text{ s}$

7940 s

Now, divide 7940 s by 20.

```
    397s
20)7940s
  -60↓
   194
   180↓
    140
    140
      0s
```

On converting, we get 397 seconds. Since 397 seconds are more than 60 seconds, we divide 397 by 60 to convert them to minutes.

```
    6 min
60)397s
  -360
    37s
```

Answer = 6 min 37 seconds

Example 18: Divide 13 h 14 min 40 s by 4

```
   3h  18 min  40 s
4 )13   14     40
   12
    1→60          (1 h = 60 min)
     +14
      74
      72
       2→120      (2 min = 2 × 60 s
          +40                = 120 s)
          160
          160
            0
```

Answer = 3 h 18 min 40 s

Exercise 12.3

1. Add the followings units of time.

a. 35 s + 50 s + 43 s

b. 45 min + 24 min + 65 min

c. 75 h + 12 h

d.

	min	s
	12	35
+	30	10

e.

	h	min
	5	35
+	12	20

f.

	h	min	s
	2	15	43
+	5	12	10

g.

	min	s
	8	47
+	15	25

h.

	h	min
	9	45
+	10	35

i.

	h	min	s
	4	49	20
+	8	12	40

2. Add 34 min 23 s and 12 min 45 s.
3. Add 2 h 45 min 34 s and 6 h 30 min 52 s
4. Add 2 days 12 h 36 min 15 s and 3 days 22 h 43 min 45 s.
5. **Solve the following.**

a.

min	s
52	45
− 24	30

b.

min	s
42	25
− 15	45

c.

h	min
52	45
− 24	30

d.

h	min
20	30
− 9	45

e.

h	min	s
12	53	49
− 8	35	24

f.

days	h	min	s
9	12	15	25
− 2	28	30	15

6. Subtract 25 min 12 s from 32 min 42 s.
7. Subtract 35 h 26 min from 45 h 20 min.
8. Subtract 2 days 12 h 53 min 46 s from 9 days 3 h 40 min 35 s.
9. **Solve the following.**

a.

h	min
3	25
×	2

b.

h	min
12	24
×	9

c.

min	s
4	23
×	2

d.

min	s
6	25
×	8

e.

h	min	s
12	12	30
	×	2

f.

h	min	s
3	15	12
	×	10

10. **Divide the following.**

a. 24 h by 4 h

b. 3 h 32 min by 20

c. 2 h 12 min 35 s by 24

d. 14 h 18 min 40 s by 18

12-hour Clock

One day is equal to 24 hours. Each day begins at 12 midnight and ends at 12 midnight the next day. The clock we normally use is called the 12-hour clock.

In this clock, from 12:01 after 12 midnight to 11:59 during the day we write **a.m.** with the time.

12 in the afternoon is written as 12 noon; we use neither a.m. nor p.m. with it.

From 12:01 after 12 noon till 11:59 at night, we write **p.m.** with the time.

12 at night is called 12 midnight; we do not use a.m. or p.m. with it.

After 12 midnight, the next day starts and we again use a.m. with the time.

24-hour Clock

Time can also be read using the 24-hour clock. In this system, we do not use a.m. or p.m. with the time.

Example: 2:00 a.m. in the 24 hours clock is 2 00 hours.

From 12:01 a.m. (that is, after 12 midnight) to 12:59 p.m., numbers in the 24-hour clock remain the same as the 12-hour clock.

After 12:59 p.m. is 1:00 p.m. and 1:00 p.m. onwards, we add 12 to the hours in the 24-hour clock.

The following figure will help explain the relationship between the 12-hour clock and the 24-hour clock.

1	2	3	4
13	**14**	**15**	**16**
5	6	7	8
17	**18**	**19**	**20**
9	10	11	12
21	**22**	**23**	**24**

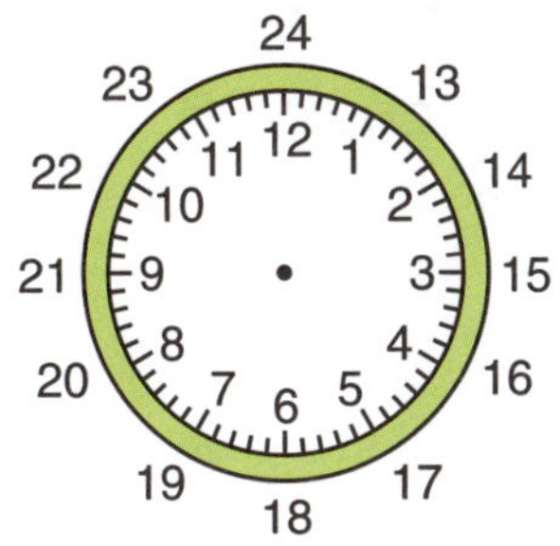

The inner reading is of the 12-hour clock and the outer reading is its equivalent in the 24-hour clock.

Example:

12-hour clock	**24-hour clock**
2:00 a.m.	2 00 hours
11:50 a.m.	11 50 hours
12:00 noon	12 00 hours
12:35 p.m.	12 35 hours
12:59 p.m.	12 59 hours
1:00 p.m.	13 00 hours

From 1:00 p.m., we add 12 to the hours.

1:00 p.m. = 13 hours (1 + 12 = 13)

2:00 p.m. = 14 hours (12 + 2 = 14)

9:15 p.m.	21 15 hours
11:20 p.m.	23 20 hours
12:00 midnight	24 00 hours

Try These!

Write the following times in 24 hour clock.

1. 1:30 p.m. ________
2. 2:10 p.m. ________
3. 5:00 p.m. ________
4. 8:20 p.m. ________
5. 10: 50 p.m. ________
6. 11:45 p.m. ________

Converting Time from 24-hour Clock to 12-hour Clock

From 0:01 a.m. (that is, after 12 midnight) to 12:59 p.m. the numbers are the same.

Note

Till 11 59 hours (that is, before 12 noon), we write a.m. with our time in the 12-hour clock.

At 12 00 hours, we use 12:00 noon in the 12-hour clock.

After 12 00 hours (that is, from 12 01 hours), we use p.m. in our 12-hour clock. From 13 00 hours, we subtract 12 from the hour, that is, 13 hours become 13 – 12 = 1:00 p.m.

Example:

24-hour clock	12-hour clock
1 00 hours	1:00 a.m.
12 00 hours	12:00 noon
12 59 hours	12:59 p.m.

24-hour clock	12-hour clock
13 00 hours	1:00 p.m.
14 00 hours (14 –12 = 2)	2:00 p.m.
15 30 hours	3:30 p.m.
23 20 hours	11:20 p.m.
24 00 hours	12:00 midnight

Exercise 12.4

1. **Write a.m., p.m., noon or midnight for the following.**

   a. 2 at night
   b. 7 in the morning
   c. 11 in the morning
   d. 11:55 in the morning
   e. 12 during the day
   f. 12:15 during the day
   g. 1:10 during the day
   h. 3:30 in the afternoon

2. **Write the time in the 24-hour clock for the given timings.**

12-hour clock	24-hour clock
1:30 a.m.	________
4:25 a.m.	________
9:40 a.m.	________

12-hour clock	24-hour clock
12:00 noon	________
12:15 p.m.	________
12:55 p.m.	________

3. **Write the timings in the 12-hour clock for the given timings.**

24-hour clock	12-hour clock
2 40 hours	________
13 20 hours	________
7 15 hours	________
15 20 hours	________

24-hour clock	12-hour clock
11 40 hours	________
12 20 hours	________
12 59 hours	________
13 00 hours	________

Word Problems on Time

Example 18: If I left my house at 2 p.m. and came back at 5 p.m., for how long was I away?

Time I came back =	5
Time I left =	− 2
	3 hours

Thus, I was away for 3 hours.

We subtract the time of leaving from the time of returning. When we subtract, the time of returning is written on the top. Since both the timings are in p.m. we can subtract easily.

If one timing is in a.m. and one is in p.m., then we convert our timings in p.m. to the 24-hour clock timing and then subtract.

Example 19: I left the house at 12:30 p.m. I came back at 3:15 p.m. For how long I was away?

Here, 12:30 p.m. will be treated like an a.m. because it is before 1 p.m. and we convert 3:15 p.m. to the 24-hour clock. It will become 15:15 hours.

Now, the time of leaving is at 12:30 hours and the time of returning is 15:15 hours.

h	min		min
14	+60		
~~15~~	15		75
−12	30		− 30
2	45		45

So, I was away for 2 hours 45 minutes.

Note

In the 12-hour clock, if a timing with 12 is given with p.m. it is treated like a.m. because it is before 1 p.m.

Example 20: Jack left at 11:45 a.m. for the park and came back at 5:30 p.m. It took him 1 hour 15 minutes to go and come back. How much time did he spend in the park?

First, we calculate the total time that Jack was away and then subtract the travelling time of 1 hour 15 minutes from it.

	h	min
	16	+60
Time of leaving	~~17~~	30
Time he came back	− 11	45
Total time	5	45
Travelling time	− 1	15
	4	30

Therefore, Jack spent 4 hours 30 minutes in the park.

If the time of going and the time spent out are given and we have to find the time of arrival, then we have to just add all the given timings.

Example 21:

Ira left for school at 7:00 a.m. She took 45 minutes to go and come back. She spent 5 hours 30 minutes in the school. What time did she come back home?

h	min
7	00
	45
+5	30
12^{+1}	75
13	15

$$\begin{array}{r} 1\,h \\ 60\overline{)75\ min} \\ -60\ \downarrow \\ \hline 15\ min \end{array}$$

Thus, Ira came back at 1:15 p.m.

Exercise 12.5

1. I left the house at 10 a.m. and returned at 11:30 a.m. For how long was I away?
2. I left the house at 10:05 a.m. and returned at 3:30 p.m. For how long was I away?
3. A train leaves Meerut at 12:05 p.m. and reaches Delhi at 4:30 p.m. How long is the journey?

4. I go to school at 7:05 a.m. and come back at 3:15 p.m. I spend 30 minutes travelling. How much time do I spend in school?
5. I go to school at 7:15 a.m. I spend 45 minutes to go and 45 minutes to come back. I come back at 3:10 p.m. How much time do I spend in the school?
6. I go to school at 6:45 a.m. I spend 5 hours 30 minutes in school and take 50 minutes to travel. What time do I reach home?

Calendar

Calendar of a year consists of 12 months. All the months do not have the same number of days. Following are the names of the 12 months with the number of days in each month.

Name of the month	No. of days
January	31
February	28 or 29
March	31
April	30
May	31
June	30
July	31
August	31
September	30
October	31
November	30
December	31

When February has 28 days, there are 365 days in a year. When February has 29 days, there are 366 days in a year. Such a year is called a leap year.

Look at the picture of January 2017 in the calendar below.

2017
January

Sun	Mon	Tue	Wed	Thu	Fri	Sat
1	2	3	4	5	6	7
8	9	10	11	12	13	14
15	16	17	18	19	20	21
22	23	24	25	26	27	28
29	30	31				

Note

1 decade = 10 years
1 century = 100 years
1 millennium = 1000 years

Example 22:

a. September 1 is a Friday. What will be the date on next Friday?

Next Friday will be after 1 week, that is, after 7 days. So, we will add 7 days to September 1.

$7 + 1 = 8$

Therefore, next Friday will be September 8.

b. What will be the date after two weeks from September 1?

After two weeks, that is, after 14 days from September 1, the date will be:

$$\begin{array}{r} 1 \\ +\,14 \\ \hline 15 \end{array}$$

So, after two weeks, the date will be September 15.

Leap Year

In 1 year, there are 365 ¼ days. This is the time the Earth takes to move around the Sun. In a leap year, there are 366 days because the ¼ day every year adds up to 1 full day after 4 years.

This extra 1 day every 4 years is added to the month of February as the 29th of February. That is why 29th of February comes once in every 4 years and that year is called a **leap year**.

To identify a leap year, we divide it by 4. If it is divisible by 4, it is a leap year. If a year ends with 00, then it has to be divisible by 400 to be a leap year.

Example 23: Is 1984 a leap year?

We check if 1984 is divisible by 4. Instead of dividing 1984 by 4, we can use the method of checking divisibility of 4. If the last two digits, that is, 84, are divisible by 4, then 1984 is divisible by 4.

Since 84 is divisible by 4, 1984 is a leap year.

Example 24: Is 1985 a leap year?

Using the divisibility of 4, we realize that 1985 is not divisible by 4. Therefore, 1985 is not a leap year.

Example 25: Is 2000 a leap year?

Since the year ends with 00, we must divide it by 400.

Since 2000 is divisible by 400, it is a leap year.

Example 26: Is 1900 a leap year?

Since 1900 is not completely divisible by 400, it is not a leap year.

Word Problems on Time

Example 27: I spent 8 days in Mumbai and 12 days in Nagpur. How many weeks and days did I spend in these two places?

Remember

1 week = 7 days
1 month = 4 weeks (approx.)
1 year = 12 months
1 year = 365 days
1 leap year = 366 days
1 year = 52 weeks + 1 day

Days

$$\begin{array}{r} 8 \\ +12 \\ \hline 20 \end{array}$$

20 days is more than 7 days. So, we will divide by 7.

$$\begin{array}{r} 2 \text{ weeks} \\ 7 \overline{) 20 \text{ days}} \\ -14 \downarrow \\ \hline 6 \text{ days} \end{array}$$

So, I spent 2 weeks and 6 days in these two places.

Example 28: Out of my holiday of 2 weeks, I spent 3 days in Delhi. How many days did I spend at home?

weeks	days
1	7
~~2~~	~~0~~
–	3
1	4

When we borrow 1 week, we get 7 days. We add 7 to 0 and then subtract 3.

So, I spent 1 week and 4 days at home.

Number of Days Between Two Given Dates

Example 29: How many days are there **between** March 16 and April 5?

Total number of days in March = 31
-16 (Number of days in March)
15

Number of days between April 1 and April 5 = 5
-1
4

Total number of days between March 16 and April 5 = 15 + 4 = 19

The number of days between March 16 and April 5 is 19.

Note

When we calculate the number of days **between** two dates we do not include the first and the last date.

Number of Days from a Certain Date to a Certain Date

Example 30: How many days are there **from** March 16 **to** April 5?

Number of days in March = 31
-16
15
$+ 1$
16

We add 1 because it is **from** March 16.

Number of days **from** April 1 **to** April 5 = 5
-1
4
$+1$
5

We add 1 because it is **to** April 5.

Total number of days from March 16 to April 5 is

16
$+ 5$
21

The number of days from March 16 to April 5 are 21.

Note

We add 1 when calculating both the times because the first date and the last date are included when the question asks **from** a date **to** another date.

Example 31: How many days are there from January 2 to January 29?

$$\begin{array}{r} 29 \\ -\ \ 2 \\ \hline 27 \\ +\ \ 1 \\ \hline =28 \end{array}$$

We add 1 because the question says **from**.

There are 28 days from January 2 to January 29.

Example 32: My school Easter holidays begin on March 3. They are for 15 days. On what date will the school reopen? On what date will my holidays end?

$$\begin{array}{r} 3 \\ +15 \\ \hline 18 \end{array}$$

The school reopens on the March 18. The holidays end on (18 – 1) March 17.

Example 33: Christmas holidays begin on December 22. They are for 3 weeks.

a. When does the school reopen?

b. What is the last day of the holidays?

$$\begin{array}{r} 22 \\ +21 \\ \hline 43 \\ -31 \\ \hline 12 \end{array}$$

(Total number of days in December)

a. The school reopens on January 12.

b. The last holiday is on (12 – 1 = 11) January 11.

Exercise 12.6

1. **Which of the following years are leap years?**

   2012 1999 1800 2100 2000 1600

2. How many months are there in a year?
3. How many weeks and days are there in a year?
4. September 6 is a Thursday.

   a. What is the date on next Thursday?

   b. What is the date after 2 weeks?

   c. What is the date after 3 weeks?

5. How many months are there in 5 years 3 months?
6. How many months are there in 7 years 5 months?
7. Convert 48 months to years and months.
8. I spent 18 days in London, 15 days in Paris and 8 days in Frankfurt. How many weeks and days did I spend in all in these 3 places?
9. I went to my sister's house for 14 days and my brother's house for 12 days. How many weeks and days did I spend in total at both their homes?
10. It takes me 1 week 2 days to do my maths project, 2 weeks to do my English project and 4 weeks 3 days to do my science project. How many weeks and days do I need to do all my projects?
11. How many days are there between
    a. July 4 and July 16?
    b. September 9 and October 5?
12. How many days are there from
    a. April 5 to April 21?
    b. September 23 to October 2?

Revision Exercise

1 Choose the correct options.

a. 5 h 25 min = _____ min

i. 325 min　ii. 525 min　iii. 300 min　iv. 25 min　☐

b. 52 min 7 s = _____ s

i. 3120 s　ii. 3127 s　iii. 420 s　iv. 472 s　☐

c. 3 days 2 hours 10 minutes = _____ minutes

i. 4440 minutes　ii. 4450 minutes　iii. 900 minutes　iv. 310 minutes　☐

d. 4900 s = _____ h _____ min _____ s

i. 21 h 1 min 40 s　ii. 40 h 21 min 1 s　☐

iii. 1 h 21 min 40 s　iv. 81 h 40 min 1 s

e. 5 h 42 min + 3 h 35 min

i. 5 h 42 min　ii. 3 h 35 min　iii. 9 h 00 min　iv. 9 h 17 min　☐

f. February 2012 had _____ number of days.

i. 28　ii. 29　iii. 30　iv. 31　☐

g. A millennium has _____ years.

i. 10　ii. 100　iii. 1000　iv. 10,000　☐

h. What will be the date 2 weeks after January 5?

i. January 12　ii. January 19　iii. January 26　iv. January 31

i. Is 1700 a leap year?

i. Yes　ii. No　☐

j. 9 years 2 months = _____ months

i. 110　ii. 108　iii. 65　iv. 272　☐

2 Fill in the blanks.

a. There are _____ months in a year.

b. January always has _____ days.

c. In a leap year, February has _____ days.

d. 1 decade = _____ years

e. If September 6 is a Wednesday, then the date on the next Wednesday will be _____.

f. A leap year has _____ days.

g. 1 year and 1 month = _____ months

h. 1 century = _____ year

i. The number of days between August 3 and August 10 are _____.

j. The number of days from August 3 to August 10 are _____.

3 7 hours = _____ minutes

4 15 min 7 s = _____ s.

5 1 day 3 hours 25 minutes = _____ minutes

6 5923 s = _____ h _____ minutes _____ s

7 **Solve the following.**

day	h	min	s
3	10	12	49
− 2	15	52	35

8 **Solve the following.**

day	h	min	s
9	23	13	52
− 7	11	49	12

9 **Solve the following.**

h	min	s
3	15	20
	×	15

10 Divide 13 h 15 min 48 s by 12.

11 Radha started watching a movie at 11 a.m. After the movie, she walked back home. She reached home at 2:30 p.m. How long did she take to walk back?

12 I left by car from Dehradun to Delhi at 7:30 a.m. I drove for 6 hours 45 minutes. On the way, I stopped for 35 minutes to eat food. What time did I reach Delhi?

13 **Which of the following years are leap years?**

2000 2002 2008 2012 2014

14 **If the first Wednesday of March is the 6th, then what is the date on the following?**

a. The second Wednesday b. The third Wednesday c. The fourth Wednesday

15 **A year has 365 ¼ days. The ¼ adds up to become 1 extra day in 4 years.**

a. In which month is this extra day added and as what date?

b. What is this kind of a year called?

16 **Solve the following.**

a. 7 years 2 months = _____ months b. 32 months = _____ years _____ months

c. 5 weeks 2 days = _____ days d. 24 days = _____ weeks _____ days

17 For my school tests, I spent 12 days studying maths, 8 days studying science and 7 days studying English. How many weeks and days did I study in total for my school tests?

18 Radha is 5 years 4 months old. Her brother is 2 years 8 months older than her. How old is her brother?

19 Sanjana is 18 years 2 months old. Her brother is 10 years 7 months younger than her. How old is her brother?

20 How many days are there between July 24 and August 19?

Worksheet

1. **If 1 min = ________ s, then 10 min = ________ s.**
2. **1 h = ________ min = ________ s**
3. **1 h 5 min = ________ s**
4. **5 min = ________ s**
5. **9 h = ________ min**
6. **Fill in the blanks.**
   a. To convert hours to minutes, we multiply by ________.
   b. To convert hours to seconds, we multiply by ________.
   c. To convert seconds to minutes, we ________ by 60.
7. **State whether the following statements are true or false.**
   a. 6:00 a.m. is six in the evening.
   b. 9:15 p.m. in the 24-hour clock is written as 21 15 hours.
   c. 12 30 in the afternoon is written as 12:30 a.m.
   d. The time duration from 12:30 p.m. to 1:00 p.m. is 30 minutes.
8. a. Chhavi reaches the theatre at 17:35. The film starts at 18:30. How long must she wait before the film starts?
   b. The film lasts for 120 minutes. At what time does it finish? Answer as per the 24-hour clock.

For the Curious Mind

Do you know that when we travel straight from America to India, we lose a day?

If we leave America on July 7, then after a journey of about 14 to 18 hours, we will reach India on July 9.

Geometry

13

Let's Get Started

Geometry is a part of mathematics which deals with the properties of points, lines, surfaces and solids. Geometry can be divided into the following two parts.

1. Plane geometry is about two-dimensional shapes like lines, circles and triangles, which are flat shapes and can be drawn on paper.
2. Solid Geometry is about three-dimensional objects like cubes, cones, cylinders and pyramids.

Plane: A plane is a flat surface that extends in all directions.

For example, a tabletop, a sheet of paper or a wall.

A tabletop is a horizontal plane.

A wall is a vertical plane.

Point: A point is an exact location or place on a plane. It is usually represented by a dot.

Line: A line is a collection of points that forms a straight path and can extend in both directions. We give a name to a line by writing two capital letters at any two points on the line.

Example:

We can call this line AB or line BA and can be written as $\overleftrightarrow{AB}$ or $\overleftrightarrow{BA}$.

> **Note**
> A straight line is the shortest distance between any two points.

Vertical Line: A vertical line stands straight from top to bottom.

Example:

Horizontal Line: A horizontal line lies flat.

Example:

> **Note**
> The arrows on both the sides show that the line can be extended in both the directions.

Diagonal Line: A diagonal line moves in any direction other than vertical and horizontal.

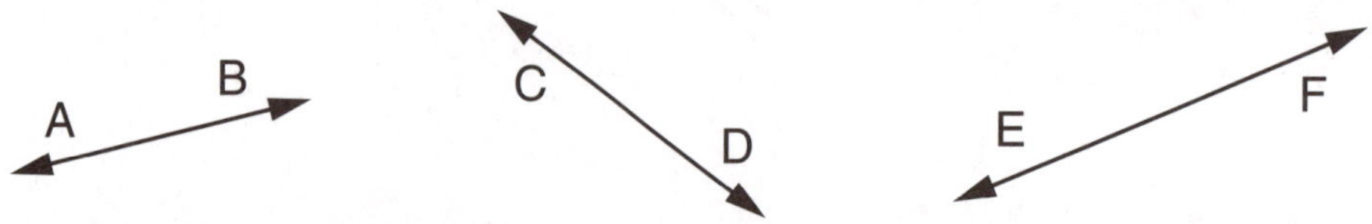

Line Segment: A line segment is a part of a line. It has two end points. The difference between a line and a line segment is that a line can extend on both the sides, whereas a line segment cannot extend on any side and cannot increase in size.

Example: AB is a line segment.

It is represented as $\overline{AB}$.

The rectangle below is made up of line segments AB, BD, DC and CA.

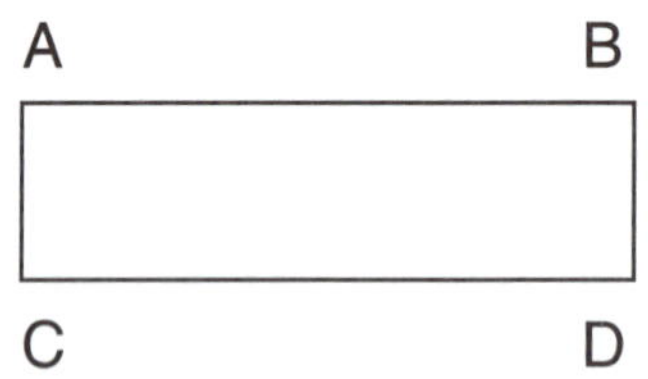

Ray: A ray has one endpoint and extends indefinitely at the other end.

Examples:

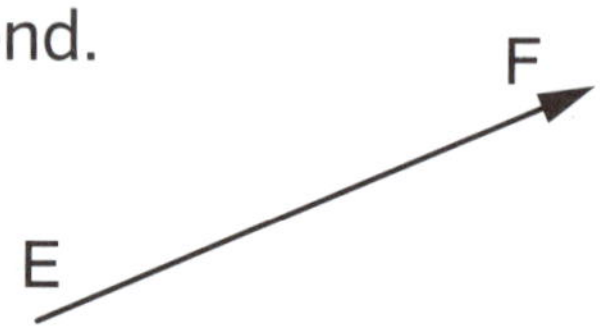

The above rays can be represented as $\overrightarrow{AB}$, $\overrightarrow{DC}$ and $\overrightarrow{EF}$.

Curve: A curve is a collection of points that do not follow a straight path.

Examples:

Remember

Point . X

Line

Line Segment

Ray

Vertical Line

Horizontal Line

Diagonal Line

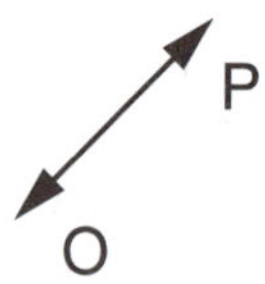

Curve

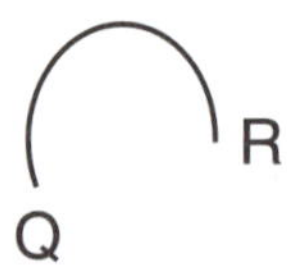

A plane is a flat surface that extends in all directions.

Exercise 13.1

1. **Classify the following as vertical, horizontal or diagonal lines.**

   a. 

   b. 

   c. 

2. 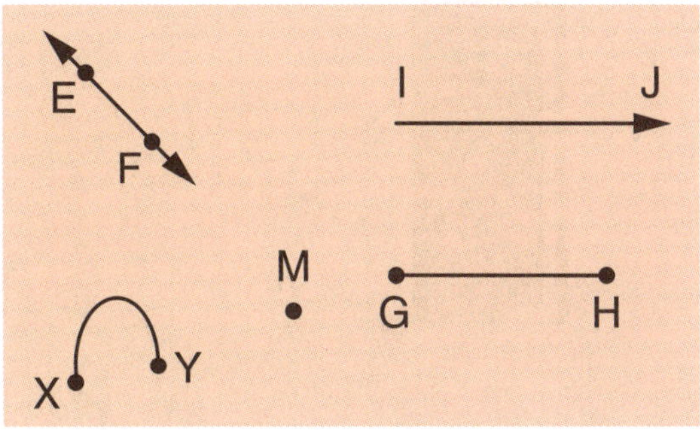

   Look at the figures and fill in the blanks.

   a. XY is a ____________.

   b. IJ is a ____________.

   c. EF is a ____________.

   d. GH is a ____________.

   e. M is a ____________.

3. **Name the line segments that make the pentagon given below.**

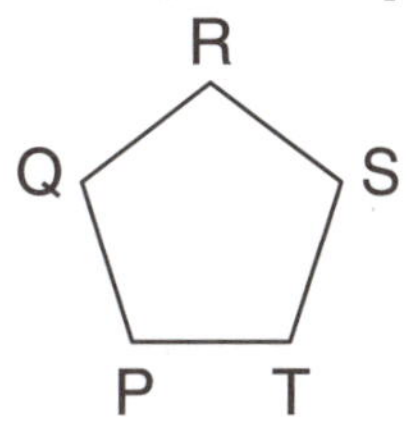

Angles

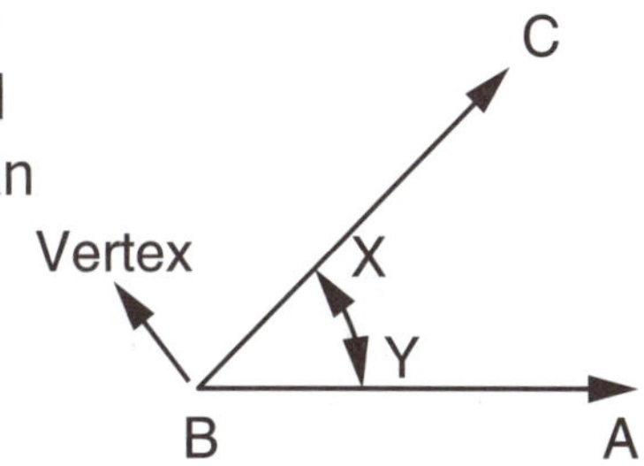

An angle is formed when the endpoints of two rays meet at one point. The point where they meet is called the **vertex**. The plural of vertex is vertices. The rays are called the **arms** of the angle. An angle is represented by the symbol ∠.

The rays BA and BC meet at point B, which is called the vertex. The rays BA and BC are called the arms of the angle. The space between BA and BC(or amount of turn between BA and BC) is the angle.

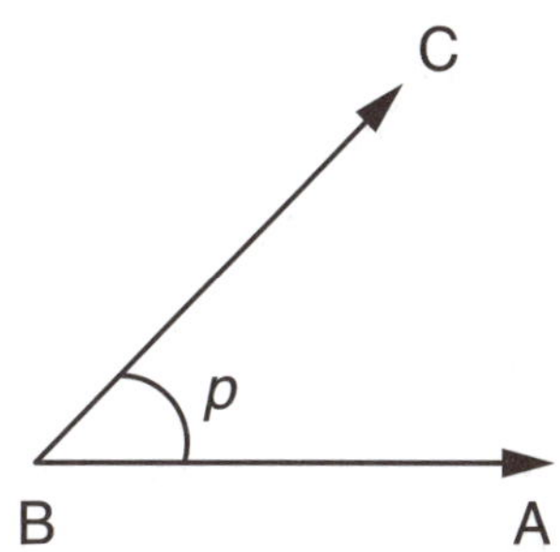

This angle can be named in four ways.

We can write the capital letters A, B, C in such a way that B (which is the vertex) always comes in the middle.

In this case, we can write ∠ABC or ∠CBA.

Since the curve inside the angle has the small letter *p*, we can write the angle as ∠*p*.

We can also call it ∠B (because that is the letter used at the vertex).

Thus, the above angle drawn can be written as ∠ABC, ∠CBA, ∠*p* or ∠B.

An angle can be drawn towards the left from the baseline as shown in Figure 1.

It can also be drawn towards the right from the baseline as shown in Figure 2.

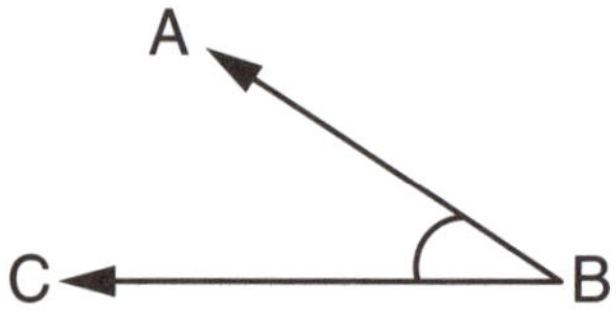

Figure 2

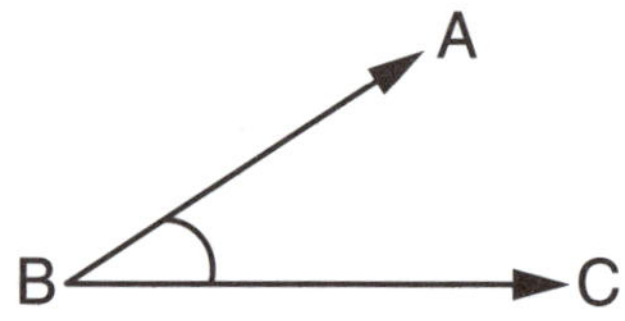

Figure 1

Angles Found in Everyday Life

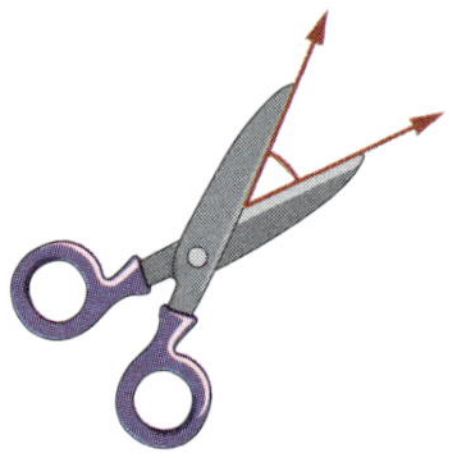

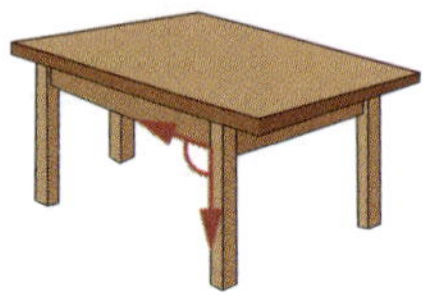

Exercise 13.2

1. In the given angle,
   a. name the vertex of the angle.
   b. name the arms of the angle.
   c. name this angle in four different ways.

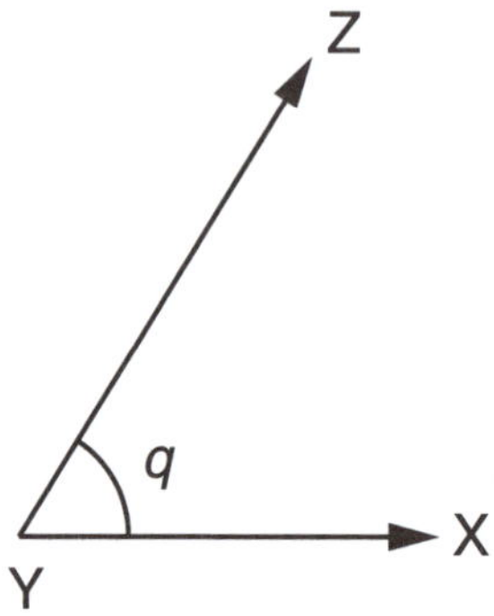

2. **Study triangle PQR and then answer the questions given below.**
   a. The triangle is made up of three line segments. Name them.
   b. In triangle PQR, there are three angles. They are ∠P, ∠Q, ∠R. Name ∠Q in three ways.
   c. Name the two arms of ∠P.
   d. Name the three vertices of triangle PQR.

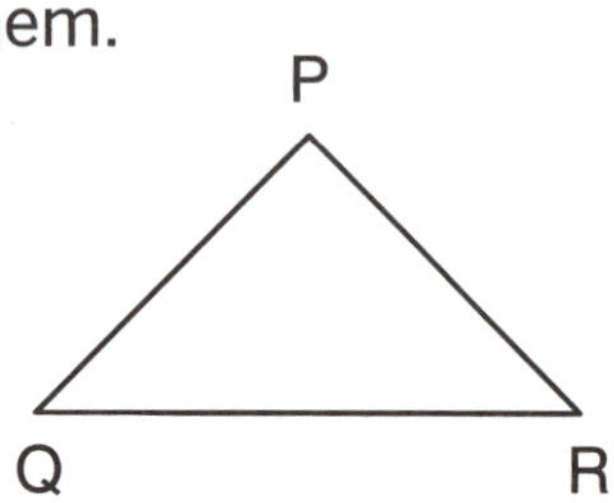

Measuring an Angle

Have you seen a D-shaped instrument in your geometry box? It is called a **protractor** and is used to measure the angles. Take the protractor from your geometry box and observe it carefully. You can see that there are two rows of measurements from 0° to 180° going in opposite directions. They are called **scales**. One is an **inner scale** and the other is an **outer scale**. There are 180 divisions between 0 and 180. Each division represents **one degree**. The bottom line is known as the **base line**. The point where the base line and the line corresponding to 90° are meeting is known as the **centre point**.

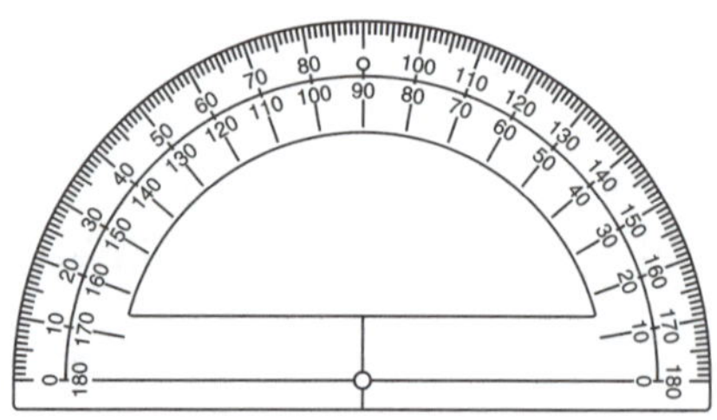

Measuring Angles Using Protractor

Let us measure the ∠XYZ using the protractor. Here, XY and YZ are the arms of the angle and Y is the vertex of the angle. Follow the steps given below for measuring the ∠XYZ.

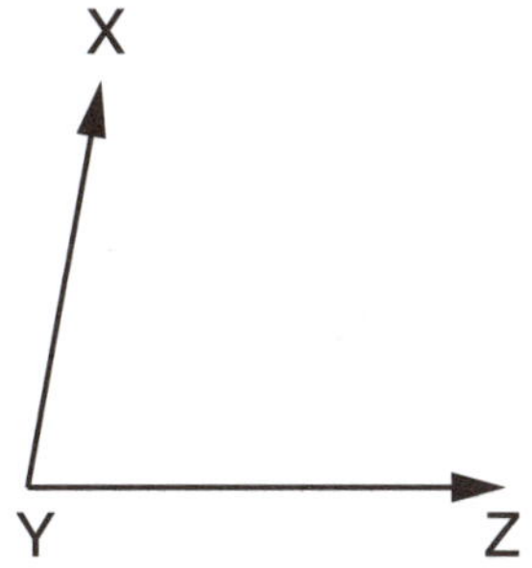

Step1: Place the protractor over the angle to be measured; say ∠XYZ, such that the centre point of the protractor coincides with the vertex of the angle, that is, Y.

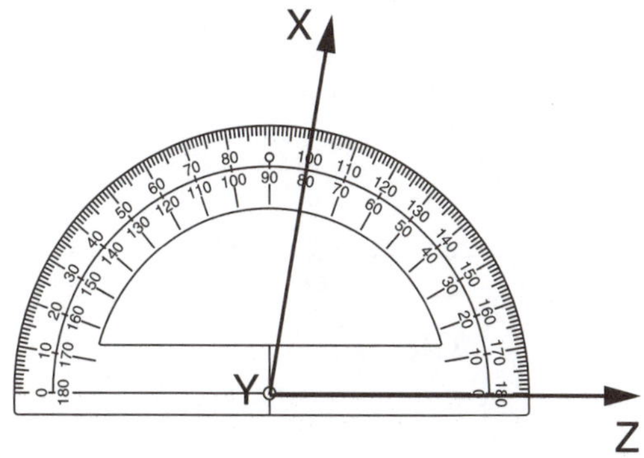

Step 2: Adjust the protractor such that the base line of the protractor coincides with the arm YZ of the protractor. Make sure that the vertex and the centre of the protractor lie on the same point.

Step 3: Choose the scale (inner or outer) to be used. Look at the scale where the baseline arm is pointing to 0°. In this case it is the inner scale.

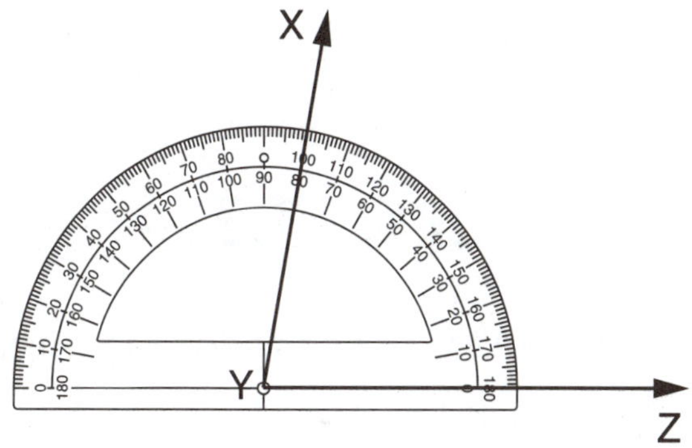

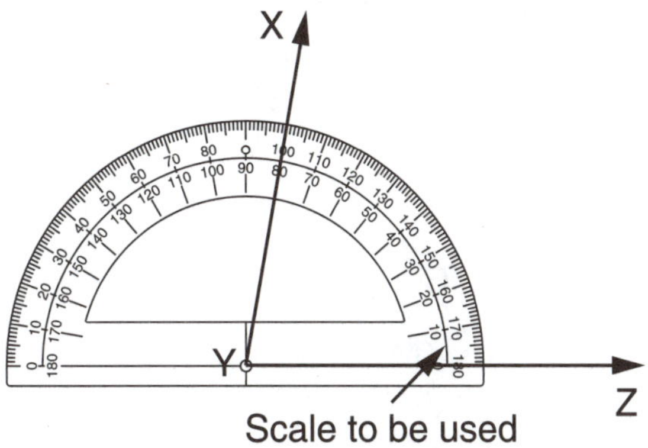

Angle Measurement

Step 4: Now, read the measure of the angle by seeing to which degree the other arm, that is, XY is coinciding. Here, XY is coinciding with an 80° line on the inner scale. Hence, the measure of the ∠XYZ is 80°.

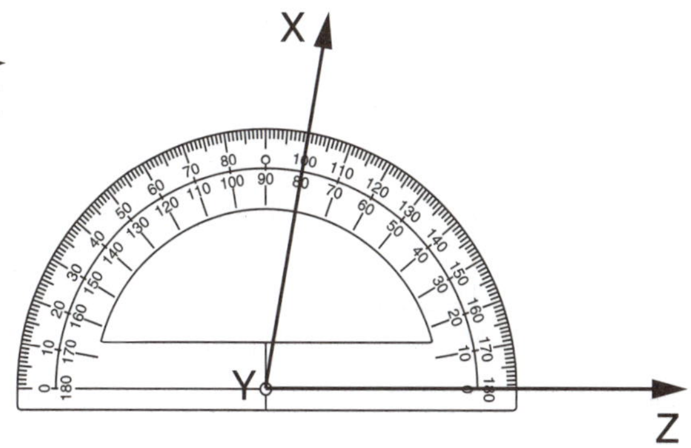

Drawing Angles

To draw an angle, we again use the protractor. To draw ∠PQR = 70°, we first draw the baseline (which is one of the arms of the angle).

Note

This angle could have been drawn in either of the following two ways using the same method.

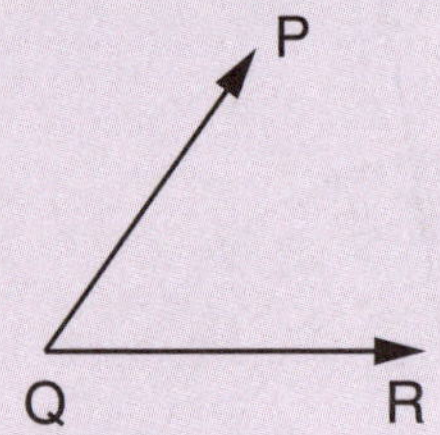

OR

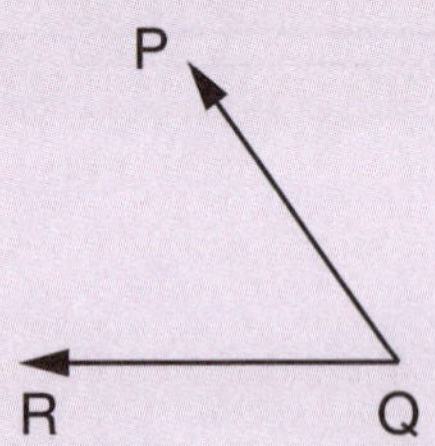

In ∠PQR, Q is the vertex of the angle since it is written in the middle (∠PQR). We place the protractor on line QR such that the baseline coincides with QR and Q lies on the centre point.

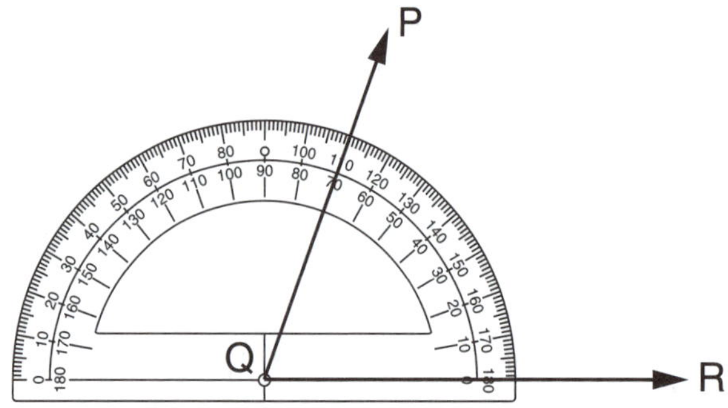

Since QR coincides with 0° on the inner reading, we look for 70° on the inner reading. Then, we join the point of 70° on the inner reading to point Q. We call the 70° point P.

Thus, ∠PQR = 70°.

Exercise 13.3

1 **Measure the following angles with a protractor.**

a. ∠ABC = ____________

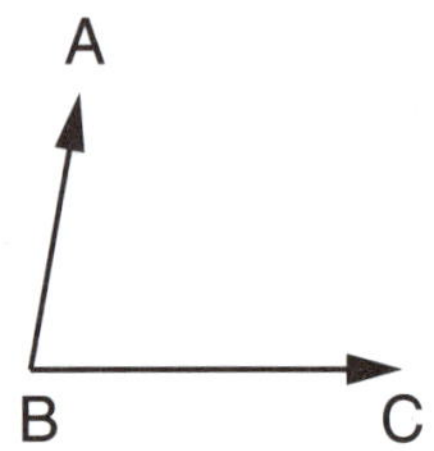

b. ∠ABC = ____________

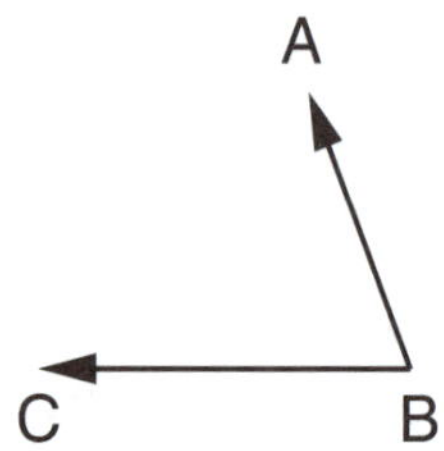

c. ∠XYZ = ____________

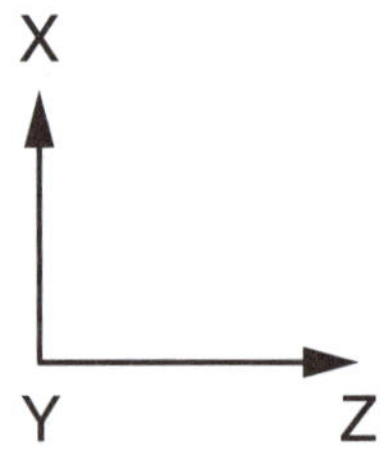

d. ∠MON = ____________

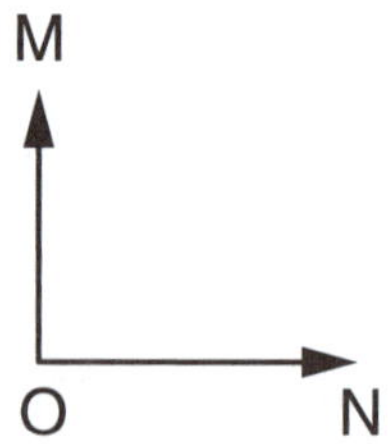

e. ∠LMN = ____________

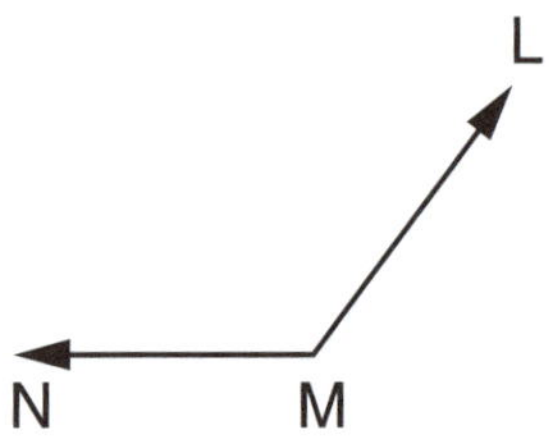

f. ∠DEF = ____________

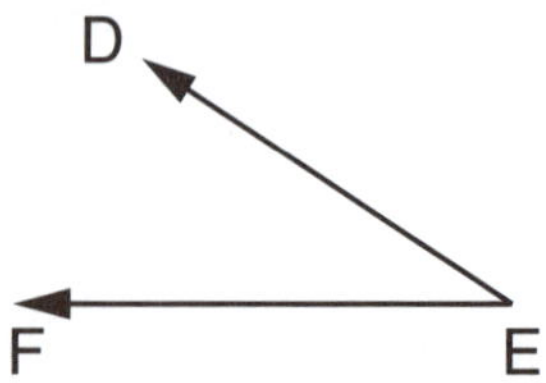

g. ∠JKL = ________

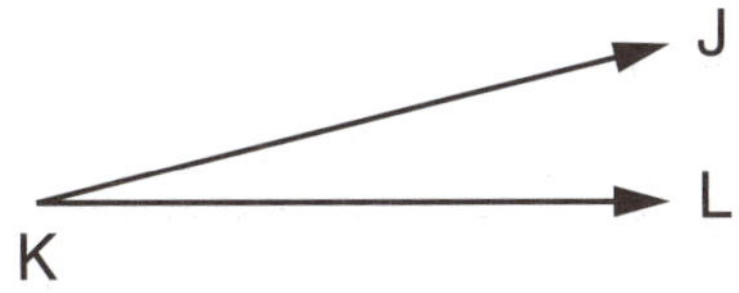

h. ∠ABC = ________

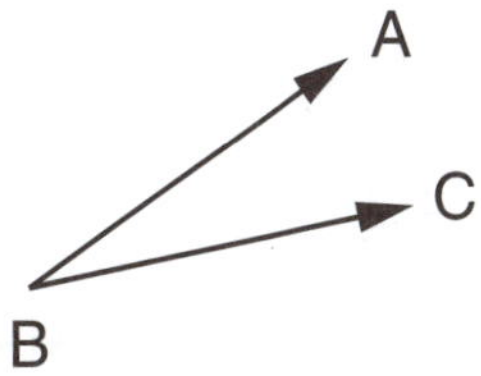

i. ∠XYZ = ________

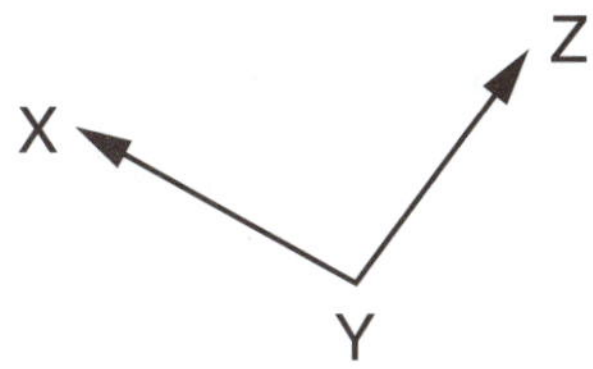

2 **With the help of a protractor, draw the following angles.**

a. 60° on the left b. 60° on the right c. 135° on the left

d. 135° on the right e. ∠ABC = 25° f. ∠XYZ = 145°

g. ∠MNO = 75° h. ∠PQR = 120°

3 **With the help of a protractor, find the value of each angle in the rectangle given below.**

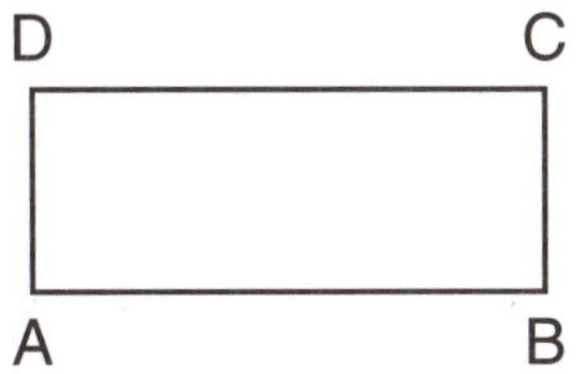

4 **With the help of a protractor, find the value of each angle in the triangle given below.**

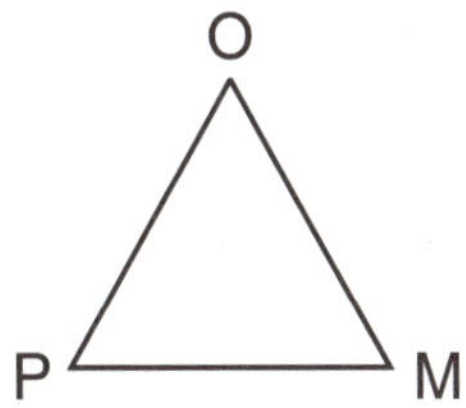

Kinds of Angles

We name angles according to their measurements. Understand the kinds of angles given below and learn them.

1. Zero Angle

When both the arms of an angle fall on one another, that is, there is no gap between them, then that angle is called a zero angle.

Example:

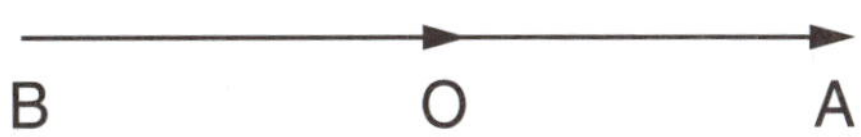

∠AOB = 0°

2. Right Angle

When an angle is equal to 90°, it is called a right angle.

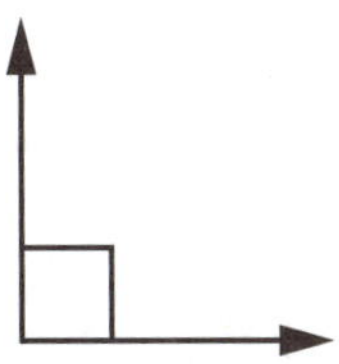

Sign of a right angle

If the above given sign of a right angle is marked and no value is given, then we have to understand that the angle is equal to 90°.

Examples:

∠AOB = 90° ∠XYZ = 90° ∠PQR = 90° ∠LMN = 90°

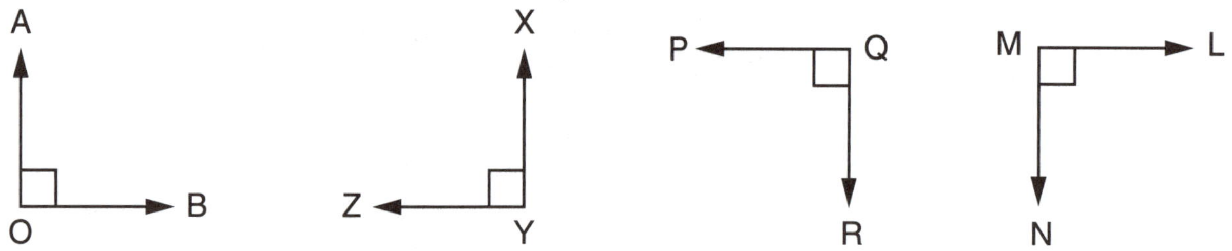

3. Acute Angle

If an angle is greater than 0° and less than 90° (that is, it is between 0° and 90°), it is called an acute angle.

Examples:

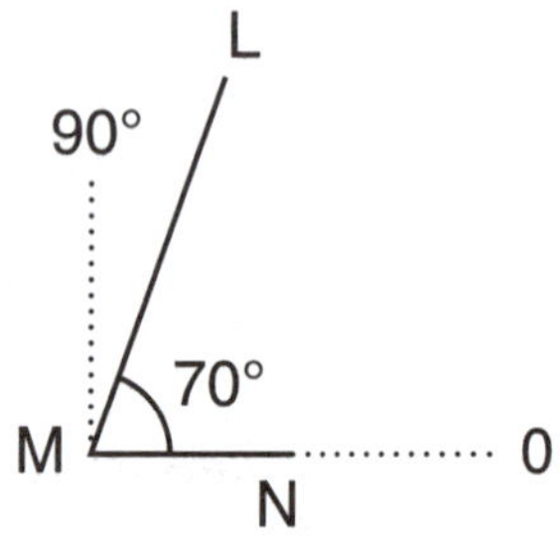

∠LMN = 70°
is an acute angle.

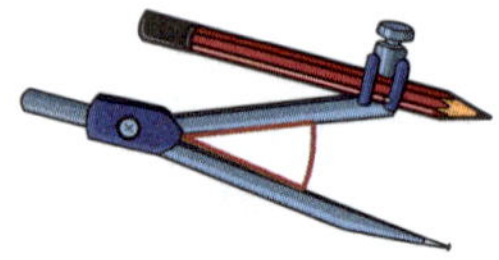

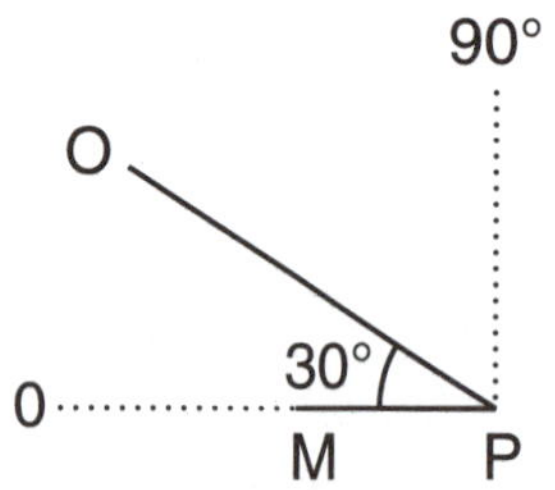

∠OPM = 30°
is an acute angle.

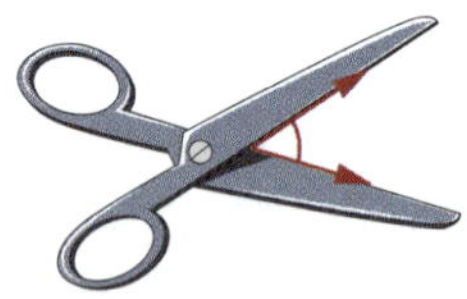

4. Straight Angle

A straight angle is equal to 180° and always looks like a straight line, that is, both the arms of the angle form a straight line.

Examples:

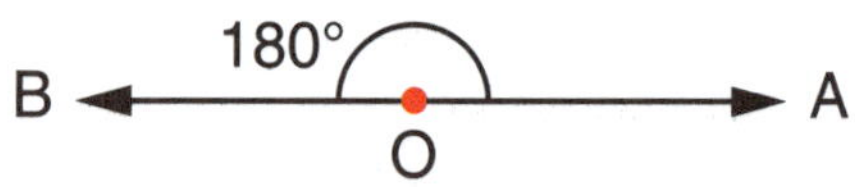

∠AOB = 180°

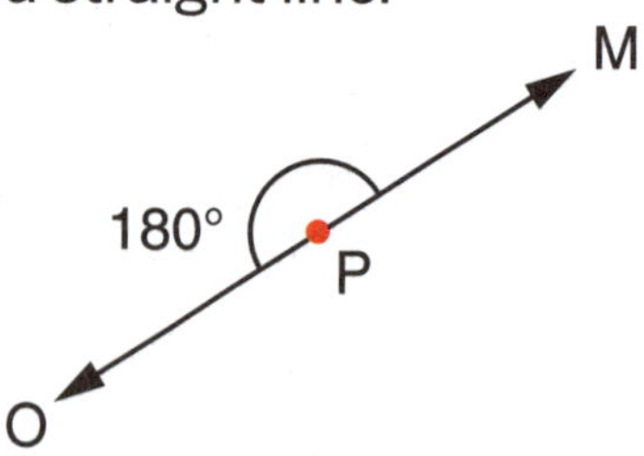

∠OPM = 180°

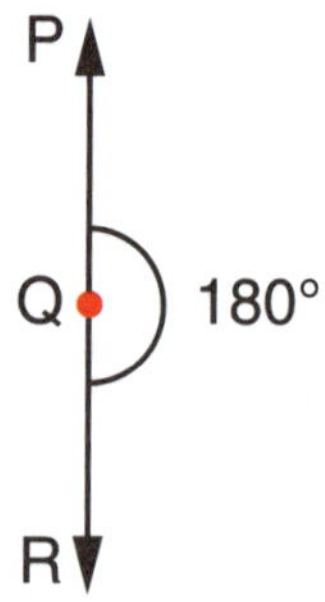

∠PQR = 180°

Note

A straight angle is always equal to 180°.
Whenever an angle forms a straight line, it is equal to 180°.

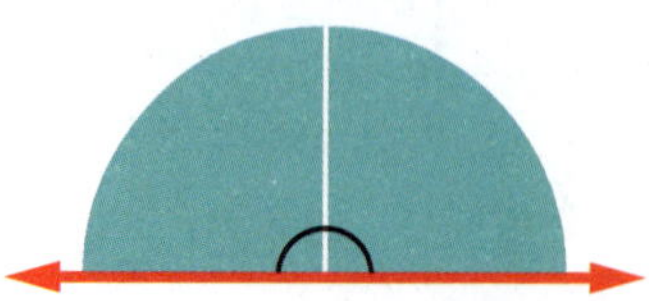

5. Obtuse Angle

If an angle is greater than 90° and less than 180° (that is, it is between 90° and 180°), it is called an obtuse angle.

Example:

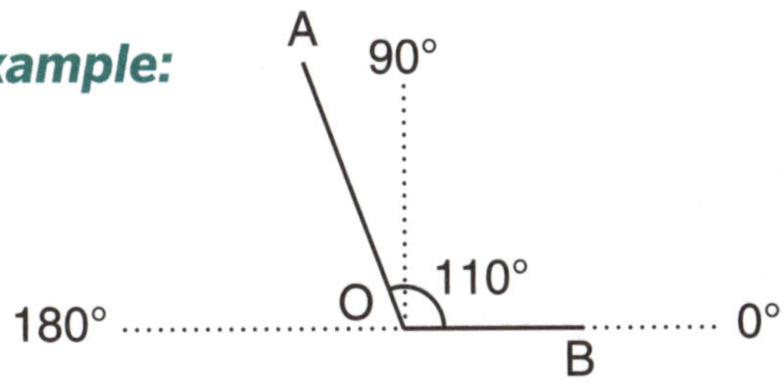

∠AOB = 110° is an obtuse angle.

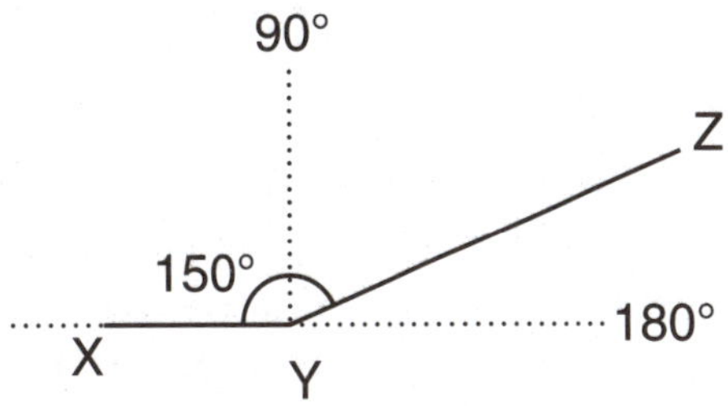

∠XYZ = 150° is an obtuse angle.

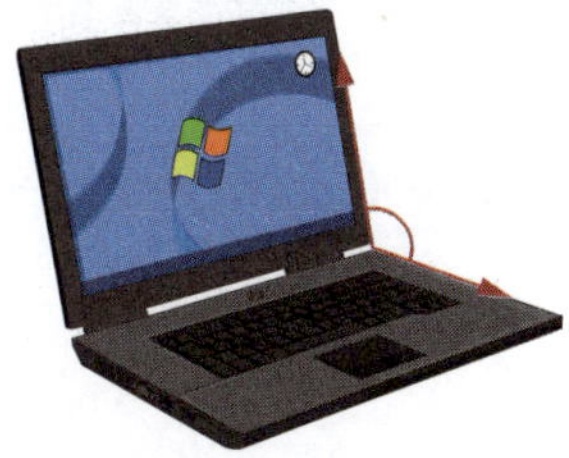

6. Complete Angle

A complete angle is equal to 360° and always completes a full circle, that is, one arm lies straight and the other arm rotates fully, completes a circle and comes and lies on top of the first arm.

Note

Whenever an angle completes a circle or a rotation it is equal to 360°.

Examples:

Complete Angle

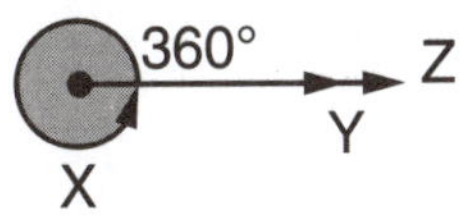

Angle equal to 360°

∠ZXY = 360°

7. Reflex Angle

If an angle is greater than 180° and less than 360° (that is, it is between 180° and 360°), it is called a reflex angle.

Examples:

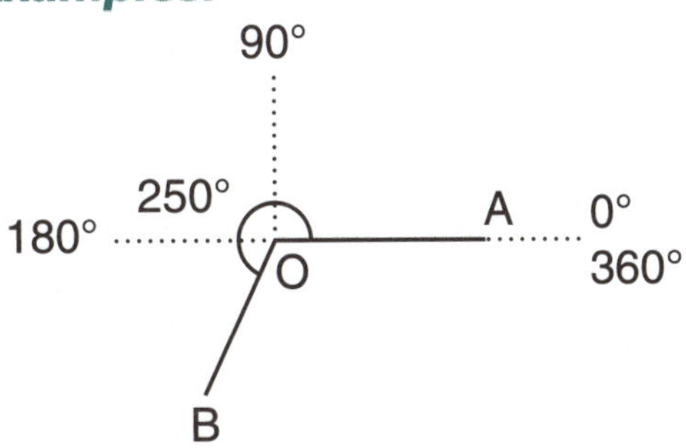

∠AOB = 250° is a reflex angle.

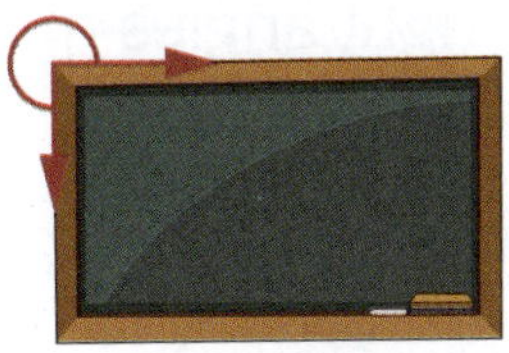

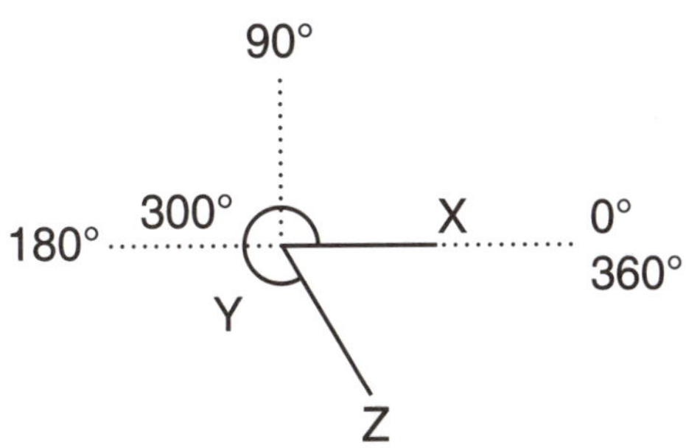

∠XYZ = 300° is a reflex angle.

Try These!

Identify and mark the different types of angles in the adjacent figure. A few have been done for reference.

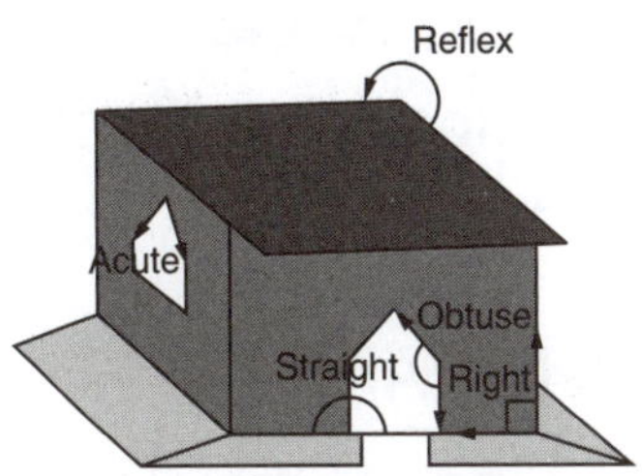

Here, ∠AOB makes two angles. One is reflex angle ∠AOB = 250° and the other is obtuse angle ∠AOB = 110°.

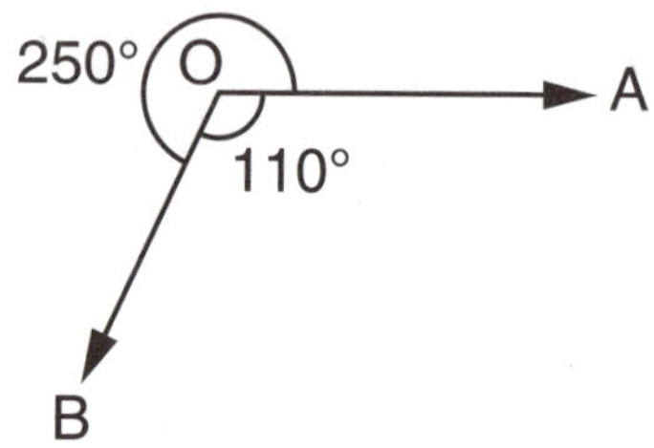

When we want to talk about the reflex angle we must mention it. In the above case, ∠AOB refers to the obtuse angle, that is, ∠AOB = 110°.

Reflex ∠AOB refers to the reflex angle, that is, ∠AOB = 250°.

Remembering Angles

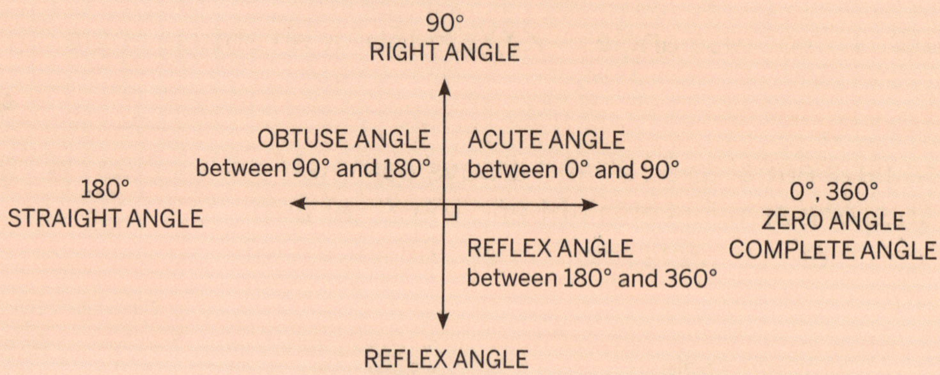

Examples of Angles on a Clock Face

1. Zero Angle

At 12 o'clock, both the hands of a clock make 0°.

2. Complete Angle

At 12 o'clock, both the hands also make an angle of 360° after the minute hand has gone around the clock and come back to 12.

3. Right Angle

The clocks here show the various right angles made by the hands of the clock at different times.

4. Acute Angle

In the clock shown here, the hands make an acute angle (more than 0° and less than 90°).

5. Obtuse Angle

In the clock shown here, the hands make an obtuse angle (more than 90° and less than 180°)

6. Reflex Angle

The hands of the clock shown here make a reflex angle.

Exercise 13.4

1 Fill in the blanks.

a. A zero angle is equal to ______ degrees.

b. An acute angle is greater than ______ degrees and less than ______ degrees.

c. A right angle is equal to ______ degrees.

d. An obtuse angle is greater than ______ degrees and less than ______ degrees.

e. A straight angle is equal to ______ degrees.

f. A reflex angle is greater than ______ degrees and less than ______ degrees.

g. A complete angle is equal to ______ degrees.

2 Identify the following angles.

a. ∠ABC = ________

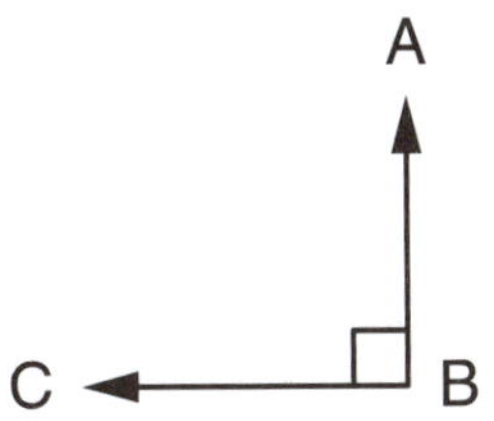

b. ∠PQR = ________

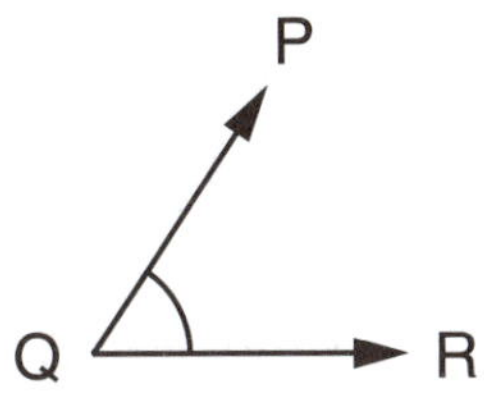

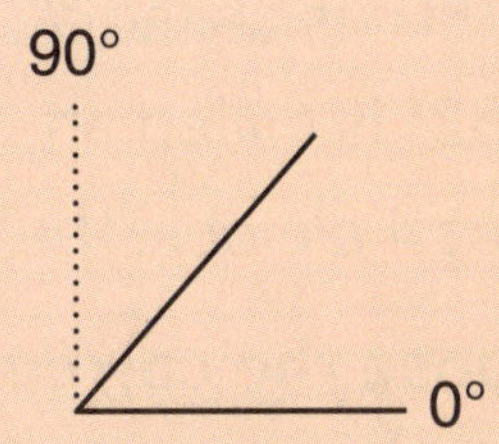

Hint: The angle falls between 0° and 90°.

c. ∠OPM = ________

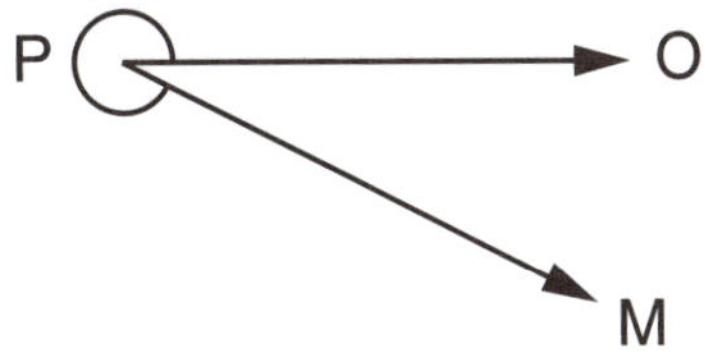

d. ∠LMN = ________

e. ∠CDE = ________

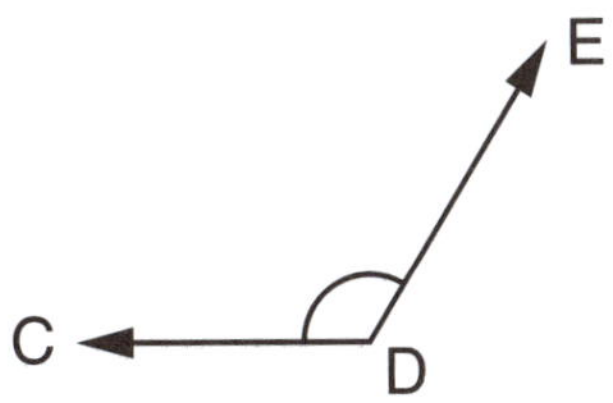

Hint:

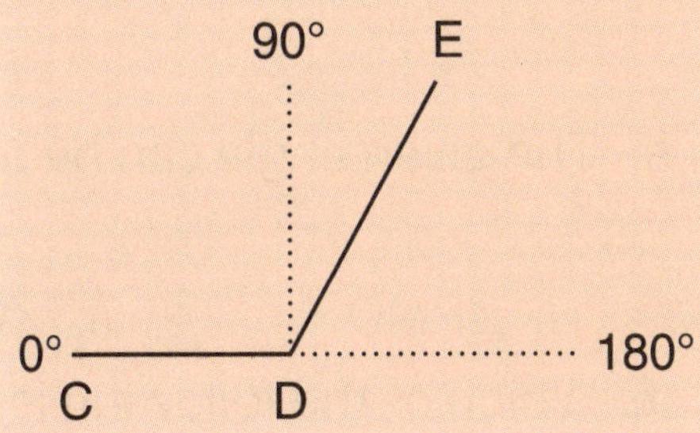

Revision Exercise

1 Fill in the blanks.

a. A line segment A———B is represented by ________.

b. A collection of points which do not follow a straight path is called a ________.

c. ↕ is a ________ line, while ↔ is a ________ line .

d. In Y 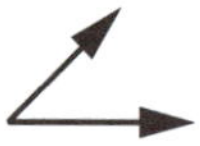

Z the vertex is ________.

e. In Y 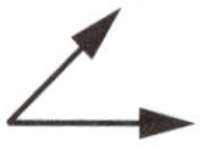

Z the arms of the angle are ________ and ________.

f. 180° is called a ________ angle.

g. 53° is called an ________ angle.

h. At 4 o'clock, the hands of a clock make an ________ angle.

2 Choose the correct option for each of the following.

a.  is a

i. vertical line ii. horizontal line iii. diagonal line iv. line segment ☐

b. A flat surface which extends in all directions is called a

i. flat ii. plane iii. table iv. wall ☐

c. Ray AB is written as

i. $\overline{AB}$ ii. $\overleftrightarrow{AB}$ iii. $\overrightarrow{AB}$ iv. AB ☐

d.  is a

i. line ii. line segment iii. curve iv. ray ☐

e. The given angle can be named

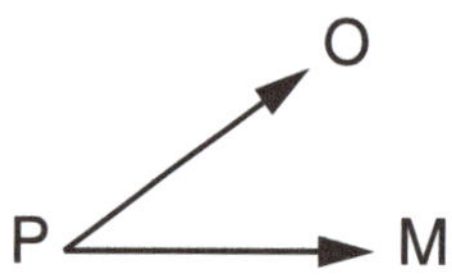

i. ∠PMO ii. ∠O iii. ∠MPO iv. ∠MOP ☐

f. Which of the following is an acute angle?

i. 90° ii. 0° iii. 75° iv. 135° ☐

g. Which of the following is a reflex angle?

i. 181° ii. 180° iii. 90° iv. 360° ☐

h. ∠ABC as shown is

i. an acute angle ii. an obtuse angle

iii. a right angle iv. a reflex angle

☐

3 **Draw the following angles in your notebook.**

a. 70° b. 150° c. 25° d. 85°

4 **Measure the following angles and classify them as Acute, Obtuse, Right, Zero and Complete angle.**

a. ∠XYZ ____________

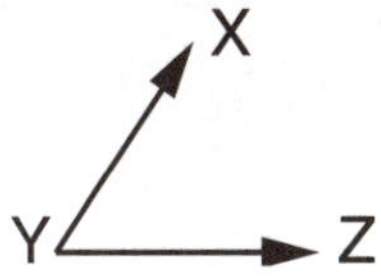

b. ∠ABC ____________

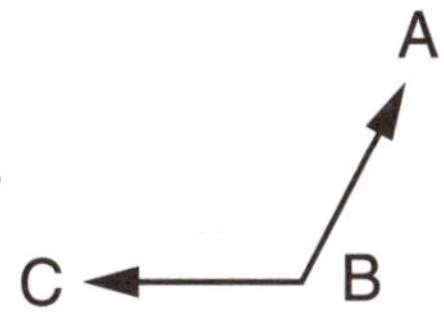

c. ∠LMN ____________

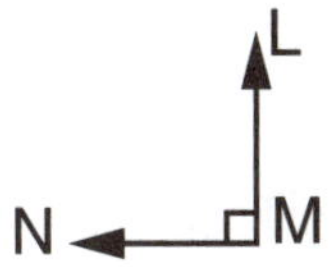

d. ∠AOB ____________

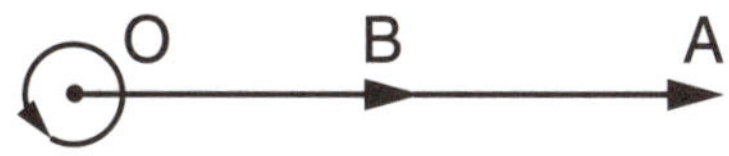

e. ∠PQR ____________

5 **State whether the following statements are True or False.**

a. ABCD is a plane.

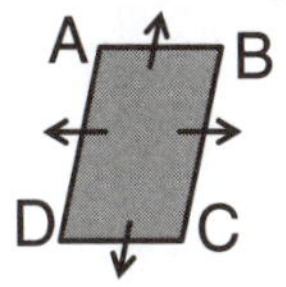

b. AB is a vertical line.

c. The edge of a table is an example of ray.

d. This is a curve.

e. This is a diagonal line.

f. This is a line segment.

g. An acute angle is equal to 90°.

h. An obtuse angle is greater than 90° and less than 180°.

i.

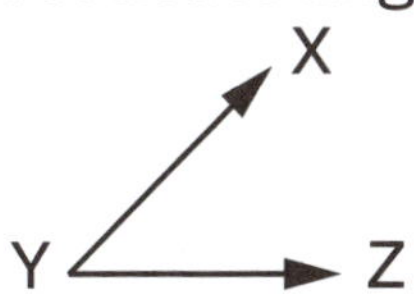

i. XY and ZY are the arms of ∠XYZ.

ii. Y is the vertex of ∠XYZ.

j. A complete angle is equal to 360°.

For the Curious Mind

Fill the given grid with numbers from 1 to 9. Number 7 is already placed for you.

1. 5 is above 7 and to the left of 3.
2. 1 is to the right of 7 and above 2.
3. 2 is to the right of 6.
4. 9 is above 4 and to the left of 7.

	7	

Geometric angles are used to construct buildings. Architects use angles extensively in their design of buildings!

Polygons

14

Polygons

A **polygon** is a closed figure made up of line segments. A polygon must have at least 3 sides for it to be a closed figure.

Closed Figures

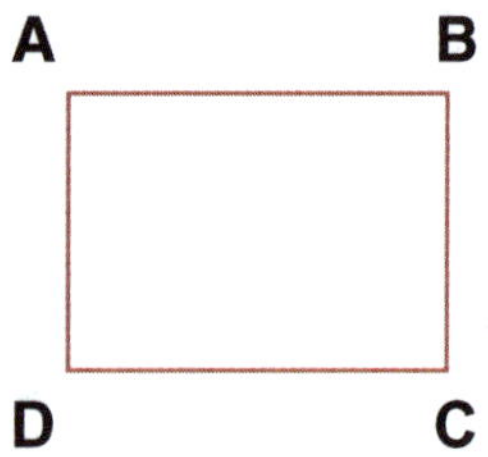

The figure given here is made up of 4 line segments—AB, BC, CD and DA. It is a closed figure.

Open Figures

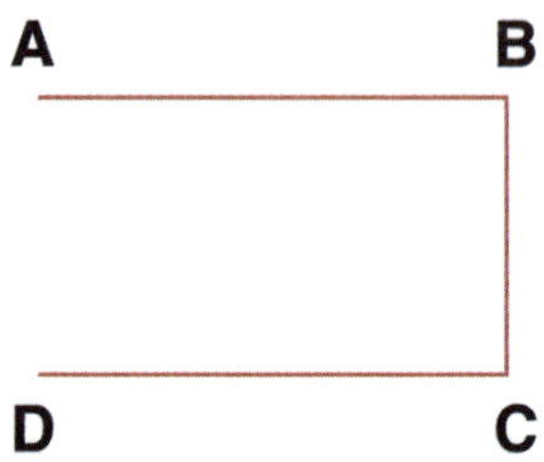

In the given figure, the line segments AB, BC and CD are joined, but DA is not joined. So, it is an open figure.

If there is only one side, the figure will not be closed and thus, we cannot call it a polygon.

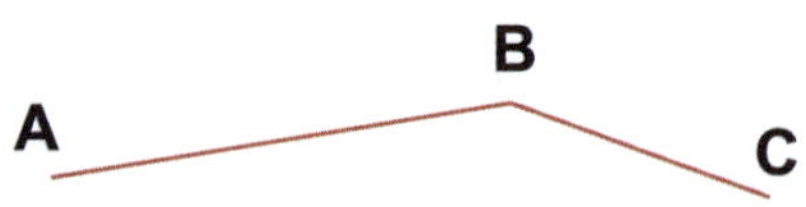

If the figure has only two sides, then too it will not be closed and we cannot call it a polygon.

Thus, closed figures with 3 or more sides are called polygons. These polygons have specific names.

Read the table below and learn the names of the common polygons.

No. of sides	Name	Figures
3	Triangle *Note: Tri means 3.*	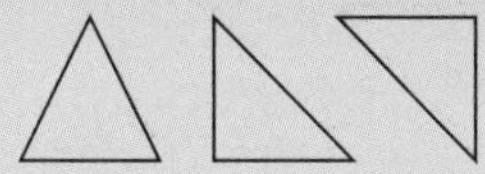
4	Quadrilateral *Note: Quad means 4.*	
5	Pentagon *Note: Penta means five*	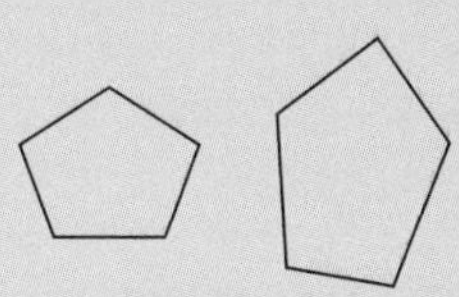
6	Hexagon *Note: Hexa means six.*	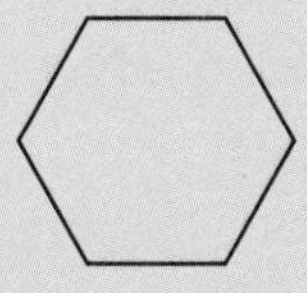
7	Heptagon or Septagon	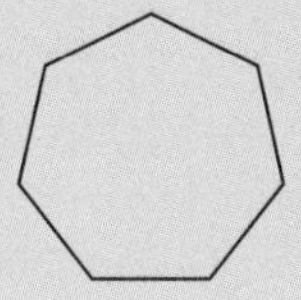
8	Octagon	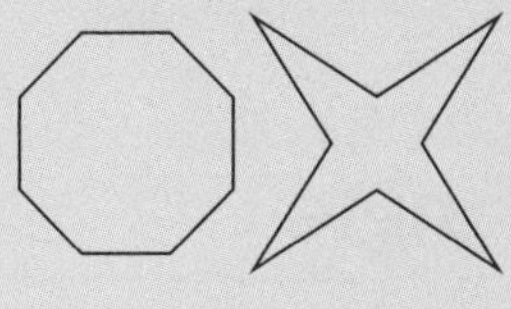
9	Nonagon	
10	Decagon	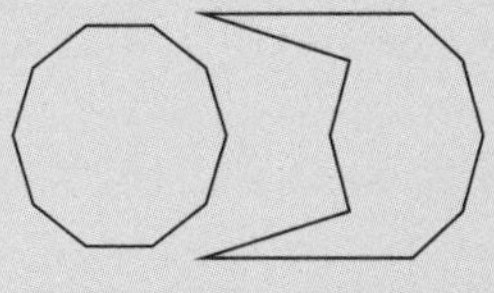
11	11-gon	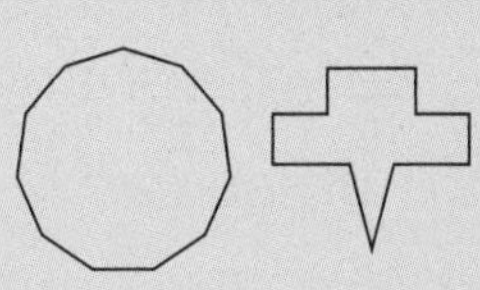
12	Dodecagon or 12-gon	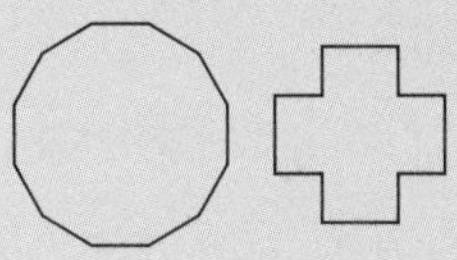

Exercise 14.1

1 Fill in the blanks.

a. A polygon is a ________ figure made up of line segments.

b. A polygon must have at least _______ sides.

2 Which of the following shapes are polygons?

a. 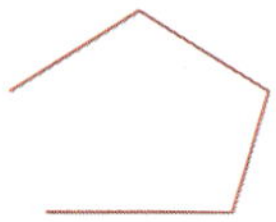

b. 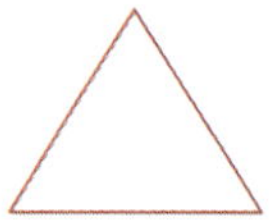

c. 

d. 

e. 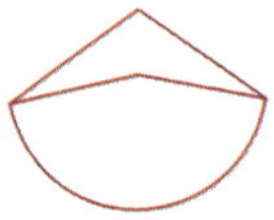

f. 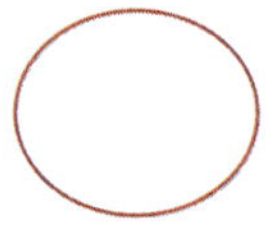

3 Write the names of the polygons with the following number of sides.

No. of sides	Name of the polygon
a. 6	____________
b. 7	____________
c. 8	____________
d. 9	____________
e. 10	____________

Triangle

Triangle is a polygon made up of 3 line segments.

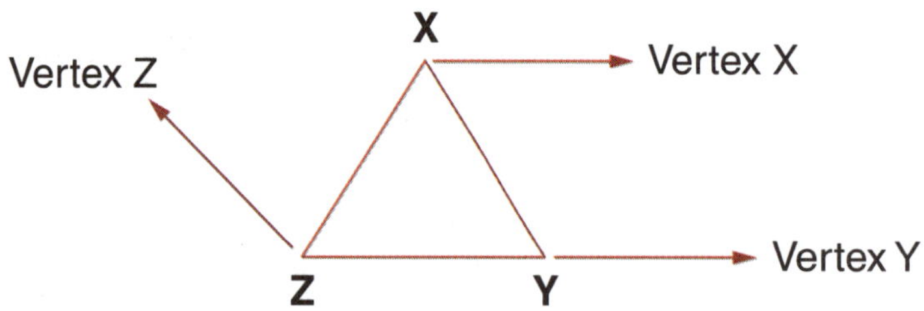

In the above triangle, the three line segments are XY, YZ and ZX. These are also called the sides of a triangle. The symbol for a triangle is Δ.

This triangle can be called ΔXYZ, ΔXZY, ΔYXZ, ΔYZX, ΔZXY or ΔZYX.

The point where two line segments meet is called a vertex. The plural of vertex is vertices.

In a triangle there are 3 vertices. In this triangle, the vertices are X, Y and Z.

Triangles can be classified according to their sides or according to their angles.

Classification of Triangles According to Their Angles

1. **Acute-angled triangle**

   A triangle in which **all** the angles are acute is called an acute-angled triangle.

   In ΔABC, ∠a, ∠b and ∠c are acute angles. So, it is an acute-angled triangle.

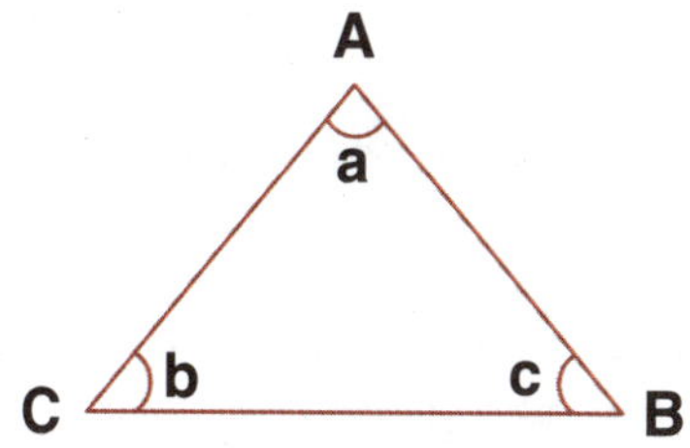

2. **Obtuse-angled triangle**

   A triangle in which **one** angle is obtuse is called an obtuse-angled triangle.

   In ΔABC, ∠b is an obtuse angle, and ∠a and ∠c are acute angles. So, it is an obtuse-angled triangle.

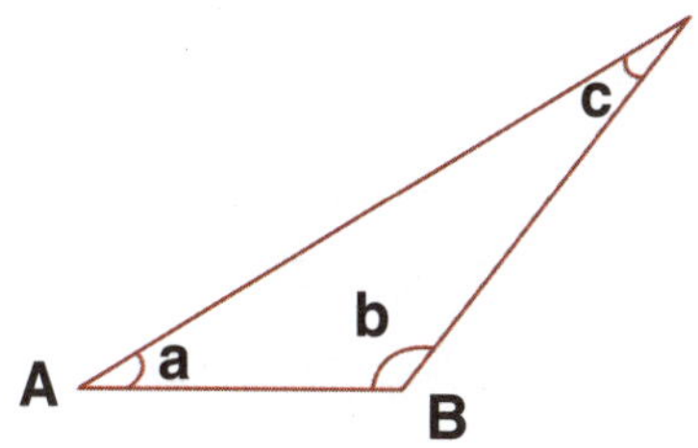

3. **Right-angled triangle**

   A triangle in which **one** angle is 90° is called a right-angled triangle.

   In ΔABC, ∠b = 90°.

   So, it is a right-angled triangle.

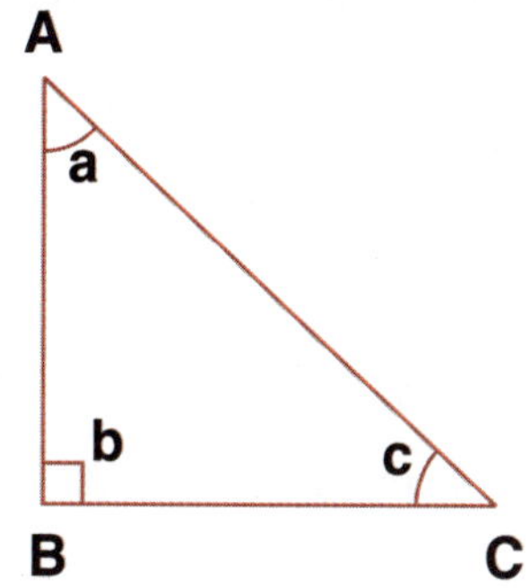

Classification of Triangles According to Their Sides

1. **Equilateral triangle**

   An equilateral triangle is a triangle in which **all** the sides are equal.

   In ΔABC, AB = BC = AC.

   Therefore, it is an equilateral triangle.

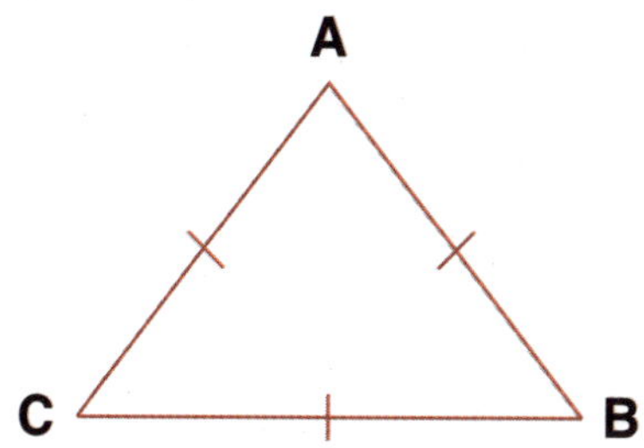

2. **Isosceles triangle**

   An isosceles triangle is a triangle in which only **two** sides are equal.

   In ΔABC, AB = AC. So, it is an isosceles triangle.

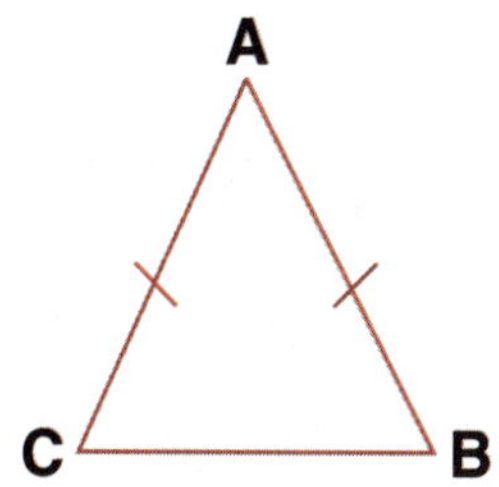

3. **Scalene Triangle**

   A scalene triangle is a triangle in which **no** two sides are equal.

   In ΔABC, no two sides are equal.

   So, it is a scalene triangle.

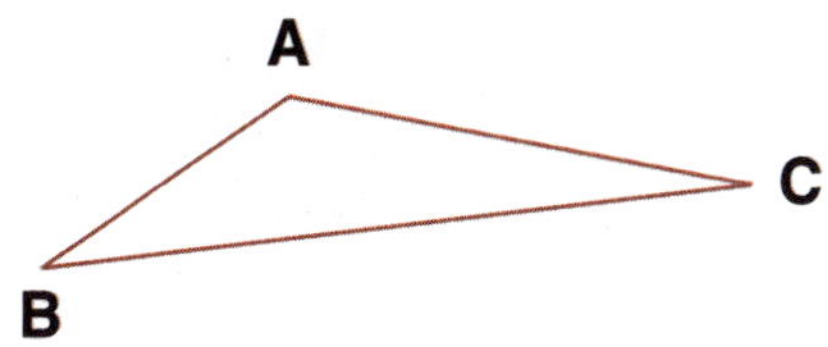

Quadrilateral

Note

A quadrangle is a square or rectangular space or courtyard enclosed by buildings.

Quadrilateral is a polygon made up of four line segments.

In the above quadrilateral, the four sides are AB, BC, CD and DA. The four vertices are A, B, C and D. The quadrilateral can be named ABCD, BCDA, CDAB, DABC, ADCB, DCBA, CBAD or BADC.

Following are some common quadrilaterals.

1. **Square**

   A square is a quadrilateral in which **all** the sides are equal and **each** interior angle is 90°. In the given quadrilateral,

   AB = BC = CD = DA and $\angle A = \angle B = \angle C = \angle D = 90°$.

   Therefore, ABCD is a square.

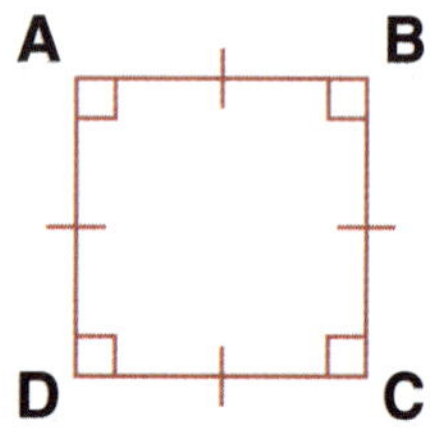

2. **Rectangle**

   A rectangle is a quadrilateral in which the **opposite** sides are equal and **each** interior angle is 90°.

   In the given quadrilateral, AB = CD and BC = AD, and $\angle A = \angle B = \angle C = \angle D = 90°$.

   Therefore, ABCD is a rectangle.

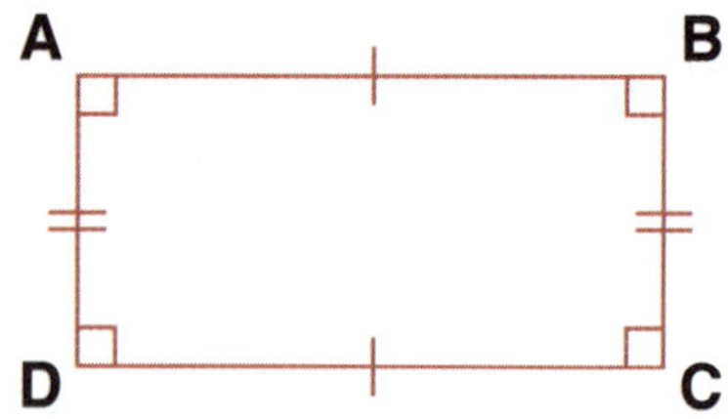

3. **Rhombus**

   A rhombus looks like a tilted square.

   All the sides of the rhombus are equal in length, like those of a square.

   The difference between a square and a rhombus is that each interior angle of a square is 90°, but each interior angle of a rhombus is not 90°.

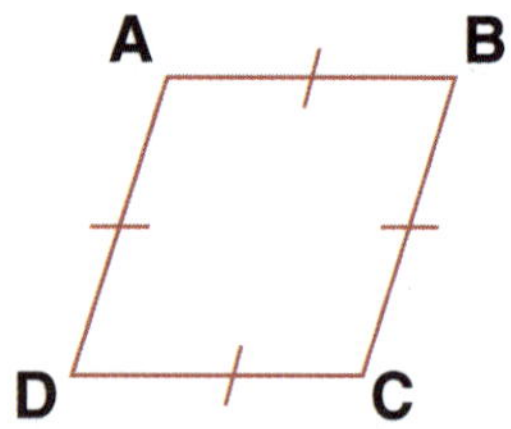

Note

A square can be called a rhombus but a rhombus cannot be called a square.

Square

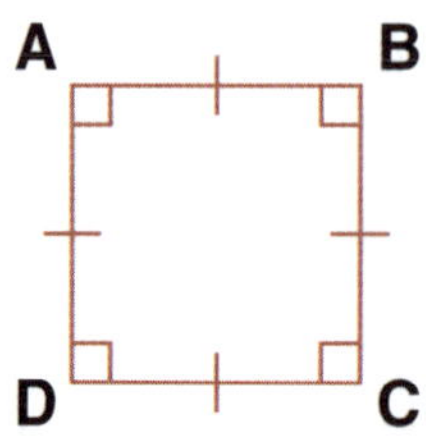

Rhombus

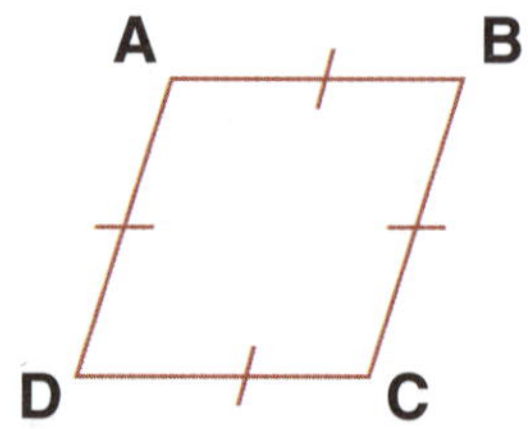

4. **Parallelogram**

The opposite sides of a parallelogram are equal, like those of a rectangle.

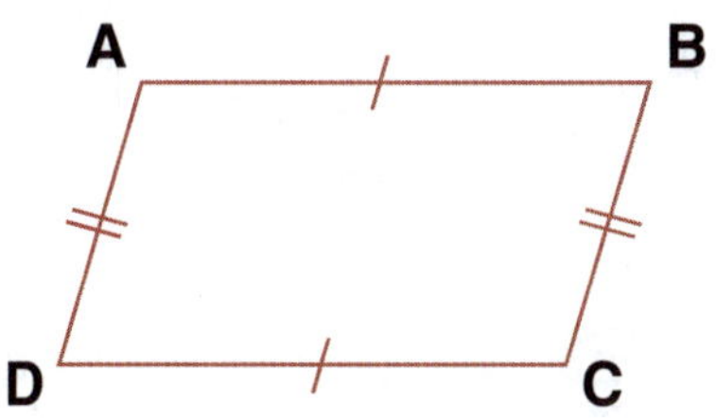

The difference between a rectangle and a parallelogram is that each interior angle of a rectangle is 90° but each interior angle of a parallelogram is not 90°.

Rectangle

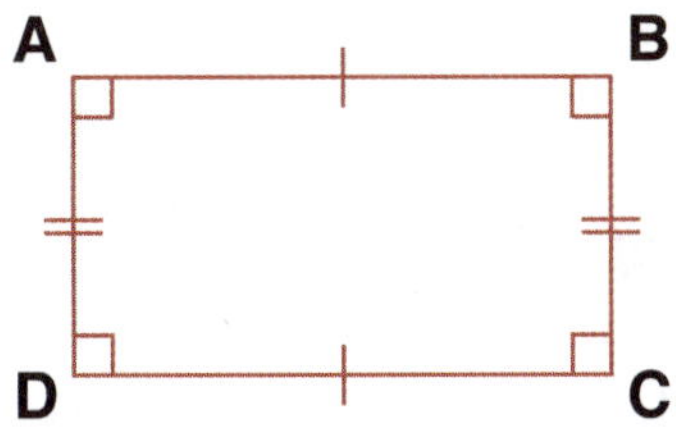

Parallelogram

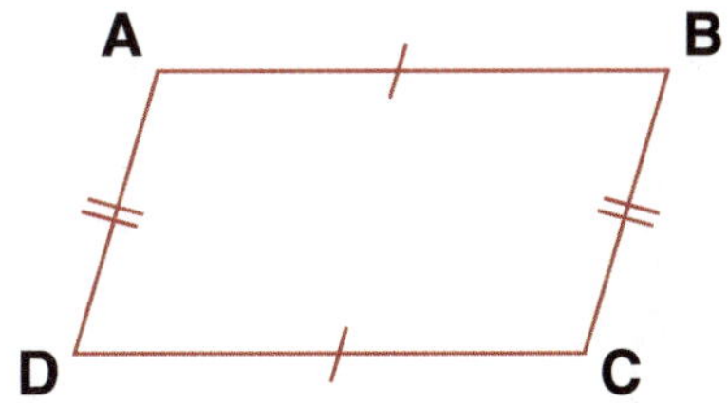

Note

A rectangle can be called a parallelogram but a parallelogram cannot be called a rectangle.

Pentagon

A pentagon is a polygon with 5 sides.

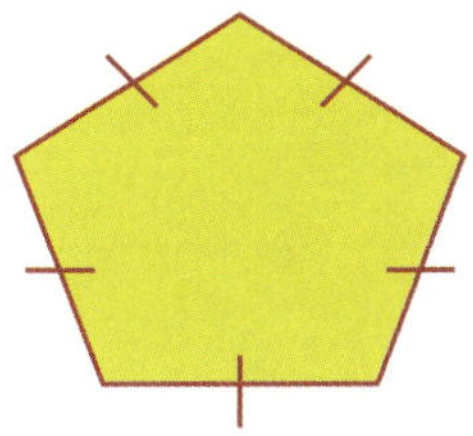

A pentagon with all sides equal and all angles equal is called a regular pentagon.

The United States Department of Defense is in Washington DC. The building has 5 sides and is called the Pentagon.

Note

Any polygon with all sides equal is a regular polygon. An octagon with all sides equal is called a regular octagon.

Exercise 14.2

1 Fill in the blanks.

a. A triangle is a polygon made up of ______ line segments.

b. Triangles can be classified according to their ______ or sides.

c. All the angles of a/an ______ triangle are equal.

d. An obtuse-angled triangle has ______ obtuse angle.

e. A right-angled triangle has ______ right angle.

f. A/An ______ triangle has all the 3 sides equal.

g. A/An ______ triangle has 2 equal sides.

h. A/An ______ triangle has no sides equal.

i. A quadrilateral is a polygon made up of ______ line segments.

j. A square is a quadrilateral in which all the four sides are ______ and each interior angle is ______ .

2 **Write the names of the figures given below.**

a.

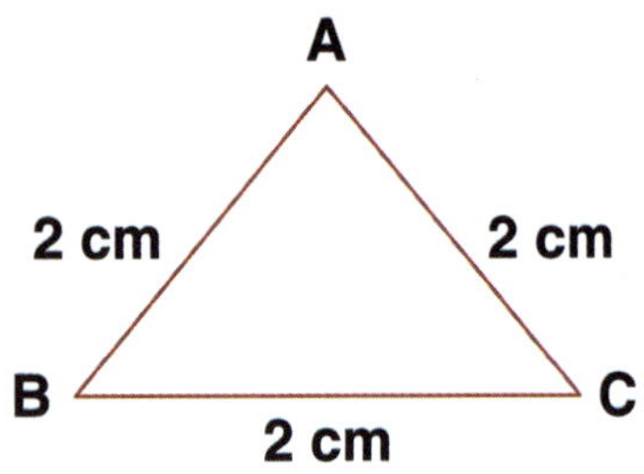

____

b.

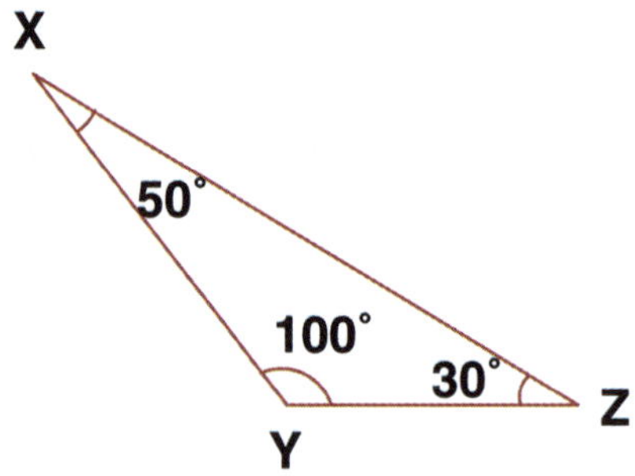

____

c.

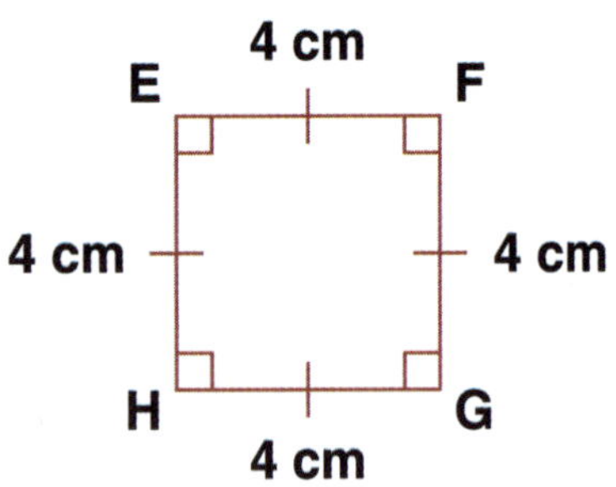

____

d.

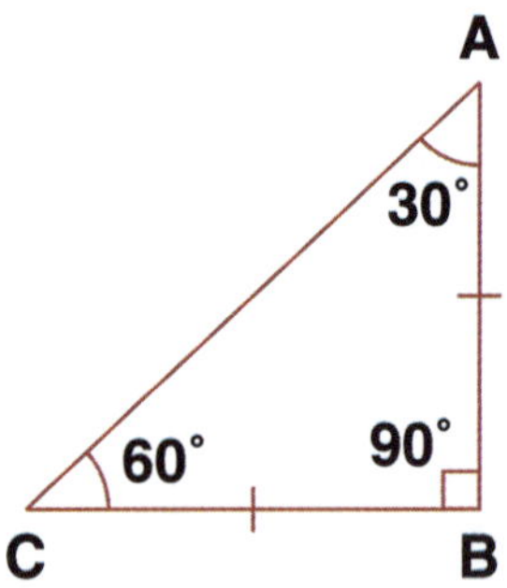

____

e.

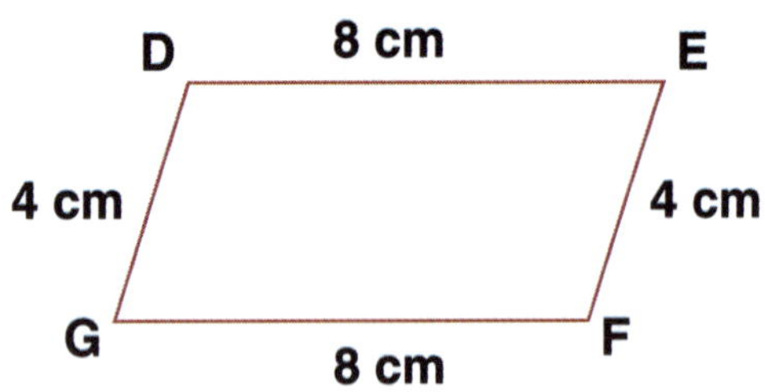

____

f.

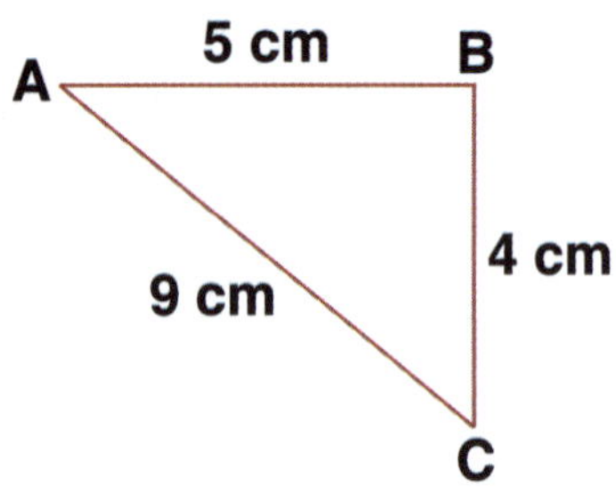

____

Revision Exercise

1 Choose the correct option for each of the following.

a. A pentagon is a polygon made up of ______ line segments.

i. 3 ii. 4 iii. 5 iv. 6 ☐

b. A heptagon is also called a/an ______.

i. pentagon ii. septagon iii. octagon iv. nonagon ☐

c. A polygon made up of 8 line segments is called an a/an ______.

i. octagon ii. nonagon iii. decagon iv. hexagon ☐

d. A decade is equal to 10 years and a decagon is a polygon made up of ______ line segments.

i. 1 ii. 100 iii. 10 iv. 1000 ☐

e. An obtuse-angled triangle has ______ obtuse angles.

i. 0 ii. 1 iii. 2 iv. 3 ☐

f. An acute-angled triangle has ______ acute angle(s).

i. 0 ii. 1 iii. 2 iv. 3 ☐

g. A triangle with two equal sides is called ______.

i. an equilateral triangle ii. an isosceles triangle ☐
iii. a right-angled triangle iv. an obtuse-angled triangle

h. All the sides of a ______ are equal.

i. square and a rectangle ii. square and a rhombus ☐
iii. rhombus and a rectangle iv. parallelogram and a rhombus

i. Each interior angle of a ______ are equal to 90°.

i. square and a rectangle ii. square and a rhombus ☐
iii. rhombus and a rectangle iv. parallelogram and a rhombus

j. All sides of ______ are equal.

i. a rectangle ii. a parallelogram iii. an isosceles triangle iv. a rhombus ☐

2 Write the names of polygons with the following number of sides.

No. of sides	Name of the polygon
5	
10	
7	
3	

No. of sides	Name of the polygon
9	
6	
4	
8	

Perimeter and Area

15

Perimeter

Perimeter is the distance covered along the boundary of a polygon or figure when you go around it once.

In other words, **perimeter** is the sum of all the sides of a polygon. Thus, to find the perimeter, we add all the sides of a polygon.

Example 1: Perimeter of Fig. 1 = 3 cm + 4 cm + 5 cm = 12 cm

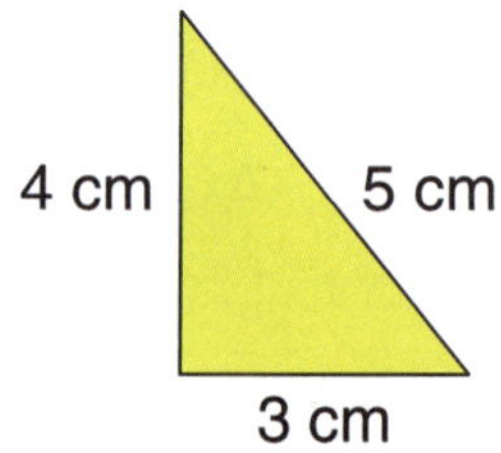

Fig. 1

Example 2: Perimeter of Fig. 2 = 5 cm + 5 cm + 5 cm + 5 cm = 20 cm

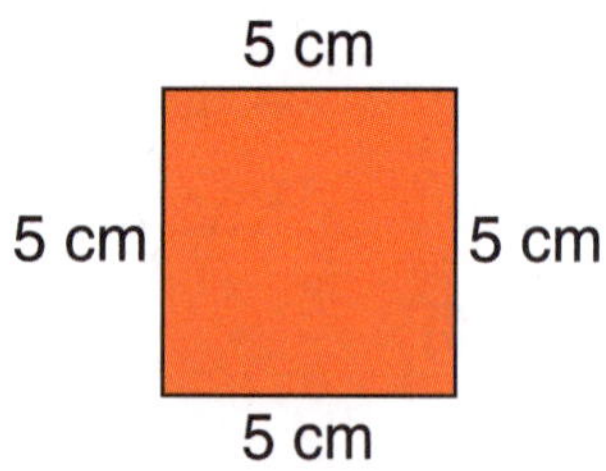

Fig. 2

Example 3: Perimeter of Fig. 3 = 2 cm + 6 cm + 2 cm + 6 cm = 16 cm

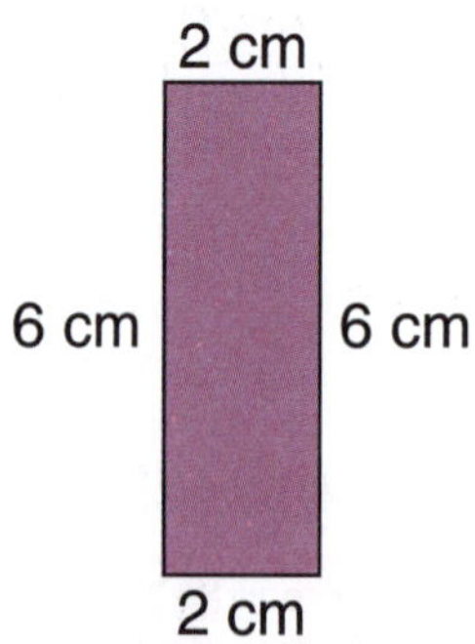

Fig. 3

Example 4: Perimeter of Fig. 4 = 4 cm + 5 cm + 5 cm + 4 cm + 6 cm = 24 cm

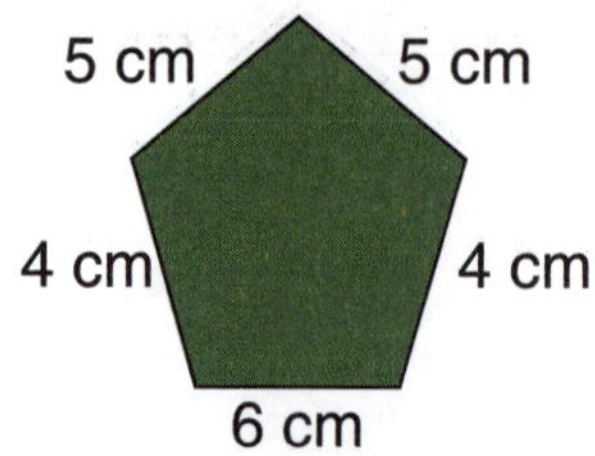

Fig. 4

Exercise 15.1

Find the perimeters of the following shapes.

1. 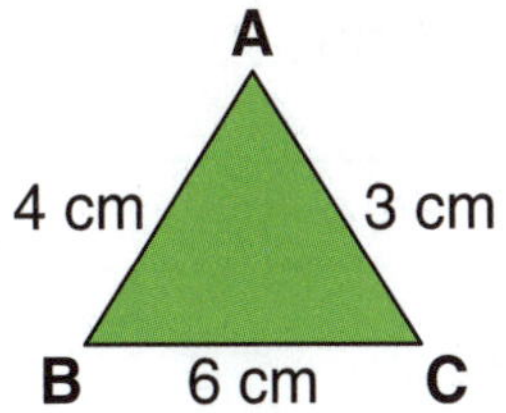

2. 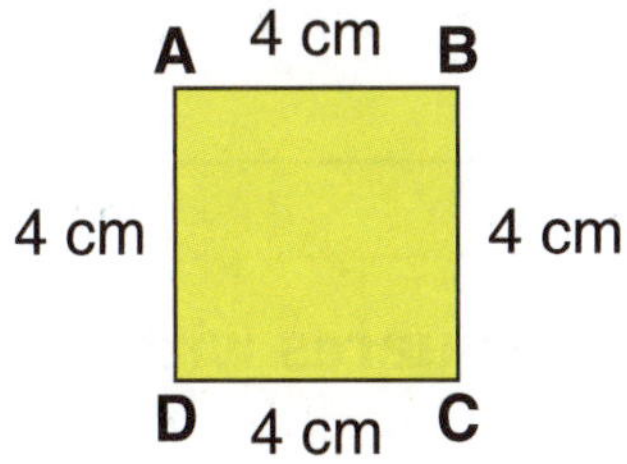

3. 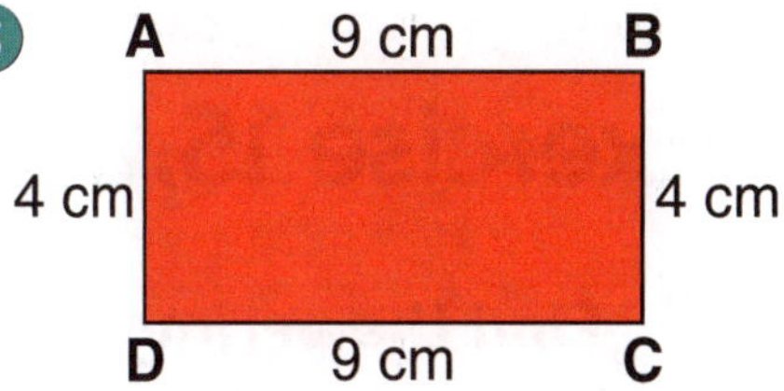

4. 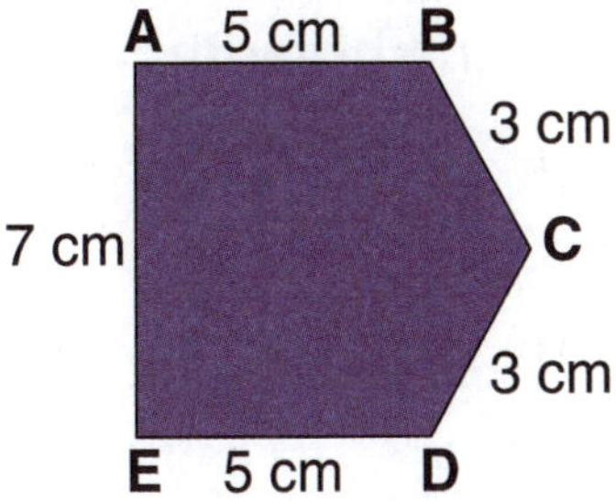

5. 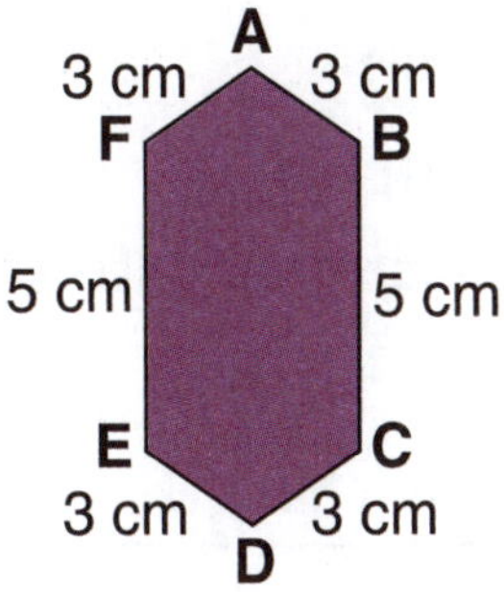

6. 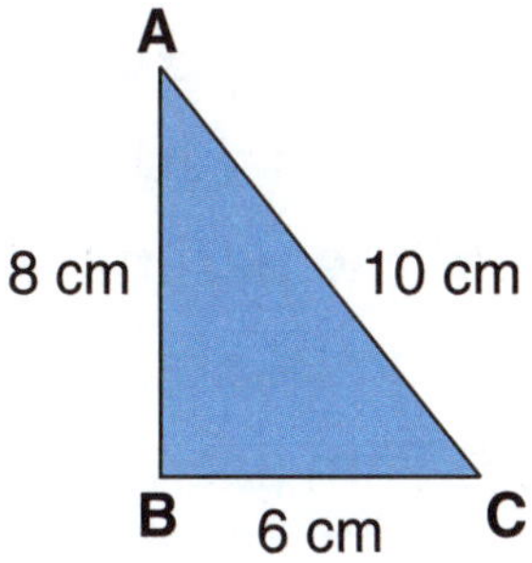

Perimeter of a Square

A square has four equal sides. Therefore, to find its perimeter, we multiply the side (s) by 4.

P = side + side + side + side

P = 4 × side = 4s

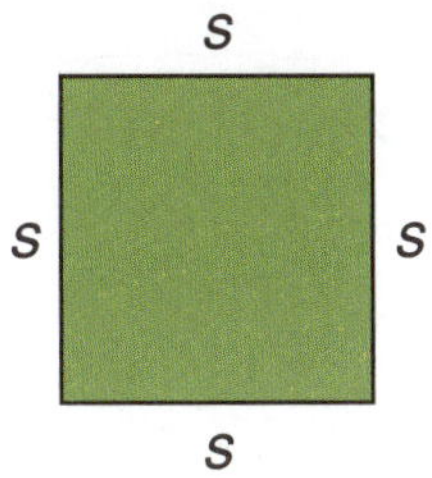

Each side of the clock = 50 cm

So, the perimeter = 50 cm + 50 cm + 50 cm + 50 cm

= 4 × 50 cm = 200 cm

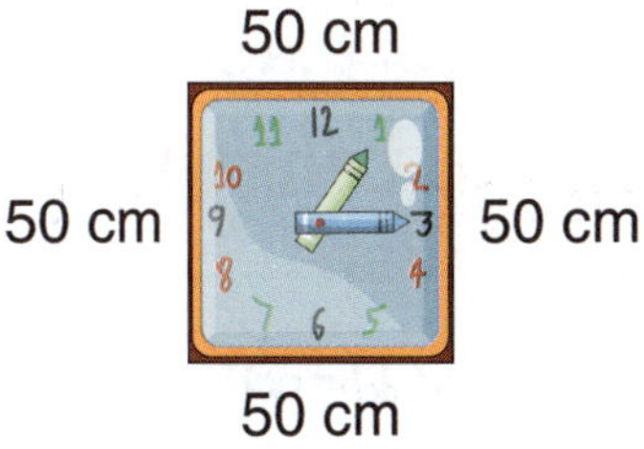

Perimeter of a Rectangle

The opposite sides of a rectangle are equal. Therefore, to find the perimeter, we can use the following formula.

P = length + breadth + length + breadth

∴ P = 2 length + 2 breadth

= 2 (length + breadth)

= 2 (l + b)

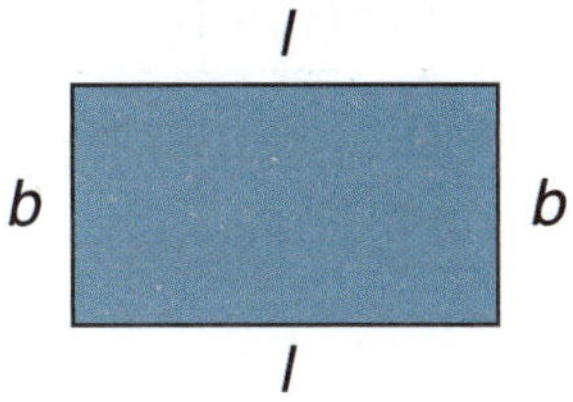

Note

The longer side of a rectangle is called the length (l) and the shorter side of a rectangle is called the breadth (b) or width.

The length or l of the rectangle = 6 cm
The breadth or b of the rectangle = 2 cm
So, the perimeter = 2 (6 cm + 2 cm)
= 2 (8 cm) = 16 cm

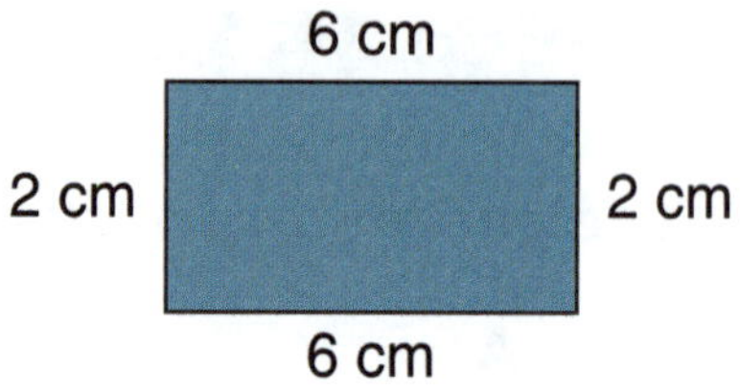

Exercise 15.2

1. **Find the perimeters of the squares with the given sides.**
   a. 3 cm b. 5 cm c. 12 m d. 20 m
2. **Find the perimeters of the rectangles with the given lengths and breadths.**
   a. Length = 6 cm, breadth = 3 cm b. Length = 5 cm, breadth = 2 cm
   c. Length = 10 m, breadth = 8 m d. Length = 12 m, breadth = 10 m
3. **Find the perimeters of the triangles with the given sides.**
   a. 3 cm, 4 cm, 5 cm b. 7 cm, 9 cm, 15 cm
   c. 12 cm each d. 18 cm each

Finding the Sides of a Square If the Perimeter is Given

A square has 4 equal sides. To find each side, we divide the perimeter by 4.

$$P = 4 \times \text{side}$$

$$\text{So, } \frac{P}{4} = \text{side}$$

Example 5: The perimeter of a square is 20 cm. Find each side.

$$\text{Each side} = \frac{P}{4} = \frac{20}{4} = 5 \text{ cm}$$

So, each side of the square is 5 cm.

Finding the Length or Breadth of a Rectangle If the Perimeter and One Side are Given

We know $P = 2\,(l + b)$
$P = 2l + 2b$

Case 1: When Perimeter and breadth are known

$P - 2b = 2l$

$$\therefore l = \frac{P - 2b}{2}$$

Case 2: When perimeter and length are known.

$P - 2l = 2b$

$$\therefore b = \frac{P - 2l}{2}$$

Example 6: Find the length of a rectangle whose perimeter is 18 cm and breadth is 4 cm.

Here, perimeter = 18 cm and breadth = 4 cm

Using the formula, $l = \frac{P - 2b}{2}$

we get $l = \frac{18 - 2(4)}{2} = \frac{18 - 8}{2} = 5$

So, the length of the rectangle is 5 cm.

Example 7: Find the breadth of a rectangle whose perimeter is 24 cm and length is 10 cm.

Here, perimeter = 24 cm and length = 10 cm

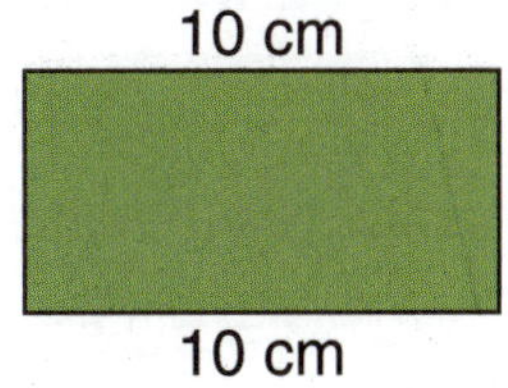

Using the formula, $b = \frac{P - 2l}{2}$

we get $b = \frac{24 - 2(10)}{2} = \frac{24 - 20}{2} = 2$

So, the breadth of the rectangle is 2 cm.

Exercise 15.3

1. **Find the sides of the squares with the following perimeters.**

   a. 28 cm b. 40 cm c. 20 cm d. 48 cm

2. **Find the lengths of the rectangles with the following perimeters and breadths.**

   a. Perimeter = 32 cm, breadth = 6 cm b. Perimeter = 40 cm, breadth = 5 cm

   c. Perimeter = 80 m, breadth = 10 m d. Perimeter = 64 cm, breadth = 12 cm

3. **Find the breadths of the rectangles with the following perimeters and lengths.**

   a. Perimeter = 46 cm, length = 12 cm b. Perimeter = 30 m, length = 5 m

   c. Perimeter = 62 cm, length = 17 cm d. Perimeter = 88 cm, length = 30 cm

Area

Area is the space covered inside the boundary of a figure or polygon.

In the rectangle ABCD, perimeter is AB + BC + CD + DA and the area is the coloured space within the rectangle.

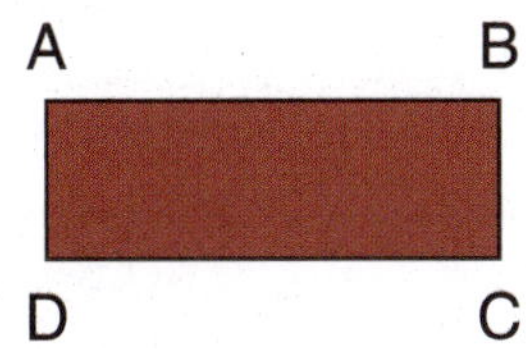

To find the distance covered on walking around a rectangular field, we need its perimeter. To find how much space is enclosed inside a rectangular floor to place tiles in it or to carpet it, we need its area.

To find the area of a rectangle, we use the following formula:

$$\text{Area of a rectangle} = \text{length} \times \text{breadth}$$

$$A = l \times b$$

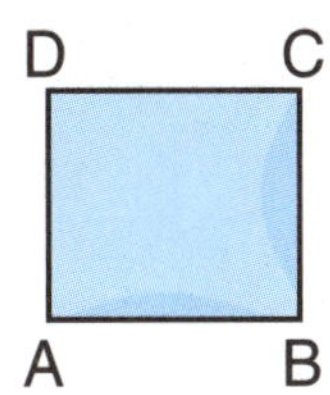

We can apply the same formula to find the area of a square. In case of a square, the length is equal to the breadth, that is, all the sides are equal. So, the same formula can be written as:

$$\text{Area of a square} = \text{side} \times \text{side}$$

$$A = s \times s$$

Once the area is calculated, the units are written with it. For example, the area can be written in sq. cm or sq. m (read as square centimetre or square metre respectively).

Example 8: Find the area of a rectangle with length 10 cm and breadth 5 cm.

Area of a rectangle = length × breadth

Area = 10 cm × 5 cm

= 50 sq. cm [Note that the unit is sq. cm.]

Thus, the area is 50 sq. cm.

Example 9: Find the area of a square with each side equal to 7 m.

Area of a square = side × side

Area = 7 m × 7 m

= 49 sq. m [Note that the unit is sq. m.]

Thus, the area is 49 sq. m.

Exercise 15.4

1. **Find the areas of the rectangles with the given lengths and breadths.**
   a. Length = 9 cm, breadth = 7 cm
   b. Length = 13 cm, breadth = 5 cm
   c. Length = 39 m, breadth = 15 m
   d. Length = 45 m, breadth = 7 m
   e. Length = 15 cm, breadth = 13 cm
   f. Length = 12 cm, breadth = 7 cm
2. **Find the areas of the squares with the given sides.**
   a. 11 cm
   b. 15 cm
   c. 43 cm
   d. 101 m
   e. 105 m
   f. 28 cm

Revision Exercise

1. **Choose the correct option for each of the following.**

   a. The perimeter of a triangle with sides 9 cm, 11 cm, 7 cm is
   i. 9 cm ii. 27 cm iii. 11 cm iv. 7 cm ☐

   b. The perimeter of an equilateral triangle in which each side is 8 cm is
   i. 8 cm ii. 24 cm iii. 40 cm iv. 64 cm ☐

   c. The area of a rectangle whose length is 10 m and breadth is 6 m is
   i. 32 sq. cm ii. 60 sq. m iii. 40 sq. m iv. 24 sq. m ☐

   d. If the perimeter of a rectangle is 40 m and the length is 12 m, then the breadth is
   i. 12 m ii. 28 m iii. 8 m iv. 52 m ☐

   e. If the perimeter of a rectangle is 36 m and the breadth is 5 m, then the length is
   i. 36 m ii. 5 m iii. 41 m iv. 13 m ☐

   f. If the perimeter of a square is 52 cm, then each side is
   i. 13 cm ii. 52 cm iii. 12 cm iv. 10 m ☐

   g. If each side of a square is 17 cm, then its area is
   i. 17 sq. cm ii. 289 cm iii. 34 sq. cm iv. 289 sq. cm ☐

   h. The area of a rectangle with length 10 cm and breadth 60 cm is
   i. 60 sq. cm ii. 600 sq. cm iii. 6000 sq. cm iv. 60000 sq. cm ☐

2. To find the perimeter of a polygon, we ________ all the sides.

3. **Find the perimeters of the following figures.**

   a. 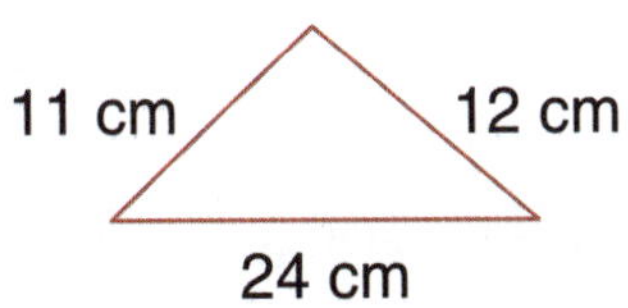

   b. 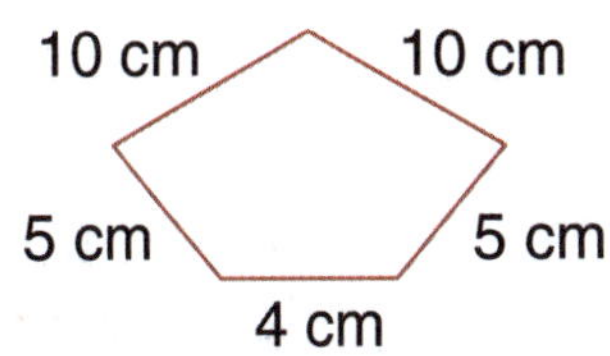

4. Find the perimeter of a square with each side equal to 15 cm.

5. Find the perimeter of a rectangle with length 18 cm and breadth 6 cm.

6. Find the perimeter of a pentagon with its sides equal to 9.45 cm, 12 cm, 3.2 cm, 8.1 cm and 11.3 cm.

7. What is the length of each side of a square if its perimeter is 76 cm?

8. Find the length of a rectangle whose perimeter is 19 cm and breadth is 2.5 cm.

9. Find the area of a rectangle whose length is 17 cm and breadth is 9 cm.

10. Find the area of a square whose each side is 14 cm.

11. Find the length of each side of a square if the perimeter is 56 cm.

Mental Maths

Fill in the blanks.

1. To find the perimeter of a square, we multiply 4 by its ________.
2. The formula to find the perimeter of a rectangle is ________.
3. The formula to find the area of a rectangle is ________.
4. The formula to find the area of a square is ________.
5. **Find the perimeters of the following figures.**

a.

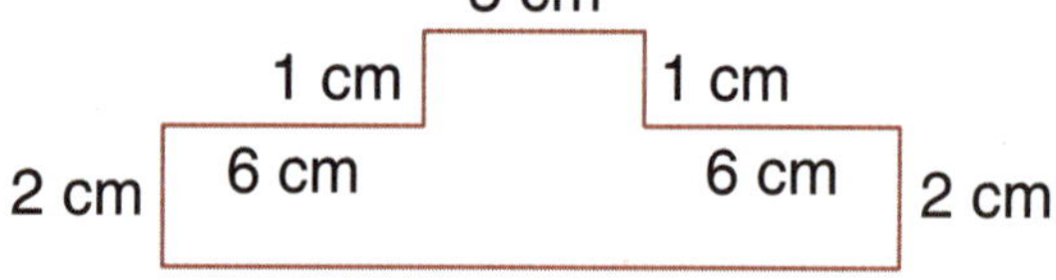

b.

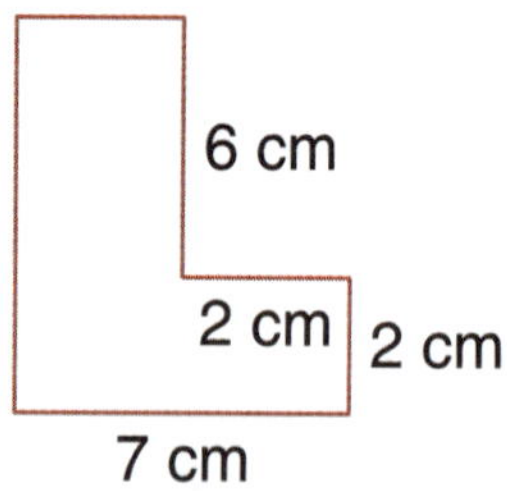

For the Curious Mind

What has a bigger area—a square with each side equal to 4 cm or a rectangle with length 6 cm and breadth 2 cm?

16 Symmetry

Let's Get Started

When one half of a figure is the mirror reflection of the other half, the figure is called **symmetrical**. That is, if we divide a symmetrical shape along the middle, then one half of the shape falls exactly on the other half. The line in the middle of the shape is called the **line of symmetry**. Therefore, the line of symmetry divides a shape into two equal halves.

Example:

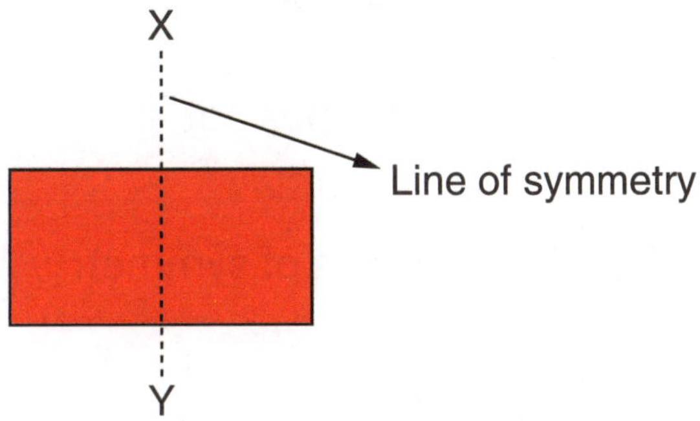

When we fold the rectangle from left to right, we find that one half of the rectangle falls exactly on the other half of the rectangle and look like this:

Thus, the line XY where the rectangle folds into two equal halves is called the line of symmetry. Shapes can have one or more lines of symmetry.

A rectangle has two lines of symmetry as shown below.

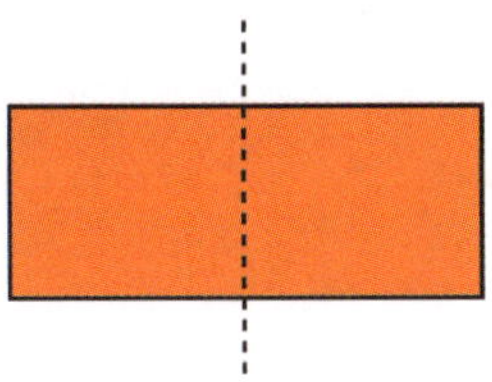

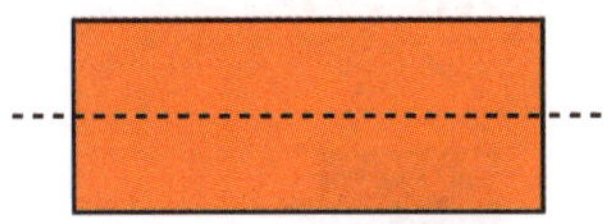

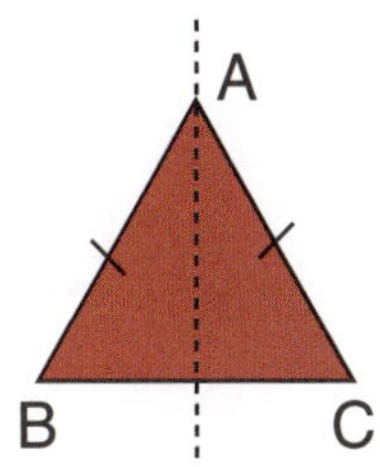

AB = AC

An isosceles triangle (in which two sides are equal) has one line of symmetry.

An equilateral triangle (in which all the three sides are equal) has three lines of symmetry. From whichever line of symmetry we fold, the triangle will get divided into two halves.

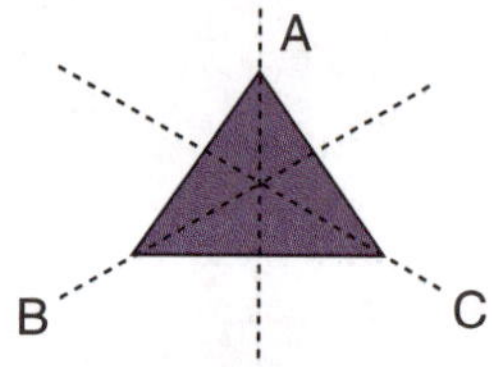

AB = BC = AC

A scalene triangle (in which no sides are equal) has no line of symmetry.

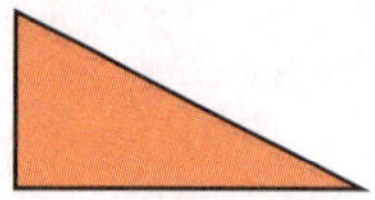

A square has four lines of symmetry.

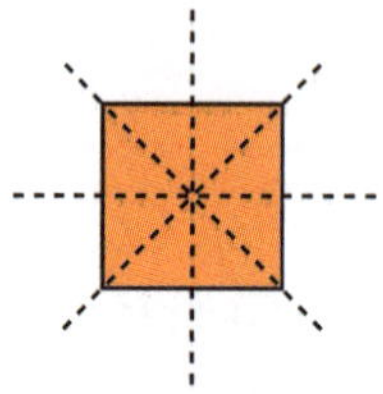

A circle has infinite lines of symmetry.

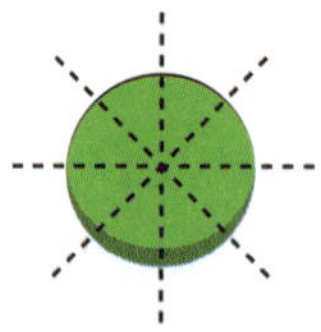

Symmetry applies not only to geometric shapes but also to other things. A face is normally symmetrical.

Below are a few more examples showing lines of symmetry.

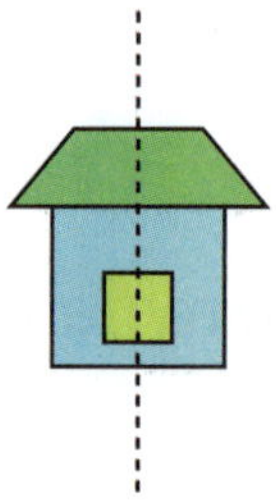

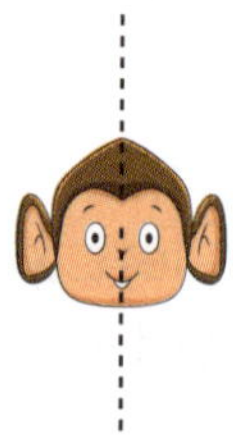

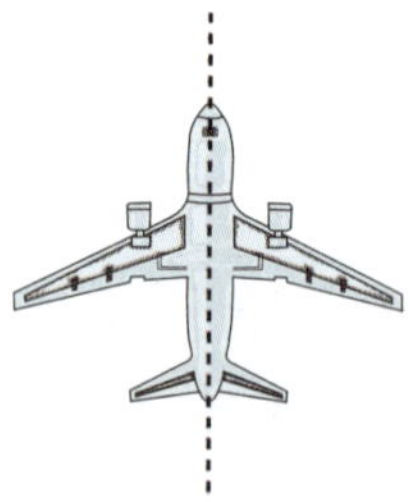

Lines of symmetry can be vertical, horizontal or diagonal. As the names suggest, these lines of symmetry divide the figures vertically, horizontally or diagonally. Some examples are given below.

Vertical Line of Symmetry

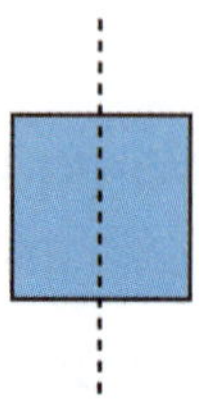

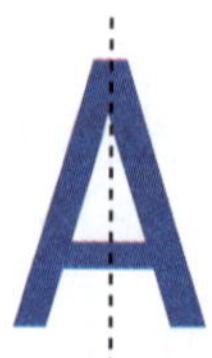

Horizontal Line of Symmetry

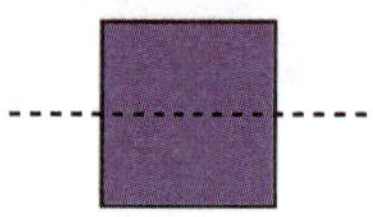

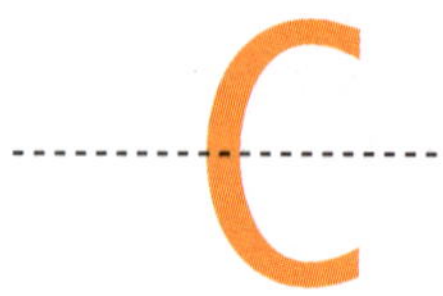

Diagonal Line of Symmetry

Remember

1. A line of symmetry divides a shape into two exact halves.
2. A line of symmetry can be vertical, horizontal or diagonal.
3. There can be one or more lines of symmetry in a shape.

For the Curious Mind

How many lines of symmetry are there in the star shown below?

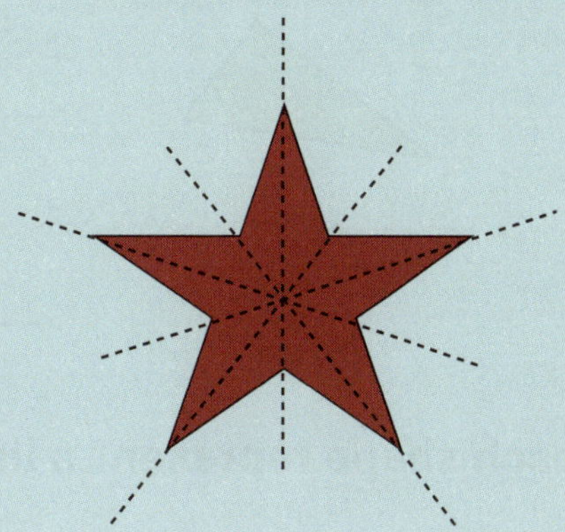

Revision Exercise

1 **Draw the line(s) of symmetry for the shapes given below. Also, write the number of lines of symmetry for each shape. One has been done for you.**

a. Rectangle 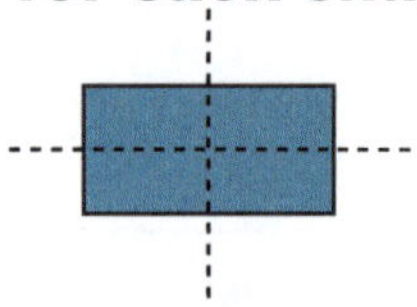 ___2___ lines of symmetry

b. Square  ________ lines of symmetry

c. Equilateral triangle 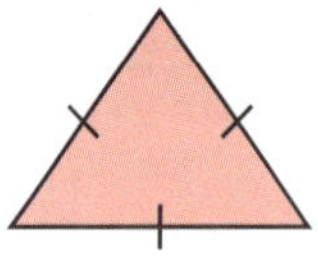 ________ lines of symmetry

d. Isosceles triangle 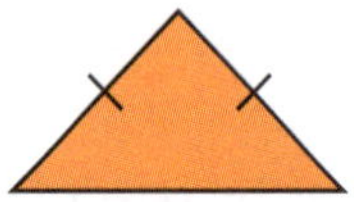 ________ lines of symmetry

e. Scalene triangle 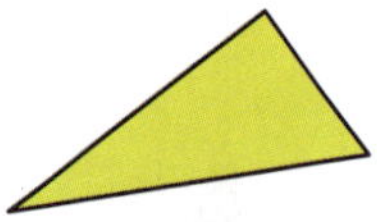 ________ lines of symmetry

f. Circle 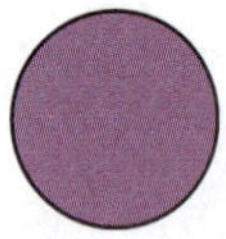 ________ lines of symmetry

2 **Does the dotted line on each shape represent a line of symmetry? Write Yes or No.**

a.  ________

b. 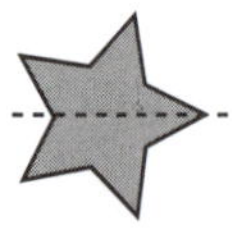 ________

c. 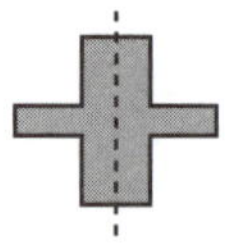 ________

d. 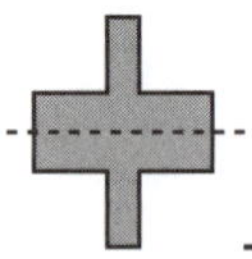 ________

e. 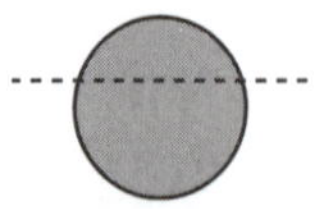 ________

f. 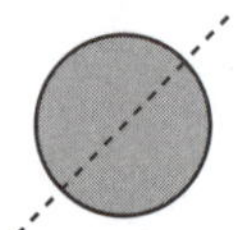 ________

3 **If the dotted line is the line of symmetry for each shape given, then complete the shapes by drawing the other half.**

a. 

b. 

c. 

d. 

Data Interpretation

17

Let's Get Started

Data is a collection of information.

We collect data to find answers to certain questions. These answers help us to understand situations and take decisions accordingly.

Pictographs and bar graphs are two ways of representing data.

Pictograph

Pictograph is a method of representing information using pictures and symbols. It has a title and shows the meaning of the symbol used.

Example 1: Given below is a pictograph representing the marks scored in mathematics by 5 students of Class 4. Study the pictograph and answer the following questions.

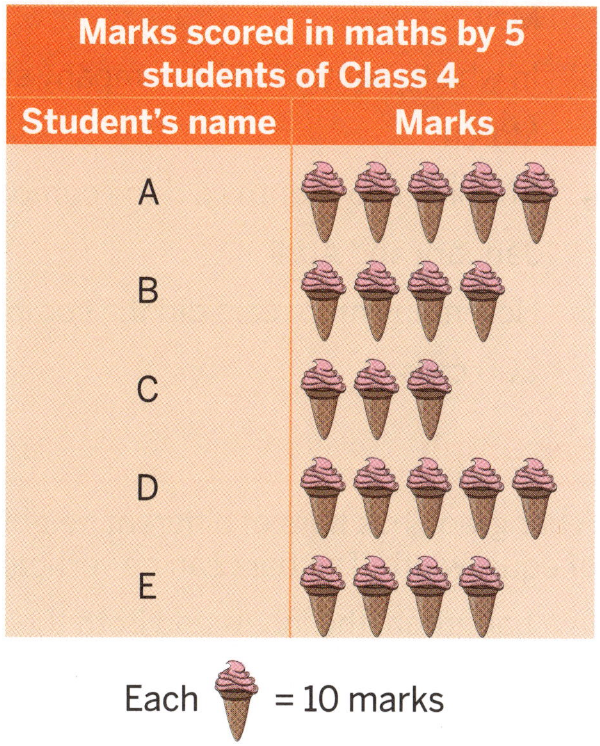

a. How much did each student score?

   Marks of A = 50, Marks of B = 40, Marks of C = 30, Marks of D = 50, Marks of E = 40

b. Which pair(s) of students scored the same marks?

   A and D; B and E

c. How many more marks than C did A score?

   50 – 30 = 20 marks

d. Who scored the lowest marks?

   C

Example 2:

The following pictograph shows the number of cars a company sold from January to May. Study the graph and answer the questions that follow.

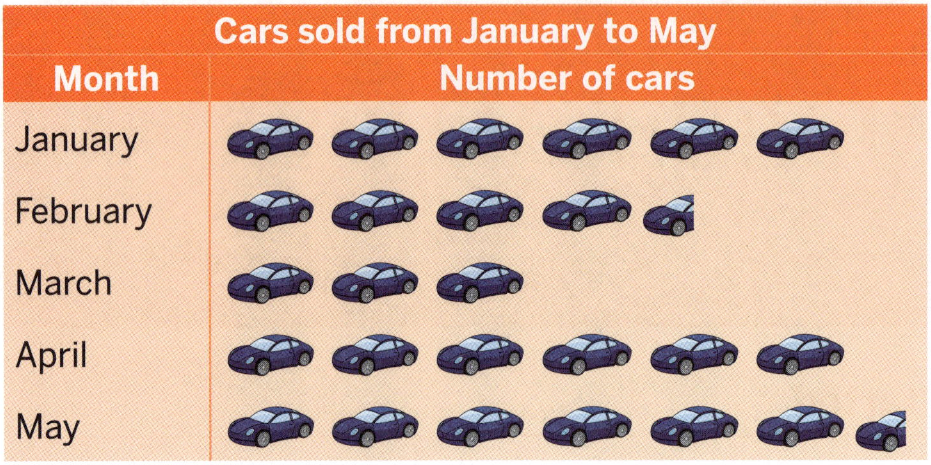

Each  = 100, Each  = 50

1. How many cars did the company sell in each month?

   Number of cars sold in January = 600 cars

   Number of cars sold in February = 450 cars

   Number of cars sold in March = 300 cars

   Number of cars sold in April = 600 cars

   Number of cars sold in May = 650 cars

2. In which month did the company sell the maximum number of cars?

   May

3. In which month did the company sell the least number of cars?

   March

4. In which two months did the company sell the same number of cars?

   January and April

5. How many more cars did the company sell in May than in February?

   200 cars

Bar Graph

A bar graph has bars of different heights conveying information. It has a title and bars of equal width. The bars can be vertical or horizontal.

In a bar graph, the labels and both the scales—vertical and horizontal—are clearly explained.

Example 3: The following bar graph shows the marks scored by 4 students out of 100 in a mathematics test. Study the graph and answer the questions that follow.

1. How many students took the mathematics test?
   4
2. Which student scored the highest marks?
   C
3. Which two students scored the same marks?
   A and D
4. How many more marks did C score than B?
   10 marks
5. How many more marks would A need to score 100 marks?
   100 – 80 = 20 marks

Marks scored by four students

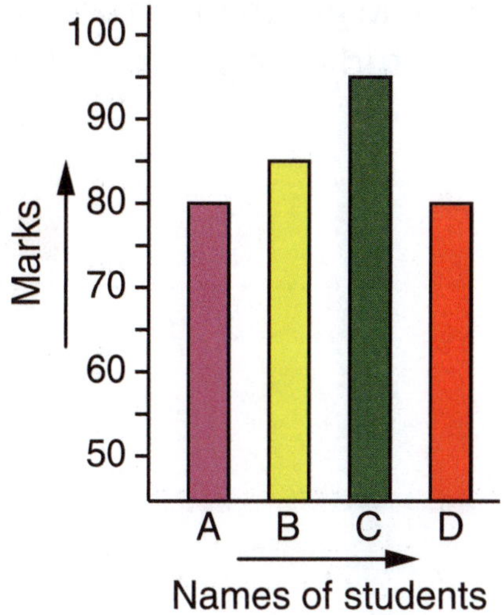

Exercise 17.1

1 The graph given below shows the number of students from Class 1 to Class 5 in a school. Study the graph and then answer the questions that follow.

Number of students from Class 1 to 5	
Classes	**Number of Students**
Class 1	
Class 2	
Class 3	
Class 4	
Class 5	

Each  = 6 students.

a. How many students are there in each of the following classes?
   i. Class 1 ii. Class 2 iii. Class 3 iv. Class 4 v. Class 5
b. Which two classes have the same number of students?
c. Which class has the least number of students?
d. How many more students are there in Class 3 than in Class 5?
e. What is the total number of students from Class 1 to Class 5?

2. The graph given below shows the population of villages A, B, C, D and E. Study the graph and then answer the questions that follow.

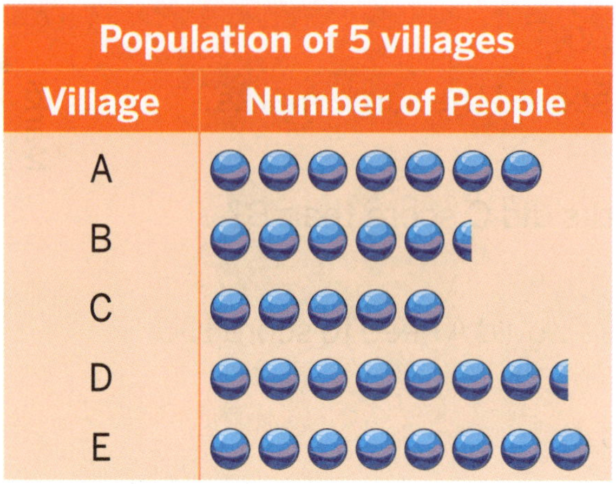

Each (icon) = 1000 people.

a. Which village has the most number of people? How many are they?

b. Which village has the least number of people? How many are they?

c. How many people live in village B?

d. How many people live in village D?

e. How many more people live in village E than in village B?

f. What is the total number of people in all the villages?

3. The given graph shows the marks scored in English by students A, B, C, D and E. Study the graph and then answer the questions that follow.

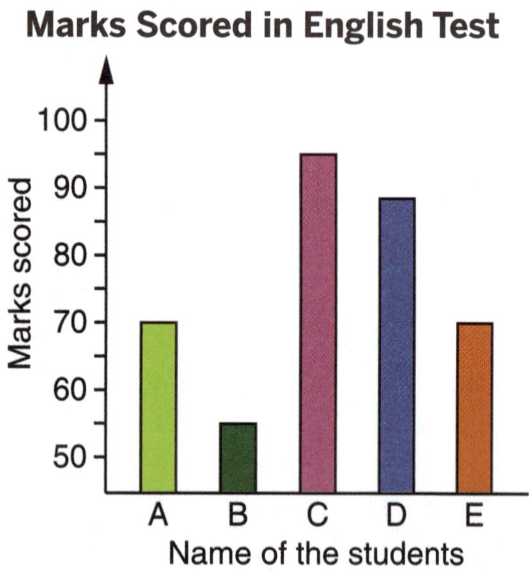

a. Who scored the highest marks?

b. Which student scored 70% marks?

c. Which two students scored the same marks? What were the marks?

d. If the minimum marks required to pass is 60, then which student did not pass?

e. How many marks less than 100 did C score?

4. The following graph shows the number of students who passed out of Sunbeam School from 2000 to 2004. Study the graph and answer the questions that follow.

a. How many students passed out of the school in each of the following years?

i. 2000 ii. 2001 iii. 2002 iv. 2003 v. 2004

b. In which year did maximum number of students pass out of the school?
c. In which two years did the same number of students pass out of the school? How many were they each year?
d. In which two years did the least number of students pass out of the school?
e. What is the total number of students who passed out of the school from 2000 to 2004?

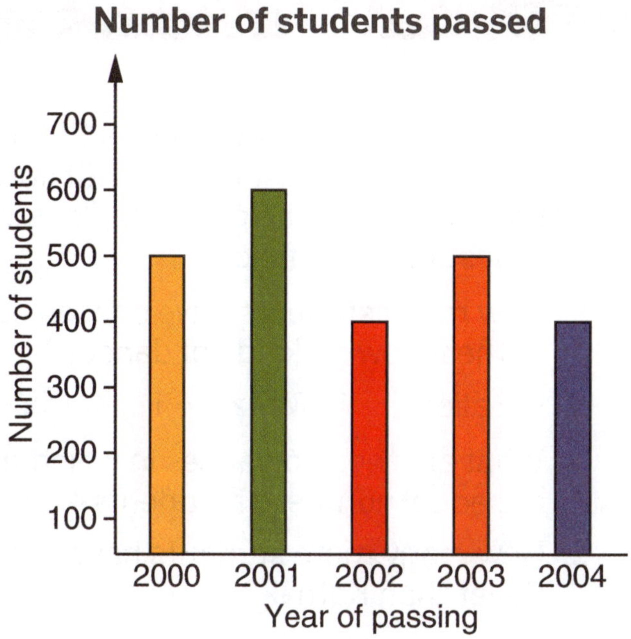

Revision Exercise

1 The following pictograph shows the different kinds of dances chosen by 72 students of Class 4 in Happy Children's School. Each image represents 9 students. Study the graph and answer the questions that follow.

a. How many students have chosen each of the following kinds of dances?

i. Ballet ii. Waltz iii. Kathak

b. What are the two dances in which there are equal number of students?

c. How many more students have chosen Ballet than Kathak?

d. How many more students have chosen Ballet than Waltz?

e. What is the total number of students who have chosen Kathak and Ballet?

Kinds of dances chosen by students of Class 4	
Kind of dance	**Number of students**
Kathak	
Waltz	
Ballet	

Each image = 9 students.

2

Saplings planted by Mrs David

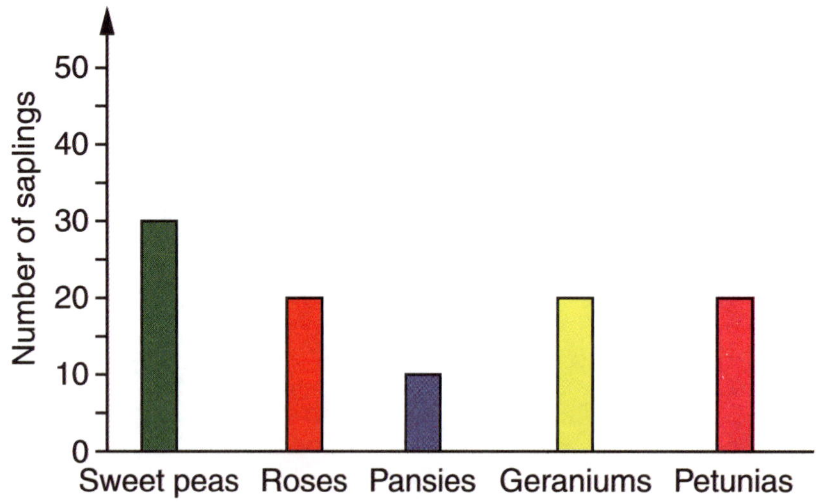

Mrs David planted 100 saplings in all. Study the bar graph and answer the questions that follow.

a. How many saplings of sweet peas did Mrs David plant?

b. Did Mrs David grow more geraniums or petunias?

c. What is the total number of saplings of roses, pansies and geraniums?

d. For which three flowers did Mrs David plant the same number of saplings?

e. Which flower did Mrs David plant in the least number?

3. The following pictograph shows the number of ice creams in different flavours sold on Monday. Study the pictograph and answer the questions that follow.

Ice creams sold on Monday	
Flavours	**Ice creams**
Chocolate	
Vanilla	
Butterscotch	
Strawberry	
Pista	

Each item = 10 ice creams

a. What is the number of ice creams sold on Monday in each of the following flavours?

i. Chocolate ii. Vanilla iii. Butterscotch

iv. Strawberry v. Pista

b. In which flavour were the maximum number of ice creams sold?

c. In which flavour were the least number of ice creams sold?

d. How many more strawberry ice creams were sold than butterscotch ice creams?

e. What is the total number of ice creams sold that day?

4. The following bar graph shows the number of holidays from January to June. Study the bar graph and then answer the questions that follow.

Number of holidays from January to June

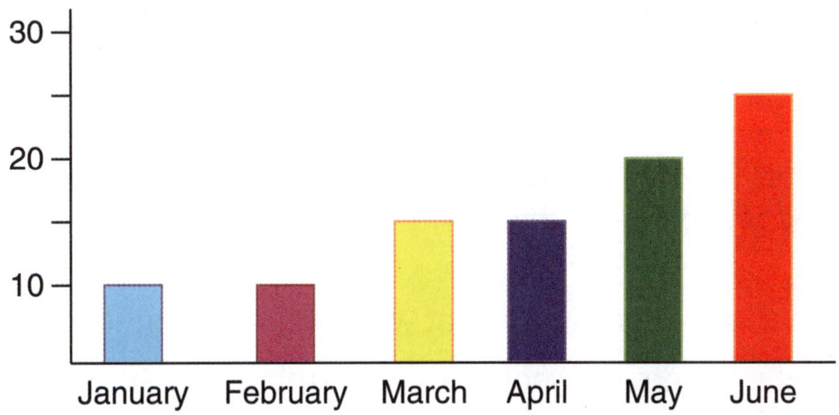

a. In which two months were the number of holidays the least?

b. In which month were the number of holidays the highest?

c. How many more holidays were there in May than in April?

d. In which months were the number of holidays 10?

e. In which months were the number of holidays 20?

Mixed Review 4

1. **Fill in the blanks.**

   a. 1 hour = ______ seconds

   b. 3 days = ______ hours

   c. 5 hours 15 minutes = ______ minutes

   d. 2 hours 35 minutes = ______ seconds

   e. 165 seconds = ______ minutes ______ seconds

   f. $\frac{1}{4}$ of 160 minutes = ______ seconds

   g. 5000 seconds = ______ hours ______ minutes ______ seconds

2. **Add the following.**

day	h	min	s
1	32	49	12
+ 2	9	31	30

3. Subtract 2 h 45 min from 7 h 19 min.

4. Multiply 3 min 14 s by 12.

5. Divide 2 h 44 min by 4.

6. **Fill in the blanks with the time in the 24-hour clock format.**

   a. 7:40 a.m. = ______
   b. 9:25 p.m. = ______
   c. 12:15 p.m. = ______
   d. 1:00 p.m. = ______

7. **Fill in the blanks with the time in the 12-hour clock format.**

   a. 2350 hours = ______
   b. 0715 hours = ______
   c. 1235 hours = ______
   d. 0249 hours = ______

8. I left my house at 11:00 a.m. and came back at 6:15 p.m. I spent 4 h 35 min in the market and rest of the time with my friend. How much time did I spend with my friend?

9. If 9th September is a Wednesday, what will be the date on the next Wednesday?

10. How many days are there between 15th September and 8th October?

11. How many days were there from 25th February to 3rd March in 2015?

12. Convert 35 months to years and months.

13. Convert 7 weeks 2 days to days.

14. Convert 25 days to weeks and days.

15 My school holidays are for 5 weeks 3 days. Out of these, 2 weeks 6 days are already over. How many more weeks and days of my holidays are still left?

16 **Fill in the blanks.**

a. An acute angle lies between ______ degrees and ______ degrees.

b. A reflex angle lies between ______ degrees and ______ degrees.

17 **Write true or false.**

a. 

is a vertical line. ____________

b. 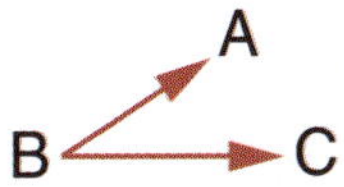

This angle can be called ∠CAB. ____________

c. A straight angle is equal to 180°. ____________

d. A ray extends only in one direction. ____________

e. The angle given here is a reflex angle. 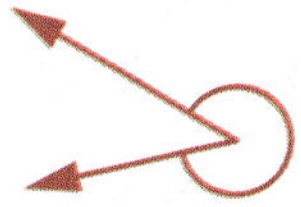 ____________

f. A scalene triangle has all sides equal. ____________

g. A complete angle is equal to 300°. ____________

h. A five-sided figure is called a hexagon. ____________

i. An octagon has 8 sides. ____________

j. An acute-angled triangle has only one angle acute. ____________

k. All the angles of a right-angled triangle are equal to 90°. ____________

l. All the sides of an equilateral triangle are equal. ____________

m. All the sides of a rectangle are equal. ____________

n. All the sides of a rhombus are equal. ____________

18 **With the help of a protractor, draw the following angles.**

a. 35° b. 75° c. 145° d. 170°

19 **Find the perimeter of the given figure.**

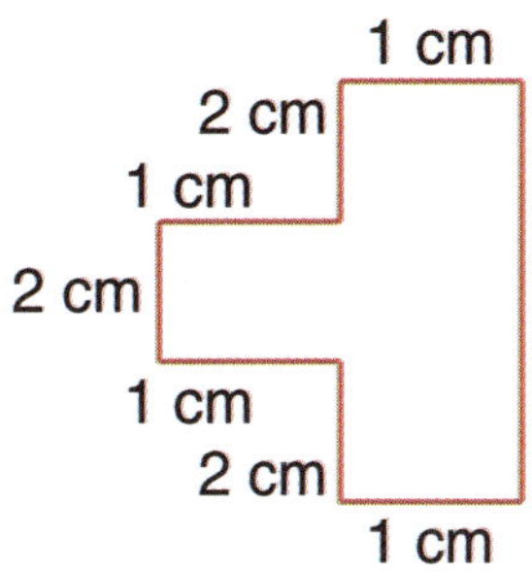

20 Find the area of a rectangle with length 13 cm and breadth 4 cm.

21 **Draw the line or lines of symmetry in the following figures.**

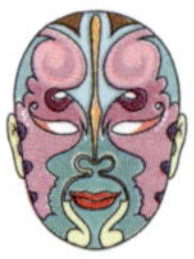

22 **If the straight lines are the lines of symmetry, then complete the figures by drawing the other half.**

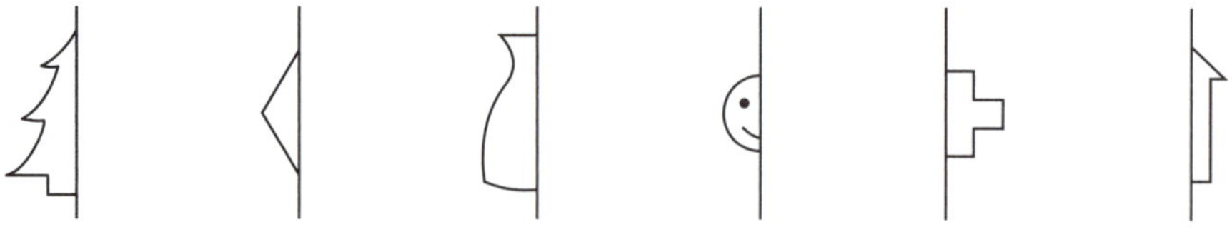

23 **The following pictograph shows the population in villages A, B, C, D and E. Study the graph and answer the questions that follow.**

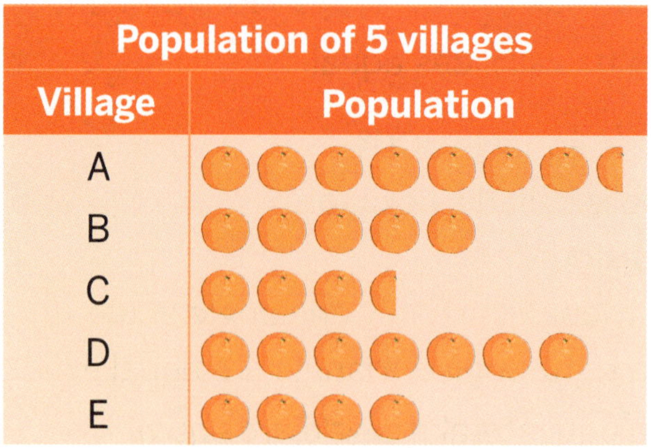

Each (orange) = 1000 persons

a. Which village has the highest population?

b. Which village has the lowest population?

c. Which village has a population of 4000?

d. Which village has a population of 1000 more than village E?

e. How much more is the population of village A than village D?

Test 1

1. **Fill in the blank with +, –, × or ÷.**

   a. 13 _____ 15 = 195.
   b. (35 _____ 5) ÷ 8 = 5.
   c. 40 – (2 _____ 3) = 34.
   d. 176 _____ 11 = 16.

2. **Fill in the blanks with the correct answer.**

   a. $\frac{2}{5}$ of 1 hour = ______ min.
   b. Find x if $\frac{30}{12} = \frac{15}{x}$.
   c. $\frac{3}{4}$ of 12 m = _______ cm.
   d. $36 \div \frac{2}{5}$ = _______.

3. a. Name two prime numbers whose sum is 18.
   b. Name two prime numbers whose product is 51.
   c. Name two even numbers with a difference of 4.
   d. Name two composite numbers with the same digits like 26 and 62.

4. Arrange the following fractions in ascending order: $\frac{5}{6}, \frac{7}{8}, \frac{1}{4}, \frac{11}{12}$

5. a. Find the LCM of 6, 10, 12.
   b. Find the HCF of 36, 48, 72.

6. a. Multiply 2793 by 608 .
   b. Divide 75634 by 184.

7. a. $\frac{2}{7}$ of a week = ________ days.
   b. $\frac{3}{4}$ of ₹2 = _______ paise.
   c. $\frac{1}{5}$ of 1 hour = _______ min.
   d. $\frac{1}{5}$ of 1 hour = _______ sec.

8. a. Take away 8 rupees 30 paisa from 11 rupees 12 paisa.
   b. Find the value of 10 + 2.65 + 18.9.

9. a. Write number name of nine million two hundred thirty-six thousand four hundred seven.
   b. Write 21,43,007 in words.

10. A man travelled 262 km 520 m by train, 139 km 120 m by bus and 17 km 25 m by car. Find the total distance travelled by him.

11. 575 sweets are distributed between 23 children. How many sweets will each child get?

12. A spelling test was given to a class of 25 students. $\frac{3}{5}$ of the students got all the spellings correct. How many students got all the spellings correct and how many did not?

13. Find the difference between 50 books at ₹25 each and 65 books at ₹45 each.

14. A man earning ₹5500 a month gets a raise of $\frac{1}{10}$th of his salary. What is his new salary?

15. Subtract 12 years 9 months from 16 years 6 months.

16. **What kind of angles are the following angles?**

Example: 45° = acute angle

a. 90° =
b. 145° =
c. 10° =
d. 0° =
e. 180° =
f. 270° =
g. 360° =

17. a. Find the area of a square whose side is 9 cm.

b. Find the perimeter of a rectangle whose length is 12.9 cm and breadth is 4.55 cm.

18. Observe the pattern and make the next shape giving it a name.

Triangle   Quadrilateral   Pentagon   ________

19. Draw the line of symmetry in the following shapes.

20. **The pictograph below shows the number of children who choose the games offered at school.**

Study the pictograph given below and answer the questions given it.

Number of children choosing different games	
Games	**Number of students**
Hockey	
Football	
Cricket	
Tennis	

Each  = 10 children

a. Which game was chosen by the maximum number of children?
b. Which game was chosen by 30 children?
c. How many more children chose Tennis than hockey?
d. What is the total number of children who chose hockey and football?

Test 2

1 **Write the following number names in numerals.**

a. Eighteen million five hundred four thousand eight hundred fifty-nine.

b. Seventy-four lakh nine thousand and nine.

2 Write the place value of the underlined digits and find their products.

8 5 $\underline{7}$ 9 8 $\underline{4}$ 2

3 Write the smallest 5-digit number which has 1 in its ones place. Write the greatest 4-digit number ending with 7. Find the difference between the two.

4 **Find:**

a. $1\frac{3}{8}$ of 5 kg 128g

b. 5.4 – 2.898

c. $\frac{35}{15} = \frac{7}{n}$. Find the value of *n*.

d. A pair of odd numbers, which add up to 20.

e. Two even multiples of 15 less than 100.

5 a. Find the HCF of 63, 105, 147.

b. Find the LCM of 12, 24, 32, 48.

6 Arrange the following fraction in ascending order.

$\frac{5}{6}, \frac{1}{3}, \frac{3}{5}, \frac{9}{10}$

7 **Simplify**

a. $3\frac{4}{5} - 2\frac{2}{3} + 4\frac{5}{6}$

b. (286.1 – 89.93) + 23.463

8 a. Solve the following:

$16\frac{2}{3} \times 8\frac{1}{10}$

b. Solve the following:

$$\frac{5\frac{5}{8}}{1\frac{9}{16}}$$

9 Add

	Days	h	min
	4	13	43
	2	19	27
+	1	22	48

10. A rectangular playground 65 metres by 50 metres is to be fenced with a wire. How much wire is needed to fence it 4 times?

11. A factory produces 5498 chocolates per day. How many chocolates will it produce in 5 weeks if every sunday is a holiday?

12. A tank can hold $5\frac{1}{4}$ litres of water. How much more water can be poured into it if it already has $3\frac{1}{3}$ litres of water in it?

13. Calculate

    3 h 18 min 12 s – 1 h 55 min 46 s

14. $\frac{1}{2}$ hour + $\frac{1}{2}$ minute = ________ seconds.

15. **Fill in the blanks.**

    A line has ________ end points while a line segment has _________ end points.

16. Identify an equilateral triangle isosceles triangle and a scalene triangle.

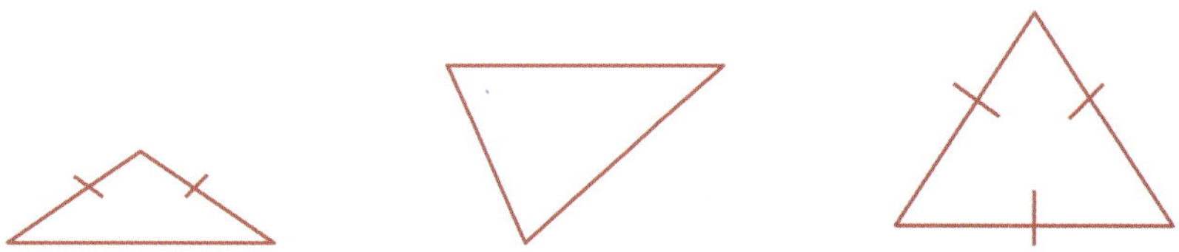

______________ ______________ ______________

17. A movie started at 5:55 p.m. and finished at 7:45 p.m. How long did the movie take to finish?

18. A train left from Delhi for Calcutta at 18 10 hours. What is this time in the 12 hour clock?

19. Seema spends $5\frac{1}{2}$ hours in school everyday. How many hours does she spend in school from Monday to Friday?

20. Construct an angle of 75° with the help of a protractor.

21. Find the side of a square whose perimeter is 48 cm.

22. Subtract 76 km 888 m from 98 km 666m.

23. Convert 8.25 p.m. to 24 hour clock.

24. Convert 275 hours into days and hours.

25. How much time is it from 8:45 a.m. to 2:30 p.m.

Test 3

1. **Fill in the blanks.**

a. $4000 \div 40 =$ ________

b. Every prime number except ________ is odd.

c. $(8 \times 1000) + (5 \times 100) + (7 \times 10) + (6 \times 1) =$ ________

d. $465 \times 293 = 293 \times$ ________

e. If $35 \times 29 = 1015$ then $1015 \div 35 =$ ________

f. $\frac{9}{36} = \frac{\square}{12}$

g. Since 18 has 6 factors, 18 is a ________ number.

h. In the figure given below, the shaded part as a fraction will be written as ______.

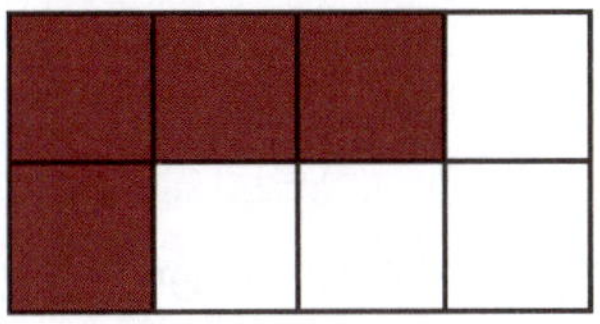

i. $5964 \times 735 \times 0 =$ ________.

j. 1 km = ________ m.

2. **Write True or False.**

a. 1 is the smallest prime number. ________

b. 88808 > 88880 ________

c. 1 is a factor of every number. ________

d. 25 is a prime number. ________

e. 28 is a composite number. ________

3. Subtract the largest 4-digit number from the smallest 5-digit number.

4. a. Write in numeral: Ninety four million seven thousand and five.

b. Write in words: 5,00,21,000

5. Write the following in ascending order.

6.835, 6.849, 6.299, 6.9

6. **Convert the following.**

a. 3 days 5 hours 13 minutes into minutes

b. 7359 mm into metres.

c. 7349 ℓ into kℓ and ℓ.

d. 6273 mg into g.

e. ₹569.25 into paise.

7. Write a pair of prime numbers with a difference of 4.

8. Write the prime factors and prime factorization of 72.

9. **Which of the following fractions are greater.**

   a. $\frac{6}{7}$ or $\frac{17}{28}$ b. $\frac{17}{20}$ or $\frac{23}{30}$

10. Write a fraction equivalent to $\frac{7}{8}$ with 96 as its denominator.

11. **Calculate the following .**

   a. $5.829 + 19.5 + 325$ b. 4 h 13 min 15 s – 1 h 40 min 25 s

   c. 60593×295 d. $57928 \div 39$

12. **Solve the following .**

   a. $7\frac{2}{9} + \frac{1}{3} + 9\frac{2}{9}$ b. $11\frac{1}{5} - 5\frac{3}{4}$

   c. $\frac{5}{12} \times 1\frac{11}{25}$ d. $4\frac{1}{3} \div \frac{26}{9}$

13. What is the least number of packets needed to keep 6297 chocolates if each packet contains 120 chocolates?

14. A factory employs 150 people. Each person receives ₹6000 a month. What is the total amount of money the factory has to give as salary in one year?

15. A piece of ribbon is $6\frac{3}{7}$ m long. If it is to be cut into 15 equal pieces, what will be the length of each piece?

16. Using the rules of divisibility find out which of the following numbers are divisible by 2, 3, 4?

   15, 28, 57, 14, 88

17. Ram's school bag weighs $3\frac{1}{2}$ kg with the books in it. If the books alone weigh $2\frac{3}{4}$ kg, what is the weight of the bag alone?

18. Samira left Delhi at 6:30 a.m. by train and reached Jaipur at 7:05 p.m. How long was her train journey?

19. Aseem spends $\frac{1}{6}$ of his salary on rent, $\frac{1}{3}$ on food, $\frac{1}{4}$ on other expenses. What fraction of his salary does Aseem spend?

20. **Reduce the following fraction to their simplest form.**

   a. $\frac{15}{25}$ b. $\frac{36}{72}$

21 **The pie chart below shows the population of towns A, B, C, D.**

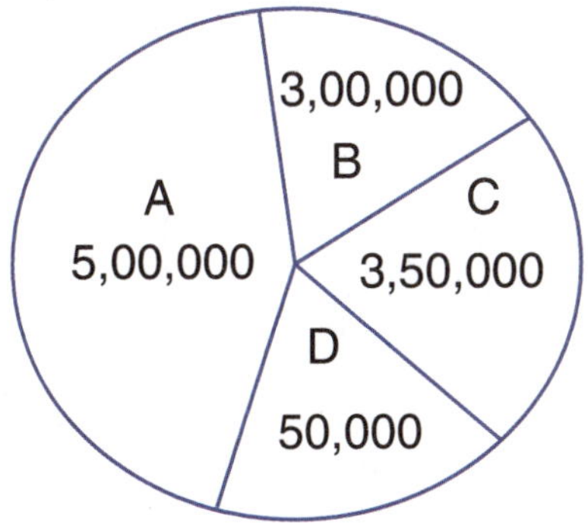

Study the pie chart above and answer the following questions.

a. Which town has the maximum population?

b. Which town has a population of 3,00,000 less than Town C?

c. Which town has a population of 1,50,000 more than town D?

d. What is the total population of town B,C and D.

22 **A train leaves Delhi at 10:00 a.m. and takes 7 hours to reach Dehradun.**

a. What time will it reach Dehradun?

b. If the train gets late by one and a half hours then what time will it reach Dehradun?

23 **The figure given below is a field.**

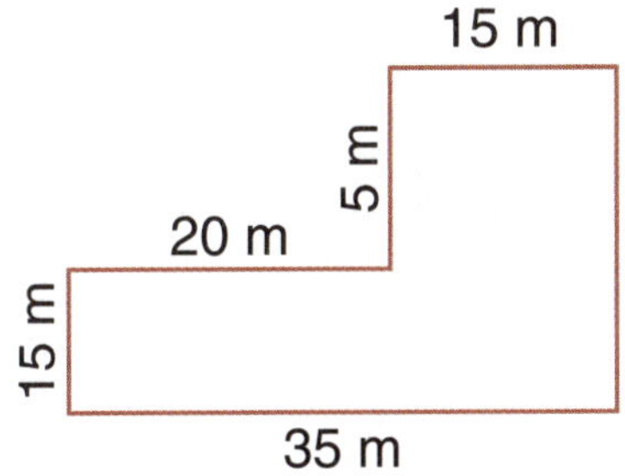

a. How much wire will be needed to fence it once?

b. How much wire will be needed to fence it 4 times?

24 **Which of the following can be called a polygon.**

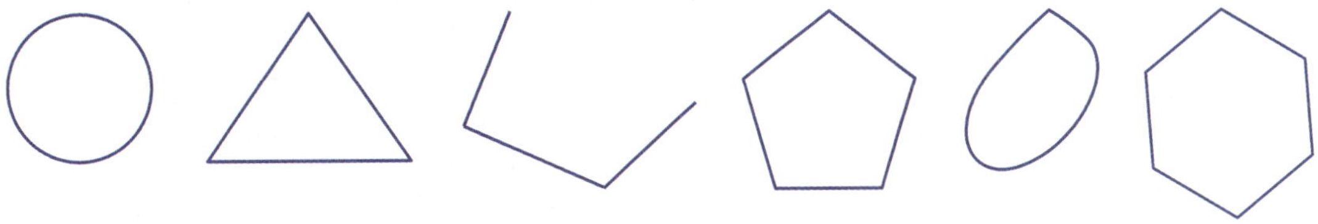

A B C D E F

25 **Match the figures from column A to column B.**

Column A	Column B
	Ray
	Line
	Line segment
	Curve
	Point

Answers

Chapter – 1

Exercise 1.1

1. a. Five lakh sixty-four thousand seven hundred sixty-nine.
   b. Twelve lakh twelve thousand nine hundred and five.
   c. Six lakh forty-eight thousand nine hundred and twenty-eight.
   d. Five lakh thirty thousand six hundred twenty-nine.
   e. Thirteen lakh forty-two thousand seven hundred.
   f. Twenty-nine lakh six thousand two hundred twenty-one
   g. Fifty lakh fifty thousand five hundred fifty
   h. Thirty-four lakh forty-nine thousand nine hundred sixty-two
2. a. 2,00,000 + 30,000 + 4,000 + 500 + 60 + 2
   b. 40,00,000 + 5,00,000 + 90,000 + 3,000 + 200 + 80 + 7
   c. 8,00,000 + 40,000 + 9,000 + 400 + 30 + 8
   d. 50,00,000 + 4,00,000 + 70,000 + 1,000 + 30 + 7
3. a. 16,294 b. 5,23,809 c. 87,53,927
   d. 96,50,781 e. 67,05,272 f. 9,00,712
   g. 17,18,000 h. 2,05,003
4. a. Four hundred sixty-eight thousand nine hundred eighty-one
   b. Five million six hundred twenty-four thousand seven hundred twenty-nine
   c. Seven hundred nine thousand four hundred
   d. Five million eight hundred thousand sixteen
   e. Three million five hundred twenty thousand one
   f. Four hundred sixty-two thousand nine hundred sixty-three
   g. Eight million eight thousand eight
   h. Nine million nine hundred ninety-nine thousand nine hundred ninety-nine
5. a. 5249 b. 3050 c. 2200
   d. 15,990 e. 9,275,620 f. 3,500,007
   g. 4,905,231 h. 2,709,001
6. a. Two lakh forty-eight thousand nine hundred seventy-four
   b. Nineteen lakh eighty-nine thousand four hundred fifty-six
   c. One million seven hundred ninety-two thousand four hundred fifty
   d. Eight hundred seventy-three thousand two
   e. Twenty nine thousand three hundred twenty-one
   f. Eight million six
   g. Nine lakh four hundred fifty-three
   h. Six million one hundred twenty-seven
7. a. 3,42,520 b. 432,520 c. 17,23,207
   d. 3,221,409 e. 90,04,005 f. 5,005,029
   g. 15,14,831 h. 1,528,362

Exercise 1.2

1. a. Place value = 8000
   Face value = 8
   b. Place value = 20,000
   Face value = 2
   c. Place value = 7,00,000
   Face value = 7
   d. Place value = 90
   Face value = 9
2. a. > b. < c. < d. < e. < f. >
   g. > h. =
3. a. 6,93,200, 6,93,212, 6,93,220, 6,93,240
   b. 7,32,844, 9,97,879, 53,21,424, 88,88,129
   c. 8,99,990, 9,00,000, 9,99,999, 99,98,998
4. a. 5,75,340, 5,75,320, 5,75,310, 5,75,300
   b. 69,32,189, 69,32,180, 6,93,219, 6,93,210
   c. 99,99,999, 9,99,999, 99,999, 9,999
5. a. 6,39,422 b. 5,70,000 c. 85,69,010
   d. 73,30,000 e. 59,60,010
6. a. 7,49,851 b. 6,38,899 c. 5,39,217
   d. 69,99,979 e. 69,98,999
7. a. Smallest: 1,35,689
   Largest: 9,86,531
   b. Smallest: 2,03,489
   Largest: 9,84,320
   c. Smallest: 1,00,679
   Largest: 9,76,100
   d. Smallest: 2,04,789
   Largest: 9,87,420

Exercise 1.3

1. a. VI b. X c. IX d. XI
   e. XVIII f. XX g. XXI h. XXV
   i. XXX j. XLI k. III l. XIII
2. a. 8 b. 16 c. 20 d. 30
   e. 39 f. 10 g. 29 h. 19
   i. 25 j. 36 k. 41 l. 28

Revision Exercise

1. a. iii b. iv c. i d. ii
   e. ii f. iv g. iv h. iv
   i. iv j. iv
2. 2,467,935; Two million four hundred sixty seven thousand nine hundred thirty five.
3. 48,48,703
4. 10,000
5. a. < b. >
6. 9,00,009, 9,00,099, 9,90,099, 90,00,999, 99,99,999
7. 9,99,791
8. 3,00,099
9. 10,99,999
10. 6,00,789
11. 8,00,000 + 90,000 + 5,000 + 300 + 20 + 1
12. 60,90,002
13. a. True b. False
14. 1 – e; 2 – c; 3 – a; 4 – b; 5 – d

For the Curious Mind

1. 100 2. 1,000

Worksheet

1. 1
2. a. 50,41,600 b. 5,400,002
3. a. Forty-nine lakh one
   b. Five million eight hundred ninety-two thousand one
4. 9000; 9
5. a. < b. < c. =
6. 1,03,459
7. 8,99,998
8. 19,99,900
9. a. 54,30,009 b. 9,00,000 + 60,000 + 400 + 2
10. a. 2**9**69921 b. 72**2**4025 c. **3**363280 d. 85**5**01597
11. a. XXX b. III
12. 2-digit 10 ; 99
    3-digit 100 ; 999
    4-digit 1000 ; 9999
    5-digit 10000 ; 99999
    6-digit 100000 ; 999999
    7-digit 1000000 ; 9999999

Chapter – 2

Exercise 2.1

1. a. 5 b. 35 c. 141 d. 2331
2. a. 25 b. 21 c. 29 d. 32
3. 997889
4. 1567788
5. 879597
6. 880999
7. 1269998
8. 1509659
9. 107928
10. 56119
11. 362830
12. 941624
13. 210241
14. 1013480
15. 774570
16. 1178395

Exercise 2.2

1. 26,424 km
2. 1,30,469 tickets
3. 18,00,639 people
4. 15,509 tables
5. ₹1,43,130
6. ₹12,60,000

Revision Exercise

1. a. ii b. i c. iv d. iii e. iv
   f. iv g. iv h. i i. iii j. iii
2. 545472
3. 664820
4. 123296
5. 316904
6. 793098
7. 1362072
8. 507123
9. 586465
10. 986000
11. 8,73,420
12. 9,01,900
13. 8,69,000
14. 12,45,500

Worksheet

1. a. 6876 b. 24421 c. 10018 d. 27019
 e. 9009 f. 100009 g. 287200 h. 19999
 i. 666666 j. 9999
2. 690000 3. c 4. b,c

For the Curious Mind

1. 9,96,809 2. ₹7,56,000

Chapter – 3

Exercise 3.1

1. a. 999999 b. 435678
2. 622514 3. 815405 4. 543646 5. 531948
6. 290001 7. 748931 8. 865571 9. 696988
10. 670601 11. 861930 12. 853062 13. 400001

Exercise 3.2

1. 2,13,020 2. 76,036 3. 1,11,130 4. 9,19,442
5. 6,49,150 6. 3,85,800 7. 4,56,000 8. 94,660
9. 3,71,898 10. 15,900

Revision Exercise

1. a. iv b. iii c. ii d. iv
 e. ii f. iv g. ii h. ii
 i. iv j. iii
2. a. 91000 b. 170000
3. 223045 4. 793476 5. 699441 6. 871278
7. a. 799851 b. 580000 8. 2,47,500 9. 2,99,001
10. 3,10,540 11. 63,100 12. 1,06,400
13. 1,20,000 14. 51,500

For the Curious Mind

457

Mixed Review 1

1. a. Fifteen lakh seventy-five thousand two hundred nine
 b. Ninety lakh one
2. a. Four million six hundred eighty-one thousand two hundred ninety-two
 b. Eight million twenty thousand seven
3. a. 18,00,503 b. 3,000,051
4. 2002
5. 195684, 45685, 5684, 23456, 932
6. 1010 7. 3067 8. 9,00,072
9. ₹8,30,000 10. ₹1,47,540 11. 1,46,917
12. ₹2,36,300 13. 2,98,631 14. 3,58,120 people

Chapter – 4

Exercise 4.1

1. a. 0 b. 0 c. 366 d. 593
 e. 0 f. 473 g. 0 h. 0
 i. 294 j. 240 k. 0 l. 381
2. a. product b. does not c. 1
3. a. 5 b. 7 c. 12 d. 9

Exercise 4.2

1

	by 10	by 100	by 1000	by 10,000
a	90	900	9000	90,000
b	160	1600	16,000	1,60,000
c	200	2000	20,000	2,00,000
d	350	3500	35,000	3,50,000
e	920	9200	92,000	9,20,000
f	300	3000	30,000	3,00,000
g	400	4000	40,000	4,00,000
h	500	5000	50,000	5,00,000

2. a. 840 b. 1600 c. 870 d. 8640
 e. 6520 f. 48,690 g. 1,35,700 h. 4,69,800
 i. 15,70,200 j. 65,16,000 k. 1,43,04,000 l. 8,61,000

Exercise 4.3

1. a. 996 b. 2,965 c. 2916 d. 4,844
 e. 3,558 f. 2,487 g. 8,580 h. 27,972
 i. 26,945 j. 38,680 k. 83,403 l. 10,003
 m. 70,296 n. 4,78,051 o. 1,03,863 p. 6,26,568
 q. 2,59,764 r. 6,24,114
2. a. 11,319 b. 15,444 c. 29,326 d. 14,445
 e. 10,395 f. 11,221 g. 1,22,567 h. 7,09,004
 i. 3,06,390 j. 7,23,927 k. 2,23,896 l. 6,06,190
3. a. 45,792 b. 98,820 c. 3,22,411
 d. 33,60,126 e. 15,46,280 f. 34,64,175

Exercise 4.4

1. 21 days 2. 120 hours
3. 540 seconds 4. 240 minutes
5. 10,800 seconds 6. ₹34,800
7. 10,600 flags 8. 17,280 people

Revision Exercise

1. a. iv b. ii c. i d. ii e. iv
 f. ii g. iii h. iv i. iii j. i
2. a. 0 b. 0
3. a. 4693 b. 827
4. a. 390 b. 3,900 c. 39,000 d. 3,90,000
5. a. 12 b. 84
6. a. 10,26,000 b. 1,17,200 c. 6,17,000 d. 62,910
7. 2,74,015 8. 3,23,568 9. 15,60,900 people
10. a. ₹9800 b. ₹10,150
11. ₹75,20,000
12. a. 7843 loaves b. 7590 loaves
13. 1,83,000 passengers 14. ₹6,86,400 15. ₹39,79,550
16. ₹67,200 17. ₹1,45,035
18. ₹1,26,72,250 19. ₹43, 500
20. ₹2,34,000 21. 1505 seats

Worksheet

1. a. i. 1679 ii. 16790 iii. 167900 iv. 1679000
 b. i. 672 ii. 67200
 c. i. 96 ii. 960 iii. 9600
 d. 4,48,000 e. 0
2. 0 3. 3251 4. 0 5. 84307
6. ₹10,950 7. 850 8. 1694000
9. 73850000 10. 240 11. 4500
12. 4,48,000 13. 18,568 14. 49 days

For the Curious Mind

₹457

Chapter – 5

Exercise 5.1

1. a. 3174 b. 854 c. 312 d. 425
 e. Q = 629, R = 1 f. Q = 1862, R = 2
 g. Q = 3697, R = 1 h. Q = 325, R = 2
 i. 1107 j. 1204 k. 205 l. 504
2. a. 1528 b. 834 c. 201
 d. Q = 341, R = 5 e. Q = 426, R = 1
 f. 1140 g. 210 h. 800 i. 500
 j. 2001 k. Q = 501, R = 1 l. 1003

Exercise 5.2

1. 24314 2. Q = 11411, R = 1 3. Q = 11336, R = 1
4. 14320 5. 2490 6. Q = 2560, R = 5
7. 4908 8. 7029 9. Q = 8306, R = 2
10. Q = 9608, R = 1 11. 12446 12. 2031
13. Q = 2001, R = 1 14. Q = 1247, R = 2
15. Q = 11419, R = 2 16. Q = 10705, R = 1

Exercise 5.3

a. i. 9 ii. 27 iii. 9 iv. 8 v. 8
 vi. 9 vii. 200 viii. 400
b. i. Q = 3, R = 5 ii. Q = 38, R = 9
 iii. Q = 11, R = 39 iv. Q = 18, R = 19

v. Q = 25, R = 46 vi. Q = 102, R = 17
vii. Q = 103, R = 1 viii. Q = 101, R = 38

Exercise 5.4

1. a. 36 b. 23 c. 37 d. 28 e. 48 f. 35
g. 103 h. 302 i. 107 j. 105 k. 102 l. 201
2. a. Q = 46, R = 3 b. Q = 23, R = 17 c. Q = 26, R = 2
d. Q = 6, R = 9 e. Q = 33, R = 14 f. Q = 25, R = 2
g. Q = 85, R = 5 h. Q = 58, R = 7 i. Q = 102, R = 1
j. Q = 203, R = 4 k. Q = 581, R = 10 l. Q = 89, R = 4

Exercise 5.5

1. 18 rows 2. 56 sweets 3. 65 buses 4. 4 books, ₹29 left
5. 45 buckets were filled and 9 gallons of water was left
6. 68 bags 7. 335 houses 8. 32 boxes
9. ₹30 10. ₹15,000

Revision Exercise

1. a. iii b. ii c. i d. i
e. iii f. ii g. iii h. iv
2. 130 books
3. Each child will get 5 litres and 63 litres will get left.
4. 49 boxes 5. 11 bags

Worksheet

2. 0 b. 187 3. 29; 15
4. a. one b. divide

For the Curious mind

250; 50; 12; 2

Chapter – 6

Exercise 6.1

1. a, c, f, h are divisible by 2. b, d, e, g are not divisible by 2.
2. a, b, e, f, g are divisible by 5. c, d, h are not divisible by 5.
3. b, d, g, h are divisible by 10. a, c, e, f are not divisible by 10.

Exercise 6.2

1. a, d,e, f, g are divisible by 3. b, c, h are not divisible by 3.
2. a, b, c, g are divisible by 9. d, e, f, h are not divisible by 9
3. b, d, f, h are divisible by 4. a, c, e, g are not divisible by 4.
4. a, c, e, h are divisible by 8. b, d, f, g are not divisible by 8.
5. b, d, h are divisible by 6. a, c, e, f, g are not divisible by 6.

Exercise 6.3

1. Even numbers are 0, 14, 290, 6752, 9384, 2340.
Odd numbers are 9, 147, 635, 139, 6843.
2. a. Yes b. No c. Yes d. Yes
e. Yes f. Yes g. No
3. a. 1, 2, 3, 4, 6, 12 b. 1, 2, 3, 6, 9, 18
c. 1, 2, 3, 4, 6, 8, 12, 24 d. 1, 2, 4, 7, 14, 28
e. 1, 2, 3, 5, 6, 10, 15, 30 f. 1, 2, 4, 8, 16, 32
g. 1, 2, 6, 7, 21, 42 h. 1, 2, 3, 4, 6, 8, 12, 16, 24, 48
i. 1, 2, 3, 4, 5, 6, 10, 12, 15, 20, 30, 60
j. 1, 3, 9 k. 1, 2, 4, 8, 16 l. 1, 5, 25
m. 1, 2, 3, 4, 6, 9, 12, 18, 36 n. 1,3 o. 1, 17 p. 1, 13

Exercise 6.4

1. Prime numbers are 2, 3, 5, 7, 11, 13, 17, 19, 23, 29
Composite numbers are 4, 6, 8, 9, 10, 12, 14, 15, 16, 18, 20, 21, 22, 24, 25, 26, 27, 28, 30
2. a. False b. False c. True d. True
e. True f. False g. False
3. a. Prime numbers are 31, 37, 41, 43, 47
Composite numbers are 30, 32, 33, 34, 35, 36, 38, 39, 40, 42, 44, 45, 46, 48, 49, 50

Exercise 6.5

1. Prime factors are 2, 3
Prime factorisation is 2×3
2. Prime factors are 2, 5
Prime factorisation is 2×5
3. Prime factors are 2,3
Prime factorisation is $2 \times 2 \times 3$
4. Prime factors are 2, 3
Prime factorisation is $2 \times 3 \times 3$
5. Prime factors are 2, 5
Prime factorisation is $2 \times 2 \times 5$
6. Prime factors are 2, 3
Prime factorisation is $2 \times 2 \times 2 \times 3$
7. Prime factors are 2, 3, 5
Prime factorisation is $2 \times 3 \times 5$
8. Prime factors are 2, 3
Prime factorisation is $2 \times 2 \times 3 \times 3$
9. Prime factors are 2, 3, 7
Prime factorisation is $2 \times 3 \times 7$
10. Prime factors are 2, 3
Prime factorisation is $2 \times 2 \times 2 \times 2 \times 3$
11. Prime factors are 2, 13
Prime factorisation is $2 \times 2 \times 13$
12. Prime factors are 2, 3, 5
Prime factorisation is $2 \times 2 \times 3 \times 5$

Exercise 6.6

1. 6, 9, 12; 3
2. a. 6, 12, 18, 24, 30 b. 7, 14, 21, 28
3. a. 2, 4, 6 b. 5, 10, 15 c. 7, 14, 21 d. 9, 18, 27
4. a. 3, 6, 9,12 b. 4, 8, 12, 16 c. 6, 12 18, 24
d. 10, 20, 30, 40
5. a. factor b. number
6. a. 2, 4, 6, 8, 10, 12, 14, 16, 18, 20 b. 25, 30, 35, 40
7. a. 3, 7, 21 b. 21, 3,7
8. 6, 12, 18, 24 9. 20, 25, 30 10. 14, 21, 28, 35

Exercise 6.7

1. a. 4, 8, 12, 16, 20, 24, 28
2. a. 12, 24 3. 6 4. 14
5. Multiples of 3 are 3, 6, 9, 12, 15, 18, 21, 24, 27, 30.
Multiples of 5 are 5, 10, 15, 20, 25, 30.
The first common multiple of 3 and 5 is 15.

Revision Exercise

1. a. ii b. iv c. ii d. ii e. iii
f. ii g. iv h. iv i. iii j. iii
2. Yes, because the last two digits are divisible by 4
3. No, because 5594 is divisible by 2 but not 3.
4. 439, 2405, 47389
5. The prime numbers are 2, 5, 7, 11, 13, 31.
The composite numbers are 15, 18, 21, 25, 27, 35, 36, 39.
6. 1, 2, 3, 4, 6, 8, 12, 16, 24, 48
7. 3 and 4
8. Prime factorisation of 60 is $2 \times 2 \times 3 \times 5$.
Prime factors of 60 are 2, 3, 5
9. 3, 9 10. 4, 8, 12

Worksheet

1. a. prime number b. composite number
c. 1 d. 2
2. a. 12 b. 8 c. 4 d. 5
3. a. 45 b. 48
4. (3, 6) 5. 6 6. 2 7. 33 8. 60

For the Curious Mind

1. 32 and 3 2. 71 and 2

Mixed Review 2

1. ₹3552
2. a. 28,000 b. 24,000 c. 72,000
3. 9 4. 25 5. ₹4,85,000
6. She can buy 8 pairs of earrings and ₹21 will be left over.
7. a. ₹12,37,500 b. ₹1,48,50,000
8. 47 bags 9. ₹3625
10. 21 and 351 11. 15, 21, 99 12. 21 and 2 13. 17, 23, 29
14. Prime factorisation $2 \times 2 \times 2 \times 2 \times 3$
Prime factors 2, 3
15. 12, 15, 18, 21, 24

Chapter – 7

Exercise 7.1

1. a. 9 b. 12 c. 35 d. 24 e. 30 f. 16
 g. 20 h. 80 i. 120 j. 90 k. 60 l. 150
2. a. 4 b. 3 c. 3 d. 6 e. 2 f. 3
 g. 4 h. 9 i. 5 j. 12 k. 12 l. 9

Revision Exercise

1. a. 48 b. 60 c. 120 d. 180 e. 105 f. 624
 g. 442 h. 2250 i. 504 j. 2880 k. 96 l. 1800
2. a. 4 b. 12 c. 15 d. 9 e. 1 f. 21
 g. 5 h. 34 i. 35 j. 4 k. 12 l. 13
3. a. False b. False c. False d. True
4. a. 24 b. 45 c. 30 d. 36
5. a. 6 b. 6 c. 6 d. 3

Mental Maths

LCM = 4 , HCF = 2

Chapter – 8

Exercise 8.1

1. a. $\frac{3}{4}$ b. $\frac{5}{8}$ c. $\frac{2}{3}$ d. $\frac{61}{120}$
2. b and d
3. a. 7 b. 27 c. 98 d. 92
4. a. 7 b. 9 c. 25 d. 55
5. a. $2\frac{1}{2}$ b. $5\frac{2}{3}$ c. $7\frac{3}{7}$ d. $18\frac{4}{5}$
 e. $25\frac{1}{4}$ f. $23\frac{1}{6}$ g. $25\frac{4}{5}$ h. $27\frac{3}{7}$
6. a. $\frac{13}{6}$ b. $\frac{16}{5}$ c. $\frac{59}{3}$ d. $\frac{54}{7}$
 e. $\frac{128}{9}$ f. $\frac{171}{53}$ g. $\frac{80}{7}$ h. $\frac{101}{11}$
7. a. $\frac{1}{2}, \frac{1}{2}$ b. $\frac{1}{4}, \frac{3}{4}$ c. $\frac{5}{8}, \frac{3}{8}$ d. $\frac{2}{8}, \frac{6}{8}$
8. a. 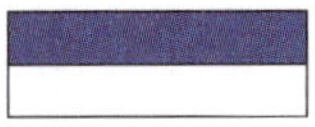 b. 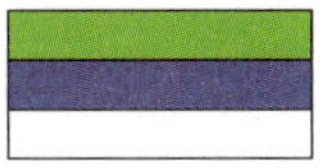
 c. 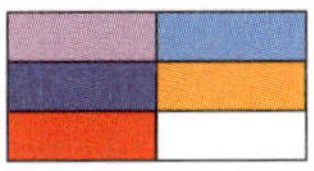 d. 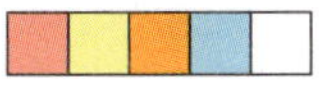
9. $\frac{2}{10}$
10. a. $\frac{3}{12}$ b. $\frac{9}{12}$
11. a. $\frac{8}{15}$ b. $\frac{7}{15}$
12.

	A	B	C	D	E	F	G
N	4	2	1	3	2	1	7
D	9	3	8	7	5	3	9

13. a. $\frac{4}{6}, \frac{6}{9}, \frac{8}{12}, \frac{10}{15}, \frac{12}{18}$ b. $\frac{2}{10}, \frac{3}{15}, \frac{4}{20}, \frac{5}{25}, \frac{6}{30}$
 c. $\frac{6}{14}, \frac{9}{21}, \frac{12}{28}, \frac{15}{35}, \frac{18}{42}$ d. $\frac{4}{14}, \frac{6}{21}, \frac{8}{28}, \frac{10}{35}, \frac{12}{42}$
14. a. $\frac{8}{12}$ b. $\frac{5}{25}$ c. $\frac{21}{49}$ d. $\frac{16}{40}$

Exercise 8.2

1. a. < b. > c. > d. >
2. a. > b. > c. < d. < e. >
3. a. > b. > c. > d. < e. <
4. a. < b. < c. > d. > e. >
 f. > g. > h. = i. > j. <
5. a. $\frac{1}{10}, \frac{2}{5}, \frac{1}{2}$ b. $\frac{1}{12}, \frac{3}{4}, \frac{5}{6}$ c. $\frac{2}{6}, \frac{12}{30}, \frac{9}{5}$
 d. $\frac{2}{12}, \frac{5}{24}, \frac{5}{8}$ e. $\frac{5}{16}, \frac{1}{2}, \frac{3}{4}$ f. $\frac{4}{18}, \frac{5}{9}, \frac{5}{6}$
6. a. $\frac{3}{4}, \frac{5}{8}, \frac{7}{12}$ b. $\frac{7}{10}, \frac{3}{5}, \frac{1}{2}$ c. $\frac{5}{6}, \frac{2}{9}, \frac{1}{18}$
 d. $\frac{3}{5}, \frac{15}{50}, \frac{1}{10}$ e. $\frac{4}{3}, \frac{5}{18}, \frac{1}{9}$

Try These

1. $\frac{4}{9}$ 2. $\frac{7}{8}$ 3. $\frac{13}{21}$

Exercise 8.3

1. $1\frac{4}{5}$ 2. 4 3. $1\frac{1}{7}$ 4. $\frac{1}{2}$
5. $\frac{1}{2}$ 6. $1\frac{1}{28}$ 7. $\frac{25}{63}$ 8. $1\frac{9}{20}$
9. $1\frac{7}{8}$ 10. $1\frac{11}{18}$ 11. $\frac{39}{77}$ 12. $1\frac{1}{30}$
13. $\frac{46}{77}$ 14. $1\frac{3}{26}$ 15. $1\frac{15}{22}$

Try These

Answer: 12

Exercise 8.4

1. $5\frac{3}{4}$ 2. $7\frac{5}{6}$ 3. 7 4. 13 5. $14\frac{1}{3}$
6. $11\frac{3}{4}$ 7. $5\frac{1}{7}$ 8. $13\frac{1}{5}$ 9. $9\frac{5}{6}$ 10. $14\frac{11}{14}$
11. $5\frac{11}{15}$ 12. $12\frac{7}{15}$ 13. $16\frac{5}{9}$ 14. $9\frac{15}{16}$ 15. $11\frac{13}{72}$

Exercise 8.5

1. $\frac{5}{14}$ 2. $1\frac{4}{9}$ 3. 2 4. $\frac{11}{40}$ 5. $\frac{33}{55}$
6. $1\frac{18}{35}$ 7. $4\frac{1}{4}$ 8. $\frac{9}{70}$ 9. $2\frac{1}{2}$ 10. $4\frac{1}{4}$
11. $8\frac{5}{7}$ 12. $4\frac{8}{9}$ 13. $7\frac{3}{5}$ 14. $6\frac{5}{8}$ 15. $\frac{5}{9}$
16. $\frac{4}{7}$ 17. $\frac{4}{11}$ 18. $\frac{1}{5}$ 19. $\frac{5}{8}$ 20. $\frac{2}{3}$
21. $\frac{1}{3}$ 22. $\frac{11}{15}$ 23. $\frac{2}{11}$ 24. $\frac{11}{13}$ 25. $1\frac{7}{24}$
26. $7\frac{4}{11}$ 27. $3\frac{1}{9}$ 28. $5\frac{1}{5}$ 29. $\frac{5}{9}$ 30. $\frac{2}{5}$

Exercise 8.6

1. $\frac{29}{35}$ 2. $\frac{13}{14}$ 3. $4\frac{1}{6}$ 4. $\frac{17}{20}$ 5. $\frac{17}{20}$ 6. 3

Revision Exercise

1. a. – ii b. –iv c. – iii d. – iii e. – iv f. – i g. – ii
2. a. 28 b. 33
3. a. > b. > c. > d. <
4. $\frac{7}{10}, \frac{3}{5}, \frac{9}{20}, \frac{1}{4}$
5. a. $\frac{1}{5}$ b. $\frac{9}{10}$ c. $19\frac{5}{8}$
6. a. $5\frac{4}{5}$ b. $\frac{71}{4}$
7. a. I b. U c. M d. P
8. a. $2\frac{2}{3}$ b. $21\frac{7}{10}$ c. $\frac{17}{10}$ d. $\frac{23}{15}$
9. a. $\frac{8}{15}$ b. $17\frac{9}{10}$ c. $\frac{1}{4}$ d. $\frac{1}{2}$
10. $16\frac{1}{4}$ 11. $\frac{4}{5}$ 12. a. 5, 9, 14 b. 9, 4

Worksheet

1. a. $\frac{11}{20}$ b. $\frac{9}{20}$
2. a. Numerator = 17, Denominator = 85
3. 35 4. 6
5. a. < b. < c. < d. =
6. $\frac{2}{5}, \frac{3}{5}, \frac{4}{5}$ 7. $\frac{7}{1}, \frac{7}{2}, \frac{7}{3}$
8. a. 1 b. Numerator; Denominator

 c. numerator, denominator d. $\frac{22}{3}$ e. $\frac{3}{5}$

 f. $\frac{5}{9}$ g. 0 h. $4\frac{3}{5}$ i. $3\frac{1}{3}$ j. 1 k. $\frac{1}{3}$

Chapter – 9

Exercise 9.1

1. a. 0.6 b. 0.04 c. 0.009 d. 0.9 e. 0.07
 f. 0.003 g. 1.5 h. 0.15 i. 0.036 j. 65.9
 k. 2.93 l. 0.189 m. 9.82 n. 0.302 o. 1.6
2. a. 1.7 b. 3.05 c. 6.6 d. 5.16 e. 5.016
 f. 6.9 g. 8.05 h. 4.67 i. 9.007 j. 2.789

Mental Maths

a. $\frac{4}{5}$ b. $\frac{19}{10}$ c. $\frac{123}{1000}$ d. $\frac{15}{4}$

Exercise 9.2

1. a. $\frac{7}{10}$ b. $\frac{9}{20}$ c. $\frac{153}{200}$ d. $\frac{9}{10}$
 e. $\frac{41}{50}$ f. $\frac{52}{125}$ g. $\frac{3}{100}$ h. $\frac{1}{200}$
2. a. $5\frac{1}{5}$ b. $2\frac{9}{50}$ c. $\frac{73}{40}$ d. $5\frac{1}{10}$
 e. $18\frac{1}{5}$ f. $134\frac{9}{10}$ g. $7\frac{4}{25}$ h. $9\frac{23}{100}$
 i. $10\frac{1}{20}$ j. $5\frac{53}{250}$ k. $9\frac{683}{1000}$ l. $14\frac{13}{125}$

Exercise 9.3

1. 5 = 5000; 2 = 200; 9 = 90; 6 = 6;
 $7 = \frac{7}{10}; 3 = \frac{3}{100}; 1 = \frac{1}{1000}; 8 = \frac{8}{10000}$
2. a. 70 b. 700 c. $\frac{7}{10}$ d. 70
 e. $\frac{7}{100}$ f. $\frac{7}{1000}$
3. a. 900 + 30 + 4 b. $900 + 30 + 4 + \frac{6}{10}$
 c. $900 + 30 + 4 + \frac{6}{10} + \frac{8}{100}$
 d. $900 + 30 + 4 + \frac{6}{10} + \frac{8}{100} + \frac{1}{1000}$
 e. $2 + \frac{4}{10} + \frac{8}{100} + \frac{3}{1000}$ f. $10 + 5 + \frac{1}{10} + \frac{9}{100}$
 g. $1000 + 300 + 90 + 5 + \frac{7}{10} + \frac{3}{100} + \frac{8}{1000}$
 h. $500 + 20 + 9 + \frac{1}{10} + \frac{3}{100} + \frac{5}{1000} + \frac{7}{10000}$
4. a. 349 b. 349.2 c. 349.27 d. 349.271
 e. 534.162 f. 206.391 g. 296.091 h. 296.301
5. a. i. Two point seven
 ii. Two and seven tenth
 b. i. Two point seven nine
 ii. Two and seventy nine hundredth
 c. i. Two point seven nine five
 ii. Two and seven hundred ninety five thousandth
 d. i. Thirty two point nine
 ii. Thirty two and nine tenth
 e. i. Thirty two point nine five
 ii. Thirty two and ninety five hundredth
 f. i. Thirty two point nine five seven
 ii. Thirty two and nine hundred fifty seven thosandth
 g. i. One fifty nine point two
 ii. One fifty nine and two tenth
 h. i. One fifty nine point two seven
 ii. One fifty nine and twenty seven hundredth
 i. i. One fifty nine point two seven five
 ii. One fifty nine and two hundred seventy five thousandth
 j. i. Five thousand seven hundred twenty six point three
 ii. Five thousand seven hundred twenty six and three tenth
 k. i. Five thousand seven hundred twenty six point three four
 ii. Five thousand seven hundred twenty six and thirty four hundredth
 l. i. Five thousand seven hundred twenty six point three four one
 ii. Five thousand seven hundred twenty six and three hundred forty one thousandth
6. a. 0.90 b. 0.900
7. a. 2.60 b. 5.20 c. 1.60
8. a. 7.800 b. 2.160 c. 19.300

Mental Maths

a. = b. < c. < d. >

Exercise 9.4

1. a and c have like decimals
2. a. 1.834, 564.600, 13.820 b. 829.56, 775.70, 2.50
3. a. < b. > c. = d. > e. >
 f. < g. < h. < i. = j. =
4. a. 4.8 b. 0.24
5. a. 5.93 b. 2.893 c. 2.8
6. a. 2.9, 4.0, 5.934, 16.2, 18.34
 b. 634.793, 634.797, 634.798, 634.799
7. a. 35.9, 35.89, 35.25, 35.13, 35.03
 b. 139.049, 139.047, 139.043, 139.042, 139.041

Exercise 9.5

1. a. 0.6 b. 0.5 c. 0.8 d. 0.9
2. a. 0.5 b. 0.75 c. 0.8 d. 0.9
 e. 0.65 f. 0.68 g. 0.22 h. 0.35

Try These

a. 9.07 b. 12.91 c. 18.44 d. 32.547

Try These

a. 11.37 b. 12.028

Exercise 9.6

1. a. 3.9 b. 5.7 c. 7.8 d. 8.9
 e. 10.7 f. 7.7 g. 6.3 h. 8.8
 i. 10.7 j. 16.1 k. 17.4 l. 12.1
2. a. 134.8 b. 1113.45 c. 2626.8
 d. 4714.43 e. 5571.79 f. 211.959

Exercise 9.7

1. a. 7.3 b. 7.5 c. 6.2 d. 4.6
 e. 4.9 f. 3.3 g. 6.6 h. 73.5
 i. 25.5 j. 578.8 k. 560.5 l. 2344.189
2. a. 264.3 b. 309.6 c. 63.4
 d. 1730.1 e. 4130.355 f. 4506.158

Exercise 9.8

1. a. 11.5 feet b. 0.7 feet
2. a. 9.9 kgs b. The first bag had more weight by 0.1 kg
3. ₹4513.96 4. ₹90.2 5. 7.08 kg 6. 10.88 kg
7. ₹64.40 8. ₹965.20 9. ₹3736.55 10. 70.3 km

Mental Maths

1. a. 0.8 b. 0.4
2. a. $\frac{9}{100}$ b. $\frac{6}{25}$
3. a. 2.6 b. 4.2
4. a. $1\frac{18}{100} = 1.18$ b. $3\frac{55}{100} = 3.55$
5. 8.2

Revision Exercise

1. a. iii b. ii c. iv d. iii e. ii
f. i g. iii h. i i. iii j. i
2. a. 0.7 b. 5.8 c. 35.3 d. 0.02
e. 0.001 f. 0.053 g. 15.07 h. 93.11
3. a. $\frac{3}{10}$ b. $\frac{73}{100}$ c. $5\frac{2}{5}$ d. $13\frac{1}{5}$
4. 9009.51 b. 748.273
5. $\frac{7}{10}$ 6. 500096.907
7. 999, 99.9, 9.999, 9.9, 9.009
8. a. 0.4 b. 0.05 c. 0.36 d. 0.11
9. 1039.51 10. 70.05 11. Robin walked more by 22.07 m
12. ₹8.25 13. a. 54.75 m b. 109.50 m

Worksheet

1. a. 0.9 b. 2.3 c. 3.86
d. 0.592 e. 3.03 f. 19.002
2. a. $\frac{7}{10}$ b. $2\frac{5}{10}$ c. $13\frac{1}{10}$
d. $3643\frac{293}{1000}$ e. $95\frac{32}{1000}$ f. $5\frac{2005}{10000}$
3. a. Five hundredth b. Five tenth
c. Five thousandth
4. a. 13.89 b. 37.83
5. 163.63 kg 6. Radha bought 0.25 kg more oranges.

For the Curious Mind

1. 13 m

Chapter – 10

Exercise 10.1

1. ₹144 2. ₹35 3. ₹27 4. 14 km
5. 13000 km 6. ₹420 7. ₹675

Revision Exercise

1. a. ii b. i c. iv d. i e. iii
2. 12 3. ₹225 4. 6 5. 6 6. 12 7. 14

Mental Maths

1. ₹50 2. ₹150 3. ₹500

Chapter – 11

Exercise 11.1

1. a. litre b. gram c. metre d. metre e. kg
2. a. 5000 b. 9000 c. 16000 d. 2500 e. 200
f. 3000 g. 20 h. 100000 i. 30000 j. 400
k. 100 l. 2163 m. 1055 n. 912 o. 509
p. 2539 q. 1095 r. 6307 s. 19002 t. 6.235
u. 6; 235 v. 4.309

Exercise 11.2

1. a. 49 kg 6 hg 1 dag 3 g b. 8 kg 5 hg 4 dag 0 g
c. 279 kg 1 hg 0 dag 8 g
2. a. 52 km 2 hm 6 dam 8 m b. 179 km 2 hm 6 dam 0 m
c. 3 km 0 hm 0 dam 8 m
3. a. 27 kℓ 8 hℓ 3 daℓ 0 ℓ b. 6 kℓ 1 hℓ 5 daℓ 4 ℓ
c. 789 kl 4 hℓ 0 daℓ 2 ℓ
4. 97 m 16 cm 97 m 1 dm 6 cm 0 mm
5. 288 m 30 cm 288 m 3 dm 0 cm 0 mm
6. 46.397 7. 5.801 8. 59.687
9. 17.012 10. 73.421 11. 3.562
12. 8.039 13. 7.146 14. 2.903
15. 4.006 16. 9.300 17. 2.085
18. 1.060 19. 135 ℓ 6 dℓ 7 cℓ 2mℓ 20. 0.952

Exercise 11.3

1. a. Sunil b. Anil c. 146.265 kg
2. 93 km 010 m 3. 211 m 4. 6 ℓ 440 mℓ 5. 9 kg 350 g
6. 59 kg 245 g 7. 6 kg 170 g 8. 160 km 250 m
9. 16 ℓ 150 mℓ 10. Geeta has 1 kg 900g more rice.

Revision Exercise

1. a. iii b. i c. ii d. ii e. iv
f. i g. ii h. ii i. iii j. i
2. a. 100 b. divide c. 1000 d. 1000
3. a. mℓ b. kg c. m d. kg e. km
4. 4500 dg < 4000 g < 5 kg < 350 hg
5. 19,000 6. 478.2 7. 36 8. 1000
9. 59,907 10. 12, 3, 4, 5 11. Anita by 0.45m 12. 5 kg

Mixed Review 3

1. a. 60 b. 504
2. a. 4 b. 19
3. $\frac{2}{6}, \frac{3}{9}, \frac{4}{12}, \frac{5}{15}$ 4. $\frac{18}{48}$
5. a. = b. > c. < d. > e. >
6. $\frac{17}{4} > \frac{3}{2} > \frac{5}{16} > \frac{1}{32}$
7. a. $\frac{28}{39}$ b. $\frac{1}{50}$ c. $9\frac{1}{3}$ d. $18\frac{3}{8}$
8. $\frac{1}{6}, \frac{1}{19}, \frac{1}{46}$
9. a. I b. I c. P d. P e. I f. I
10. $16\frac{1}{8}$
11. a. $\frac{17}{20}$ b. $1\frac{1}{24}$ c. $7\frac{5}{8}$
12. a. $\frac{13}{18}$ b. $12\frac{3}{8}$ c. $\frac{1}{12}$ d. $4\frac{3}{4}$
13. a. 9 b. $23\frac{1}{25}$ c. $6\frac{2}{3}$ d. $44\frac{1}{3}$
14. a. $1\frac{5}{16}$ b. $3\frac{1}{2}$
15. $\frac{7}{20}$ 16. I spent ₹4500 and ₹1500 was left with me.
17. a. 0.9 b. 7.38 c. 0.06 d. 5.1
e. 0.018 f. 7.001
18. a. $\frac{7}{10}$ b. $9\frac{1}{2}$ c. $168\frac{1}{5}$ d. $34\frac{179}{1000}$ e. $2\frac{14}{25}$
19. 534.978 20. 0.8, 8, 8.888, 88.8, 888.8, 8888
21. 6.98 kg 22. 623.45 km
23. a. 7000 b. 500 c. 900 d. 970
e. 8019 f. 1 kℓ 234 ℓ
24. 38 kℓ 5 hℓ 2 daℓ 4 ℓ
25. a. 86m 25cm b. 56.489 c. 4926

Chapter – 12

Exercise 12.1

1. a. 8 o'clock or 8 : 00 b. 5 minutes past 9 or 9 : 05
2. a.  b.  c. 

Exercise 12.2

1. 155 2. 80 3. 4800
4. 4210 5. 1388 6. 5100
7. 2060 8. 7332 min 9. 4 min 3 s
10. 9 h 57 min 11. 1 h 43 min 55 s
12. 1 h 11 min 29 s

Exercise 12.3

1. a. 2 min 8 s b. 2 h 14 min c. 3 days 15 h
d. 42 min 45 s e. 17 h 55 min f. 7 h 27 min 53 s
g. 24 min 12 s h. 20 h 20 min i. 13 h 2 min
2. 47 min 8 s 3. 9 h 16 min 26 s
4. 6 days 11 h 20 min 00 s
5. a. 28 min 15 s b. 26 min 40 s
c. 28 h 15 min d. 10 h 45 min
e. 4 h 18 min 25 s f. 6 days 7 h 45 min 10 s

6. 7 min 30 s   7. 9 h 54 min
8. 6 days 14 h 46 min 49 s
9. a. 6 h 50 min   b. 111 h 36 min or 4 days 15 hrs 36 min
c. 8 min 46 s   d. 51 min 20 s
e. 24 hrs 25 min   f. 32 h 32 min
10. a. 6 hrs   b. Q =10 min; R = 12 min
c. Q = 5 min 31 s; R = 11 s
d. Q = 47 min 42 s; R = 4 s

Try These

1. 13 30 hours   2. 14 10 hours   3. 17 00 hours
4. 20 20 hours   5. 22 50 hours   6. 23 45 hours

Exercise 12.4

1. a. a.m   b. a.m   c. a.m   d. a.m
e. noon   f. p.m   g. p.m   h. p.m

2.

12-hour clock	24-hour clock
1:30 a.m.	01 30 hours
4:25 a.m.	0425 hours
9:40 a.m.	0940 hours
12:00 noon	1200 hours
12:15 p.m.	1215 hours
12:55 p.m.	1255 hours

3.

12-hour clock	24-hour clock
2 40 hours	2:40 a.m.
13 20 hours	1:20 p.m.
7 15 hours	7:15 a.m.
15 20 hours	3:20 p.m.
11 40 hours	11:40 a.m.
12 20 hours	12:20 a.m.
12 59 hours	12:59 a.m.
13 00 hours	1:00 p.m.

Exercise 12.5

1. 1 hour 30 minutes   2. 5 hours 25 minutes
3. 4 hours 25 minutes   4. 7 hours 40 minutes
5. 6 hours 25 minutes   6. 1:05 p.m.

Exercise 12.6

1. 2012, 2000, 100 are leap years.
2. 12   3. 52 weeks + 1 day
4. a. 13   b. 20   c. 27
5. 63   6. 89   7. 4 years
8. 5 weeks 6 days   9. 3 weeks 5 days   10. 7 weeks 5 days
11. a. 11 days   b. 25 days
12. a. 17 days   b. 10 days

Revision Exercise

1. a. i   b. ii   c. ii   d. iii   e. iv
f. ii   g. iii   h. ii   i. ii   j. i
2. a. 12   b. 31   c. 29   d. 10   e. 13
f. 366   g. 13   h. 100   i. 6   j. 8
3. 420   4. 907   5. 1645
6. 1 h 38 min 43 s   7. 18 h 20 min 14 s
8. 2 days 11 h 24 min 40 s
9. 2 days 0 h 50 min 0 s
10. 1 h 6 min 19 s
11. 30 min   12. 2:50p.m.   13. 2000, 2008, 2012 are leap years
14. a. 13   b. 20   c. 27
15. a. In Feburary as 29 Feburary   b. A leap year
16. a. 86   b. 2 years 8 months
c. 37 days   d. 3 weeks and 3 days
17. 3 weeks 6 days   18. 8 years
19. 7 years 7 months   20. 25 days

Worksheet

1. 60, 600   2. 60, 3600
3. 3900   4. 300   5. 540

6. a. 60   b. 3600   c. divide
7. a. False   b. True   c. False   d. True
8. a. 55 min   b. 20 30 hours

Chapter – 13

Exercise 13.1

1. a. Diagonal line   b. Vertical line   c. Horizontal line
2. a. Curve   b. Ray   c. Line
d. Line segment   e. Point

Exercise 13.2

1. a. Y   b. YZ and YX
c. Angle ZYX, angle XYZ, angle q, angle Y
2. a. PQ, QR, PR   b. angle PQR, angle RQP, angle Q
c. PR and PQ d. P, Q, R

Exercise 13.3

3. Each angle = 90 degrees.

Exercise 13.4

1. a. zero   b. 0, 90   c. 90   d. 90, 180
e. 180   f. 180, 360   g. 360
2. a. Right angle   b. Acute angle   c. Reflex angle
d. Straight angle   e. Obtuse angle

Revision Exercise

1. a. $\overline{AB}$ b. curve   c. vertical, horizontal
d. Y   e. XY and ZY   f. straight
g. acute   h. obtuse
2. a. iii   b. ii   c. iii   d. iii
e. iii   f. iii   g. i   h. iii
5. a. True   b. False   c. False   d. True
e. True   f. False   g. False   h. True
i. i. True   ii. True   j. True

For the Curious Mind

8 5 3
9 7 1
4 6 2

Chapter – 14

Exercise 14.1

1. a. closed   b. 3
2. b and c are polygons.
3. a. Hexagon   b. Heptagon or septagon
c. Octagon   d. Nonagon   e. Decagon

Exercise 14.2

1. a. 3   b. angles   c. equilateral   d. one
e. one   f. Equilateral   g. Isosceles   h. scalene
i. 4   j. equal, 90 degrees
2. a. Equilateral triangle   b. Obtuse angled triangle
c. Square   d. Right angled triangle
e. Parallelogram   f. Right angled triangle

Revision Exercise

1. a. iii   b. ii   c. i   d. iii   e. ii
f. iv   g. ii   h. ii   i. i   j. iv
2. i. a. Pentagon   b. Decagon
c. Septagon or heptagon   d. Triangle
ii. a. Nonagon   b. Hexagon
c. Quadrilateral   d. Octagon

Chapter – 15

Exercise 15.1

1. 13 cm   2. 16 cm   3. 26 cm
4. 23 cm   5. 22 cm   6. 24 cm

Exercise 15.2

1. a. 12 cm b. 20 cm c. 48 m d. 80 m
2. a. 18 cm b. 14 cm c. 36 m d. 44 m
3. a. 12 cm b. 31 cm c. 36 cm d. 54 cm

Exercise 15.3

1. a. 7 cm b. 10 cm c. 5 cm d. 12 cm
2. a. 10 cm b. 15 cm c. 30 m d. 20 cm
3. a. 11 cm b. 10 m c. 14 cm d. 14 cm

Exercise 15.4

1. a. 63 sq. cm b. 65 sq. cm. c. 585 sq. m
   d. 315 sq. m e. 195 sq. cm f. 84 sq. cm
2. a. 121 sq. cm b. 225 sq. cm c. 1849 sq. cm
   d. 10,201 sq. m e. 11,025 sq. m f. 784 sq. cm

Revision Exercise

1. a. ii b. ii c. ii d. iii
   e. iv f. i g. iv h. ii
2. add
3. a. 47 cm b. 34 cm
4. 60 cm 5. 48 cm 6. 44.05 cm 7. 19 cm
8. 7 cm 9. 153 sq. cm 10. 196 sq. cm 11. 14 cm

Mental Maths

1. side 2. $2(l+b)$ 3. $l \times b$ 4. side × side
5. a. 36 cm b. 30 cm

For the Curious Mind

a square with each side equal to 4 cm

Chapter – 16

For the Curious Mind

5 lines of symmetry

Revision Exercise

1. b. 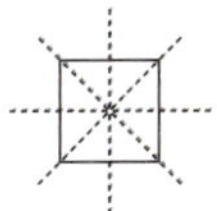 4 lines of symmetry

   c. 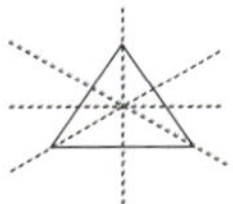 3 lines of symmetry

   d. 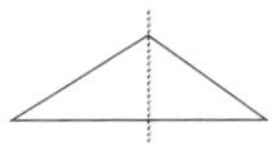 1 line of symmetry

   e. 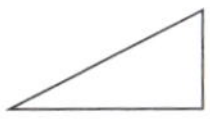 0 lines of symmetry

   f. 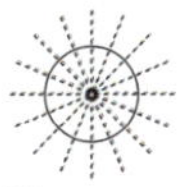 Infinite line of symmetry

2. a. Yes b. Yes c. Yes d. Yes e. No f. Yes
3. a. 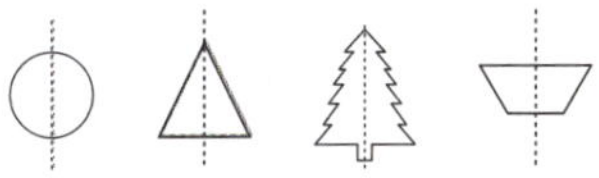

Chapter – 17

Exercise 17.1

1. a. i. 30 ii. 24 iii. 30 iv. 24 v. 18
   b. 1,3 and 2,4 c. 5 d. 12 e. 126
2. a. E, 8000 b. C, 5000 c. 5500
   d. 7500 e. 2500 f. 33000
3. a. C b. A and E c. A and E, 70 d. B e. 5
4. a. i. 500 ii. 600 iii. 400 iv. 500 v. 400
   b. 2001
   c. In 2000 and 2003, 500 students
   In 2002 and 2004, 400 students
   d. 2002 and 2004
   e. 2400 students

Revision Exercise

1. a. i. 27 ii. 18 iii. 27
   b. Kathak and Ballet c. none d. 9 e. 54 students
2. a. 30 b. the same number of both c. 50
   d. Roses, Geraniums, Petunias e. Pansies
3. a. i. 60 ii. 55 iii. 40 iv. 65 v. 35
   b. Strawberry c. Pista d. 25 e. 255
4. a. January and February b. June c. 5
   d. January and February e. May

Mixed Review 4

1. a. 3600 b. 72 c. 315 d. 9,300
   e. 2 min 45 sec f. 2,400 g. 1 hour 23 min 20 sec
2. 4 days 18 hours 20 minutes 42 seconds 3. 4 hours 34 minutes
4. 38 minutes 48 seconds 5. 41 minutes
6. a. 07 40 hours b. 21 25 hours
   c. 12 15 hours d. 13 00 hours
7. a. 11:50 p.m. b. 7:15 a.m.
   c. 12:35 p. m. d. 2:49 a.m.
8. 2 hours 40 minutes 9. 16th September
10. 22 days 11. 7 days 12. 2 years 11 months
13. 51 days 14. 3 weeks 4 days 15. 2 weeks 4 days
16. a. 0; 90 b. 180; 360
17. a. False b. False c. True d. True e. True
    f. False g. False h. False i. True j. False
    k. False l. True m. False n. True
19. 16 cm 20. 52 sq. cm
23. a. A b. C c. E d. B e. 500

Test 1

1. a. x b. + c. x d. ÷
2. a. 24 b. 6 c. 900 d. 90
3. a. 13 and 5 b. 17 and 3 c. 2 and 6 d. 24 and 42
4. $\frac{1}{4}, \frac{5}{6}, \frac{7}{8}, \frac{11}{12}$ 5 a. 60 b. 12
6. a. 16, 98, 144 b. Q = 411, R = 10
7. a. 2 days b. 150 paise c. 12 min d. 720 sec
8. a. ₹2.82 b. 31.55
9. a. 9,236,407 b. Twenty one lakh forty three thousand seven
10. 418 km 665 m 11. 25
12. 15 students got all the spellings correct, 10 did not.
13. ₹1675 14. ₹6050 15. 3 years 9 months
16. a. Right angle b. Obtuse angle c. Acute angle
    d. Zero angle e. Straight angle f. Reflex angle
    g. Complete angle
17. a. 81 sq. cm b. 34.9 cm
18. Hexagon
20. 1. Cricket 2. Football 3. 10 4. 75

Test 2

1. a. 18,504,859 b. 74,09,009
2. 70000, 40, 2800000 3. 10001, 9997, 4
4. a. 7051 g b. 2.502 c. 3
   d. 13 and 7 e. 30, 60,
5. a. 21 b. 96 6. $\frac{1}{3}, \frac{3}{5}, \frac{5}{6}, \frac{9}{10}$
7. a. $5\frac{29}{30}$ b. 219.633 8. a. 135 b. $3\frac{3}{5}$
9. 9 days 7 h 58 min 10. 920metres
11. 1,64,940 12. $1\frac{11}{12}$ 13. 1 hour 22 min 26 sec
14. 1830 sec 15. no, 2
16. Isosceles, Scalene, Equilateral 17. 1 hour 50min
18. 6:10 pm 19. $27\frac{1}{2}$ 21. 12 cm
22. 21 km 778 m 23. 20 25 hours
24. 11 days 11 hours 25. 5 hours 45 min

Test 3

1. a. 100 b. 2 c. 8576 d. 465 e. 29
   f. 3 g. composite h. $\frac{4}{8}$ i. 0 j. 1000
2. a. False b. False c. True d. False e. True
3. 1
4. a. 94,007,005 b. Five crore twenty-one thousand
5. 6.299 < 6.835 < 6.849 < 6.9
6. a. 4,633 minutes b. 7.359 m c. 7 kℓ 349 ℓ
   d. 6.273 g e. 56925
7. 3 and 7
8. Prime factors are 2,3
   Prime factorisation is $2 \times 2 \times 2 \times 3 \times 3$
9. a. $\frac{6}{7}$ b. $\frac{17}{20}$ 10. $\frac{84}{96}$
11. a. 350.329 b. 2 h 32 min 50 sec
    c. 1,78,74,935 d. Q = 1485; R = 13
12. a. $16\frac{7}{9}$ b. $5\frac{9}{20}$ c. $\frac{3}{5}$ d. $1\frac{1}{2}$
13. 53 packets 14. ₹1,08,00,000
15. $\frac{3}{7}$ m
16. Divisible by 2: 28, 14, 88
    Divisible by 3: 15, 57
    Divisible by 4: 28, 88
17. $\frac{3}{4}$ kg 18. 12 h 35 minutes
19. $\frac{3}{4}$ of his salary
20. a. $\frac{3}{5}$ b. $\frac{1}{2}$
21. a. A b. D c. none d. 7,00,000
22. a. 5p.m. b. 6:30 p.m.
23. a. 110 m b. 440 m
24. B, D, F
25. Line, Ray, Point, Line Segment, Curve

Notes

Notes